C.8

THE HISTORIC ARCHITECTURE OF SCOTLAND

THE
HISTORIC
ARCHITECTURE
OF SCOTLAND

John G. Dunbar

B. T. Batsford Ltd, London

First published 1966

© John G. Dunbar 1966

Made and Printed in Great Britain
by Jarrold and Sons Ltd, London and Norwich
for the Publishers B. T. Batsford Ltd
4 Fitzhardinge Street, London W1

CONTENTS

ACKNOWLEDGMENT

It is a pleasure to acknowledge the assistance I have received in the preparation of this book from numerous friends and colleagues. I am particularly indebted to fellow-members of the staff of the Royal Commission on the Ancient and Historical Monuments of Scotland, and also to the Commissioners for their permission to make use of certain unpublished material in the Commission's records. Dr Michael Apted, Miss Catherine Cruft, Mr Richard Feachem, Mr Alexander Fenton, Mr Geoffrey Hay, Mr Iain MacIvor, and Mr David Walker have given freely of their specialist knowledge of various topics, and Mr James Wallace has most kindly assisted with the fieldwork. The staffs of the National Library of Scotland, the National Museum of Antiquities of Scotland, the Scottish National Buildings Record and the Scottish Record Office have displayed their customary courtesy and efficiency in answering inquiries relating to material in their custody, and the Scottish Development Department have made available their unpublished Lists of Buildings of Architectural or Historic Interest.

The great majority of the sites and buildings described in the following chapters have been personally visited within the past few years, and I am especially grateful to the many owners and occupiers who allowed me access to their properties.

Finally, I should like to express my thanks to Mr Samuel Carr of B. T. Batsford Ltd for his continued help and encouragement, and to my sister, Miss Mary Dunbar, who as well as critically reading the entire text in typescript has most generously shouldered the burden of preparing the index.

The Author and Publishers would like to thank the following for permission to reproduce the illustrations appearing in this book: Robert M. Adam, for figs. 105–7; G. Douglas Bolton, for figs. 7, 22, 34, 40, 67, 125, 133, 142, 148, 152, 153 and 175; J. Allan Cash, for figs. 3, 6, 13, 21, 30, 32, 59, 86 and 184; The Gourock Ropework Co. Ltd, for fig. 156; Noel Habgood, for figs. 39, 81, 128 and 202; The Controller of Her Majesty's Stationery Office, for fig. 46 (Crown Copyright); The Controller of Her Majesty's Stationery Office, for figs. 12, 25, 35, 48, 56, 58, 69, 87, 91, 103, 160, 161, 163, 181, 187, 192, 193, 196, 201, 203 and 206–8 (Crown Copyright; photographs: Royal Commission on the Ancient and Historical Monuments of Scotland); A. F. Kersting, for figs. 80, 101, 102, 114, 115, 117, 119, 130, 136, 149 and 151; Donald B. MacCulloch, for fig. 188; Mrs Isa MacLaren, for fig. 166; Ministry of Public Building and Works, Edinburgh, for figs. 4, 5, 11, 16, 28, 31, 33, 96, 97, 100, 108 and 139 (Crown Copyright); R. Scott Morton, for fig. 169; The Trustees of The National Galleries of Scotland, for fig. 182; George Outram & Co. Ltd, for fig. 104; J. Peterson, for fig. 204; Geoffrey B. Quick, for figs. 38, 49, 50, 57, 65, 71, 72, 74, 85, 98, 116, 165 and 198; Register House, Edinburgh, for fig. 64; Charles Reid, for fig. 173; Dr J. K. St. Joseph, for fig. 2; *Scottish Field*, for figs. 37, 55 and 79; Scottish National Buildings Record, for figs. 23, 24, 29, 36, 51, 53, 54, 60, 63, 66, 73, 75, 78, 88–90, 126, 127, 134, 141, 144, 150, 157, 158, 164,

166, 168, 169, 174, 185, 193–5, 197 and 205; Scottish *Sunday Express*, for fig. 167; The Scottish Tourist Board, for figs. 140, 143 and 186; Kenneth Scowen, for fig. 138; W. Suschitzky, for figs. 15, 68, 99, 118, 129, 135, 171, 172 and 176; Valentine & Sons, Dundee, for figs. 14, 26, 70, 113, 159 and 170; Reece Winstone, for fig. 124.

The line illustrations have been specially drawn for the book by Ian G. Scott. For permission to base drawings on copyright material, the Publishers wish to thank the following: The Trustees of George Heriot's Trust, Edinburgh, for fig. 27; Country Life Ltd, for figs. 92 and 155, and for fig. 82, from *The Architecture of Robert and James Adam*, vol. II, by Arthur T. Bolton; A. Drummond and the Factor of the Kennet Estate, for fig. 84, from *Old Clackmannanshire*; The Clarendon Press, Oxford, and G. Hay, for figs. 120 and 121, from *The Architecture of Scottish Post-Reformation Churches, 1560–1843*; Oliver and Boyd Ltd and Ian G. Lindsay, for fig. 145, from *Georgian Edinburgh*; Ernest Benn Ltd, for fig. 178, from *Norse Building in the Scottish Isles*; Royal Commission on the Ancient and Historical Monuments of Scotland, for figs. 17, 19, 45, 52, 61, 94, 131, 132, 137, 147, 154, 162, 198 and 199; The Society of Antiquaries of Scotland, for figs. 9, 177 and 179; The Trustees of The National Galleries of Scotland, and the Institute of Scottish Architects, for figs. 43, 44 and 111, from *Examples of Scottish Architecture from the Twelfth to the Seventeenth Century*; The Elgin Society, for fig. 123, from *Old Moray*.

THE ILLUSTRATIONS

The line drawings, except those which bear scales, are reproduced at a standard scale at 1 in. to 32 ft.

SCOTLAND

COUNTIES & ISLANDS

MILES

KILOMETRES

SHETLAND

FAIR ISLE

ORKNEY

STROMA

CAITHNESS

SUTHERLAND

LEWIS

HARRIS

BERNERAY H.

NORTH UIST

BENBECULA

SOUTH UIST

ROSS & CROMARTY

MORAY

BANFF

SKYE

RAASAY

NAIRN

Inverness

ABERDEEN

CANNA

BARRA

SANDRAY

PABBAY

BERNERAY

EIGG

MUCK

INVERNESS

Aberdeen

KINCARDINE

COLL

TIREE

NORTH ARGYLL

LORN

ANGUS

Dundee

PERTH

Perth

IONA

MULL

Oban

CLACKMANNAN

KINROSS

FIFE

COLONSAY

MID-ARGYLL

COWAL

DUNBARTON

Stirling

STIRLING

Edinburgh

EAST LOTHIAN

ISLAY

KNAPDALE

RENFREW

Glasgow

LOTHIAN

MIDLOTHIAN

BERWICK

KINTYRE

ARRAN

LANARK

PEEBLES

SELKIRK

ROXBURGH

Ayr

AYR

DUMFRIES

Dumfries

WIGTOWN

KIRKCUDBRIGHT

RWF

INTRODUCTION

The distinctive characteristics of any national style of architecture depend in part upon endowed geographical factors and in part upon the circumstances of political and economic history. Scotland's geographical endowment, in comparison with that of many other western European countries, is a markedly unfavourable one. Small in size and remote in situation, saddled with a difficult terrain and a harsh climate, the country cannot be said to present many natural advantages for the pursuit of architecture.

One favourable circumstance is not lacking, however, namely the ready availability of plentiful supplies of good building-stone, and all Scottish historic buildings of any consequence that survive today are constructed of this material. There is little evidence from medieval Scotland of the employment of sophisticated techniques of timber construction such as are known to have been developed in contemporary England and Norway. Nor was brick used at all widely before the late Georgian era—indeed it did not become a common building-material until after the end of the First World War. Admittedly, the majority of the rural population of Scotland appears to have lived in primitive dwellings of unmortared stone, clay, wattle or turf until the end of the eighteenth century, but the minority who could afford to build lavishly (and at some periods it was a very small minority indeed) invariably built in stone and lime.

The wide variety of suitable building-stones makes for strongly marked differences of colour and texture. The dark greywacke rubble of the Upper Tweed valley, the sparkling granites of the north-east, the grey West Highland schists and the smooth regular flag-stones of Caithness and Orkney compose a regional pattern no less significant than that delimited by local political boundaries. Freestone suitable for ashlar construction and other ornamental uses is rather more difficult to obtain, however, and from early medieval times onwards it was customary to transport freestone dressings for a considerable distance from their quarry source. Imported stone was rarely, if ever, employed before the nineteenth century, except for specialised purposes, such as the construction of elaborate funerary monuments.

The famous oolitic limestone beds of England and France are absent from Scotland, where the characteristic freestone is sandstone. This material lacks the superb light-reflecting qualities of the most favoured limestones, but its diversity and strength of colour and its richness of texture make it an ideal stone for use in a relatively sunless climate. The best known of all Scottish sandstones, the fine-grained Carboniferous Craigleith stone used in the construction of the greater part of the New Town of Edinburgh, is, unfortunately, drab-coloured and rapidly darkens in response to atmospheric pollution, and the brighter hues tend to occur in the softer Triassic and Old Red Sandstones, such as those of Dumfriesshire and East Lothian.

The influence of climatic conditions is apparent in many traditional methods of building construction. The Scottish practice of harling was evolved as a means of protecting rubble facework against wind-driven rain and snow, while the use of close-jointed sarking-boards, rather than battens, in slate-roof construction evidently reflects a desire to obtain the maximum degree of interior warmth, even at the risk of increasing the rate of timber decay. In the case of small domestic structures the entire pattern of building is often directly related to local weather-conditions, the most conspicuous example of this correspondence being the older form of Hebridean 'black house', with its thick windowless walls and low rounded roof.

Not until a particular framework of historical events was imposed upon the foundations of geography, however, did a distinctive national style of architecture begin to emerge. For some 200 years after the general introduction of stone-and-lime construction at the end of the eleventh century Scotland formed part of the same cultural province as France and England, and the buildings of this latter country, in particular, supplied much of the inspiration (and provided many of the trained craftsmen) for the architectural activities of the northern kingdom. During this period the royal house of Canmore, supported by powerful Anglo-Norman immigrant families, succeeded in establishing the social and political fabric and, in consequence, the characteristic architectural pattern of western European feudalism. Motte-and-bailey castles of earth and timber were erected, followed, in due course, by stone-built manor-houses and castles of enceinte; at the same time considerable numbers of parish churches were built, and cathedrals and monasteries were established and generously endowed.

The most impressive representatives of this first great building-period of Scottish architecture, such as the fine double-transeptal abbey church of Kelso and the towering donjon of Bothwell Castle, were in all respects the equals of their English and Continental counterparts and offered great promise for the future. But this promise was never realised. The comparatively peaceful and prosperous reigns of the last two Canmore Kings were followed by the long-drawn-out Wars of Independence and, thereafter, by a no less protracted struggle for authority between the Crown and the baronage, and the resultant devastation, lawlessness and economic stagnation were such as to force the country into temporary cultural isolation and stifle artistic endeavour.

Thus the price paid for national independence and unity was as high in the aesthetic as in the political sphere, and in the circumstances it is scarcely surprising that Scottish architecture of the later Middle Ages is characterised by conservatism, insularity and extreme limitation both of form and expression. This is especially true of ecclesiastical buildings which, with one or two exceptions, appear mean in scale and coarse in detail when judged by contemporary French and English standards. The most notable native achievement of this period was the development of the tower-house, whose potentialities both for defence and for domestic comfort were explored with considerable skill and versatility.

With the dawning of the Renaissance a new and more promising chapter in the history of Scottish architecture was begun and, although Scotland remained a comparatively poor and backward country throughout the sixteenth and seventeenth centuries, two important cycles of building activity occurred during this period. The first of these was brought about by the personal intervention of James V (1513-42) who, continuing his father's policy of fosterage of the Royal Works, carried through in little more than a decade a building programme unparalleled either in interest or intensity by that of any other Scottish monarch. From the events of these few years there derive whatever grounds of substance there are in the myth that has endowed native architecture of this period with a French ancestry. But although James V's Francophil policies gave Scotland, in Falkland Palace, the earliest major Renaissance building in Britain, native architecture as a whole remained unaffected by the achievements of the court school, and all creative enterprise ceased in the Royal Works after the king's death.

The second main sequence of building activity occurred during the two generations following the Reformation, and was initiated and sustained not by the Crown, but by the nobility and baronage, a class then increasing in prosperity as a result of the acquisition of former Church lands and revenues, and through receipt of royal patronage. Two principal stylistic periods may be distinguished, the first, or Scottish Baronial phase, being marked by a vigorous flowering of the vernacular tradition, and the second, or Scottish Renaissance phase, which began soon after the Union of the Crowns (1603), being characterised by the hesitant introduction of new types of plan-form and by the widespread adoption of English fashions in decoration.

Scottish architecture continued to maintain its national identity for the best part of a century after the Restoration, but when, in consequence of the Act of Union (1707), Parliament, like the Court before it, became permanently established in London it was inevitable that English taste should exert an increasing influence in North Britain. This period saw the final abandonment of the fortified house (still the accepted form of Scottish nobleman's and gentleman's residence at the time of the Civil War) in favour of the classically derived country mansion and laird's house. Several Scottish architects of distinction now made their appearance, of whom some, like Sir William Bruce, James Smith and the elder Adam, were content to transpose current English architectural themes into Caledonian idioms, while others, such as Colen Campbell, James Gibbs and the Adam brothers, took the road to London, determined to influence the accents of the metropolis itself.

The progress of architecture in Scotland during the late Georgian and Victorian eras was directly related (for the first time since the early Middle Ages) to the development of British architecture as a whole. The fact that traditional materials and methods of construction continued to be employed ensured the survival of certain regional mannerisms, and in some spheres of activity individual native architects made important personal contributions, but Scottish architecture—at least at its higher levels—ceased to exist as a national style soon after the Forty-five. The entire period was one of intense building activity both in town and country as Scotland at last began to experience the effects of industrial and agrarian expansion. So far as country houses were concerned, Scottish architects and patrons from the first showed a decided preference for the castellated and Gothic styles, and by the beginning of Queen Victoria's reign native romanticism had inspired, in revived Scottish Baronial, an appropriate northern variation of its own. In the sphere of urban architecture the most notable achievements were the creation of the Georgian New Town in Edinburgh and the Victorian expansion of Glasgow, each in its own way an outstanding example of civic planning.

This book attempts to provide a general introduction to the historic buildings of Scotland as they exist today. It is not confined to a survey of the more familiar categories of 'ancient monument', such as ruined castles and abbeys, but gives equal prominence to certain other types of structure about which basic information has so far been hard to come by—namely lairds' houses of post-medieval date, the greater and lesser country mansions of the later Stuart and Georgian eras, urban and rural buildings of traditional character, and the architecture of the Industrial Revolution.

A good deal of historical and descriptive information has been included in the hope that the book may prove useful for purposes of reference. But architecture is not a subject which lends itself readily to armchair study and the main purpose of the book will be frustrated unless it stimulates the reader to go out and look at buildings for himself. With this in mind a selected list of sites and buildings that are specially worth visiting has been appended to each chapter to which it seems appropriate.

Since the net has been so widely cast it is inevitable that a certain amount of relevant material will have slipped through the mesh. Some of the omissions, at least, are deliberate. No attempt has been made to deal with prehistoric and Roman remains—notwithstanding the fact that a number of surviving chambered cairns and brochs have undoubted architectural qualities—nor has the survey been carried beyond the beginning of the Victorian era, although this has excluded any reference to the work of such distinguished Scottish architects as David Rhind, Alexander ('Greek') Thomson and Charles Rennie Mackintosh. Little is said about interior decoration or landscape architecture, and nothing about the organisation of the building industry or the development of architecture as a profession.

Scottish architecture has never been as accessible as it is today, when even the most distant parts of the country lie only a few hours' journey away from the main centres of population, and when many of the most outstanding buildings of the past are regularly open to public view. Equally, however, it must be acknowledged that historic buildings have never disappeared at a more rapid rate than they do at present. Much of this destruction is inevitable, and indeed desirable, under modern conditions of society, and its progress is unlikely to be significantly hindered by random, and sometimes ill-judged, protests made by various amenity-bodies and by interested private individuals. What is required, rather, is the acceptance and enforcement, at both central- and local-authority levels, of a carefully formulated policy of selective preservation. Despite the multiplicity of official and voluntary bodies directly concerned, in some way or other, with historic buildings, such a policy clearly does not exist in Scotland today, and appears to stand little chance of adoption unless in response to pressure from informed public opinion. It is hoped that this book will help to make available the raw material upon whose study and appreciation such opinion must be founded.

I CASTLES, TOWERS
AND PALACES

It is convenient to begin the history of the Scottish castle in the twelfth century. No doubt a case can be made out for the inclusion of certain structures of an earlier period such as the tall circular stone towers, known as brochs, which were the most conspicuous features of the Scottish architectural scene during the first two centuries of the Christian era. Equally it may be suggested, though it has yet to be proved, that a measure of continuity can be traced between certain classes of the native 'duns' of post-Roman times, comprising small, circular or oval enclosures surrounded by massive drystone walls, and the simple castles of enclosure characteristic of the early medieval period. But within its generally accepted definition as a fortified private residence the western European castle emerges only with the establishment of a feudal society at the beginning of the Middle Ages, and persists only for so long as that society retains its distinctive characteristics.

The establishment of military feudalism in Scotland was the result of a considered policy on the part of King David I (1124–53) and his immediate successors, and with the introduction of Anglo-Norman institutions and methods of government, and the settlement of a new French-speaking aristocracy, there appeared in Scotland castles similar in form and function to those of contemporary Norman England. The form was soon to change, and continued to change, but in their function as out-posts of royal authority, as centres of local administration and justice, and as the private strongholds of territorial magnates who were bound by ties of loyalty and service to the Crown, the earliest castles fulfilled a role that did not become obsolete for more than four centuries.

Motte-and-Bailey Castles

The castles erected by incoming Anglo-Norman lords to subdue and secure the lands granted to them by Scottish kings were primarily constructions of earth and timber and, because of the more or less temporary nature of the materials used, only very partial traces of such castles can be seen today. Moreover, the surviving remains can be quite misleading unless they are interpreted in the light of contemporary documentary and pictorial evidence as well as of that more recently obtained by excavation; but when all these sources are drawn upon a fairly clear picture of the typical motte-and-bailey castle of the twelfth century begins to emerge. The earthworks comprised a small circular mound (French *motte*) standing within, or adjacent to, a rather larger enclosure (the bailey) whose limits were defined by a ditch and cast-up bank. Upon the top of the motte, and within a strong encircling palisade, there stood a wooden tower, the citadel that formed the last refuge of the defenders. Within the bailey there were grouped buildings of a more domestic nature, some providing additional living accommodation, and others, such as stables, kitchens and storerooms, meeting the day-to-day service requirements of the lord, his family and his followers. The bailey, too, might be protected by a palisade, and both motte and bailey had their own entrance gateway, that of the former sometimes being reached by means of a flying bridge.

Such are the castles so vividly portrayed in the Bayeux Tapestry, and such, in its essential characteristics, appears to have been Somerled of Argyll's castle in Galloway as it is described in an early thirteenth-century romance, though in this case the tower was built not of timber but of forced earth and clay, its high battlemented walls effectively protecting it from assault.

The description of the surviving remains of another Galloway castle, the Mote of Urr, may serve as a guide to the principal features that are likely to be encountered by a present-day visitor to one of these sites (2). Here the motte stands towards the south end of an unusually large bailey, some 5½ acres in extent, above which it rises to a height of more than 30 ft.; the summit of the motte has an average diameter of about 85 ft. The motte is separated from the bailey by a ditch some 25 ft. in width and 8 ft. in depth, while the bailey itself is protected by a second ditch about 47 ft. in width, and of similar depth to the first. There are traces of an original entrance-causeway crossing the outer ditch on its west side. Nothing is known about the nature of the original buildings that stood within the bailey, and recent archaeological excavations on the summit of the motte have been frustrated by earlier disturbance of the occupation levels.

Excavations carried out in 1957 on the summit of a Stirlingshire motte, the Keir Knowe of Drum, were more rewarding, however, for they brought to light traces of what was probably a small timber tower about 15 ft. square, surrounded by stockades and, in one sector, by a wall. Future investigations may reveal evidence of similar structures on other Scottish mottes, but at the moment the closest parallel to the discoveries at the Keir Knowe is to be found at Abinger Motte, Surrey, where excavation showed that a square wooden tower with a surrounding palisade stood upon the summit of the motte in the first half of the twelfth century. The upper portion of such a tower, comprising the fighting platform, may alone have been enclosed, the lower part being reduced to a mere timber framework to facilitate the free movement of the defenders across the motte.

No complete inventory of motte-and-bailey castles has yet been made, but it is probable that at least 200 structures of this type still survive in Scotland either in whole or in part. The distribution of known sites is significant, for they are found predominantly in the south-west, in Dumfriesshire and Galloway, less commonly throughout other parts of southern Scotland and in central and eastern Scotland between the Forth and the Moray Firth, and hardly at all in the far north and west. They occur, that is to say, in areas where there is known to have been Anglo-Norman penetration in the twelfth and early thirteenth centuries, and they are absent, or virtually absent, from those regions where the authority of the Scottish Crown was not recognised until a much later period. Sometimes it is possible to associate a site with a grant of land to a particular individual, as in the case of the motte of Annan, Dumfriesshire, which is probably the 'castellum' referred to in David I's charter of about 1124 granting Annandale to Robert Brus. Often it was the king himself who ordered the construction of a motte to establish his authority in a particular area, and in many cases, as for example at Inverurie and Kintore, Aberdeenshire, such castles were also associated with the foundation of royal burghs—organised and specially privileged centres of trade and manufacture which looked to the near-by castle garrison for protection in times of war and insecurity. Some royal castles became, in addition, the centres of sheriffdoms, and the remains of mottes are today visible in a number of county towns, including Peebles, Selkirk and Elgin.

Because it could be constructed in a relatively short space of time, making use largely of unskilled labour and of materials that were ready to hand, the motte-and-bailey castle was an ideal offensive weapon—a point aptly made by the Bayeux Tapestry when it shows that the second command issued by William the Conqueror to his army after their arrival at Hastings (the first was to prepare dinner) was for the erection of a fortress of this type. A castle constructed entirely of earth and timber was less suitable as the permanent residence of an established hereditary aristocracy, however, and in Scotland, as in England, the advantages of building in stone and lime must always have been evident.

Indeed, both in England and Normandy a solution to the problem of providing a building suitable to this new role of the castle in society had been found before the end of the eleventh century in the erection of massive rectangular stone keeps of which the Tower of London is one of the earliest and best known examples. During the following century a number of these keeps were constructed close to the Scottish border, for example at Newcastle, Norham and Carlisle, and one or two may have been erected in Scotland itself at such important sites as Roxburgh and Edinburgh, although no traces of such structures have so far been found in the northern kingdom. Early stone castles in Scotland there were, however, just as there were early stone churches, and these must now be considered. But before doing so it is worth noting that motte-and-bailey castles did not necessarily go out of use as soon as stone castles were introduced. Some probably remained in service for generations, retaining most of their original characteristics. Others, like Urquhart, Inverness-shire, were absorbed into later stone castles, or, like Duffus, Morayshire, were refashioned in stone whilst retaining their original motte-and-bailey plans. Nor were the basic materials used in their construction neglected in later centuries, for even after it had become usual to build the outer defences of a castle in stone and lime, many of the internal buildings were still constructed of timber. Writing as late as 1578 Bishop Lesley mentions the existence of clay-built towers in the Borders (p. 45), while a slightly earlier account of the same region refers to 'stronge houses whereof—the utter sydes or walles be made of greatt sware [square] oke trees strongly bounde & Joyned together'. Earthworks, too, continued to be employed throughout the medieval period, as the formidable outworks at Hermitage Castle, Roxburghshire (3), bear witness, while with the development of artillery fortification in late medieval and post-medieval times the earth rampart assumed a new role, and one which must be discussed later in this chapter.

Simple Castles of Enclosure

Among the earliest stone castles to appear in Scotland was a group which represents one of the simplest and most universally employed methods of defence at all periods. These structures were characterised by a high curtain-wall of stone, pierced with few openings, enclosing a small courtyard around which there were ranged buildings of stone or timber. Within this general category individual castles varied a good deal in size and shape, and it will be convenient to consider firstly those that appear to be most closely related to the motte-and-bailey castle.

One of the most direct methods of improving the defences of the early Norman castle was to replace the timber palisade encircling the summit of the motte with a stout curtain-wall. The central tower or fighting platform could then be dispensed with, making room upon the summit for some of the residential buildings that had formerly been confined to the bailey. Typologically, at any rate, this 'shell keep', as it is called, was one of the earliest forms of stone castle, though it was practicable only in those cases where the summit of the motte was fairly spacious. There are many examples of this type of construction in England and Normandy, but few in Scotland, and only two of these deserve mention here. The first is the Doune of Invernochty, Aberdeenshire, a great oval motte some 250 ft. in length and 120 ft. in breadth, around whose summit there may be seen traces of a stone wall measuring up to 6 ft. in thickness. Within the curtain, excavation has exposed the foundations of two rectangular stone buildings, one of them perhaps a chapel. The second example, also in Aberdeenshire, is the Peel of Lumphanan, where there are again some scanty remains of a curtain-wall and of internal buildings. Invernochty was one of the principal castles of Mar in early medieval times, and the centre of the lordship of Strathdon, while Lumphanan, strategically placed on the Cairnamounth road, was the headquarters of the barony of Kincardine O'Neil. Here, at an earlier date, Macbeth himself made his last stand:

Thus Makbeth slew thai than
In to the wode of Lunfannan.

The designation 'shell keep' is usually reserved for structures standing upon an artificial mound, often of earlier date, but it could as well be applied to another type of simple castle of enclosure that appears in Scotland during the late twelfth and thirteenth centuries. The castles of this second class seem for the most part to have been erected upon sites where there were no earlier Anglo-Norman earthworks and, unlike the typical motte-and-bailey castle, they comprise a single defensive enclosure. Many are built upon rocky sites, already well fortified by nature, where the erection of an enclosure wall on the edge of the rock summit was the most obvious solution to the problem of defence. To the archaeologist, concerned with the origins of plan-types, such structures may perhaps be seen as the lineal descendants of the native brochs and duns, and comparison may be drawn in particular with the small insular duns of the Hebrides, some of which are probably of medieval date.

A good many of these castles are in fact found upon the western seaboard, one of the most notable examples being Mingary, which occupies the summit of an isolated rock on the Ardnamurchan coast and effectively commands the entry to the Sound of Mull and Loch Sunart. Its most impressive feature is the great enclosing wall, which still rises to a height of up to 40 ft., being pierced at ground level by two doorways, of which one was intended solely for the use of sea traffic. The original courtyard-buildings have been almost entirely replaced by later ones, but the surviving architectural detail of the curtain itself, such as the tall lancet windows, is clearly of thirteenth-century character. Upon a similar site, almost entirely surrounded by the waters of Loch Moidart, Inverness-shire, stands Castle Tioram (*4*), a structure which bears a strong resemblance to Mingary and must be contemporary with it, although the erection of later courtyard-buildings, including a massive tower-house, has considerably altered its original appearance.

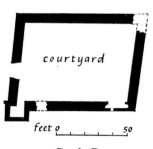

courtyard

feet 0   50

1 Castle Roy,
Inverness-shire

Another member of this group, and the one that most clearly demonstrates that basic simplicity of design that is common to all the rest, is Castle Roy, Inverness-shire (*1*), where a curtain-wall 7 ft. thick and up to 25 ft. in height, encloses a quadrangular courtyard measuring 80 ft. by 53 ft. No later structures here distract attention within the courtyard, where some traces still remain of the original timber buildings that once stood against the inner face of the curtain. At first-floor level in the west wall a semicircular-backed fireplace recess, reminiscent of Norman work, indicates the former existence of residential quarters at this level, and suggests a late twelfth- or early thirteenth-century date for the structure as a whole. The main entrance is represented by a doorway in the north wall having a high, pointed, inner arch, and there may also have been a postern in the west wall. The rectangular tower at the north-west angle does not appear to be an original feature of the design.

Further south the simple castle of enclosure is well represented by Loch Doon Castle,

Ayrshire, which stood until fairly recent years upon a small island in Loch Doon, whence it was removed stone by stone and rebuilt on an adjacent site shortly before the level of the loch was artificially raised. This ambitious and successful rescue-operation by a government department has preserved for inspection an irregular multangular enclosure, measuring up to 75 ft. by 6o ft., and surrounded by an excellently constructed (and reconstructed) wall of ashlar masonry some 8 ft. in width and 26 ft. in height. The entrance arrangements, which are unusually complete, comprise a main gateway and a postern, the former originally defended by a portcullis, together with an inner gate secured by sliding draw-bars, and the latter by a single gate and draw-bars. Similar arrangements no doubt prevailed in other castles of the group. Loch Doon was probably erected about the end of the thirteenth century and first comes on record in 1306 when it was successfully besieged by an English army.

Finally, mention may be made of one of the earliest and most remarkable buildings of this class, Castle Sween, Argyll, which takes its name from the Celto-Norse lords who ruled Knapdale in the thirteenth century. The earliest portion of the castle comprises a quadrangular curtain-wall measuring 84 ft. by 70 ft. over all, against the inner face of which three main ranges of timber buildings were originally disposed round a small court. The external elevations are unique among Scottish castles in possessing flat pilaster-buttresses at the angles, and at intermediate points on each curtain, the one in the centre of the south wall containing a semicircular-headed entrance-doorway. As long ago as 1889 Macgibbon and Ross, in their masterly survey of Scottish castellated architecture, pointed out that these features are characteristic of Romanesque work, and there seems little doubt that when Sweyn and his master-builder came to erect this stronghold about the end of the twelfth century they modelled their design in part upon one of the great rectangular keeps of England or Normandy.

Great Castles of Enclosure

By the end of the twelfth century the rectangular Norman keep was rapidly going out of fashion in its country of origin, and important new developments in the art of fortification were taking place in western Europe and the Near East. This was the beginning of a period during which elaborate, highly mechanised weapons of siege warfare, virtually unused in the West since Classical times, were revived and brought to a new measure of perfection. Long and expensive sieges took place involving the use of such weapons as movable assault-towers, stone-throwing catapults of varying size and ingenuity, and battering-rams inclosed within mobile armoured casings, as well as the silent but deadly mine, whose presence beneath the walls of a castle might be unsuspected by the defenders until the firing of the timber tunnel-supports brought the masonry tumbling about their ears. Military engineers and architects were not slow to respond to the challenge, and during the course of the thirteenth century a succession of scientifically planned fortresses of increasing complexity appeared in widely differing localities, as necessity demanded and material resources were available.

Many of the more important stone castles of the twelfth century, following the motte-and-bailey plan, comprised two principal components, the keep and the bailey, and their main defensive strength was concentrated in the keep. One of the most notable developments in thirteenth-century fortification was the strengthening of the defences of the bailey to a degree which made it unnecessary to have a separate keep, and the dual function of the keep as strongpoint and baronial residence was increasingly fulfilled by a well-defended bailey containing ample room both for residential buildings and for service quarters. The all-important curtain-wall was now frequently reinforced at base by a heavy plinth or apron, and equipped with carefully placed firing-apertures, with battlements, and with overhanging galleries of stone or timber at the wall-head; projecting towers were utilised to provide flanking fire along the wall-face and to serve as mounts for the catapults of the garrison. At the same time special care was taken to protect the weakest point in the curtain, the main entrance-doorway, and the gatehouse began to develop as a key-point in the system of defence. Another principal aim of the military architect of the thirteenth century was that of keeping the attacker sufficiently far away to frustrate the use of short-range weapons of assault. This was achieved primarily by the erection of outworks, which might include such features as palisades, forewalls, and wet or dry moats, and, if the site was suitable, these were often grouped concentrically so that an outer line of defence was itself covered by an inner one. Many of these devices had been familiar to Roman and Byzantine designers at an earlier period, but their employment in the defence of private fortresses of king, baron and military order was something new, and the great thirteenth-century castles of England and Wales, of France, and of the Lower Armenian and Frankish kingdoms are among the most considerable monuments of military architecture ever to have been erected.

Most of these features are illustrated in one or other of the great Scottish castles of enclosure. One of the most primitive, and perhaps one of the earliest in which projecting towers are associated with a curtain-wall, is Kinclaven, Perthshire, a much ruined structure situated close to the confluence of the rivers Tay and Isla. In most respects this building strongly resembles the simple castles of enclosure already described, but it differs from them in having been provided from the first with angle towers. So far as can be seen these towers were square on plan, and this suggests that the castle was erected before round towers became fashionable, an early thirteenth-century development usually associated with the greater ability of this latter form to withstand assault by mine and battering-ram. Kinclaven is on record as a royal castle in the reign of Alexander III (1249–86) and played some part in the Wars of Independence, being captured and despoiled by William Wallace, after which event, if Blind Harry is to be believed:—

In till Kynclewyn thar duelt nane agayne
Thar wes left nocht bot brokyn wallis in playne.

Two castles that well illustrate the use of circular flanking-towers in conjunction with a wall of enclosure are Lochindorb, Morayshire, and Rothesay in the Isle of Bute. The former stands upon an island in a remote Highland loch and comprises a large quadrilateral enclosure strengthened at the angles by round towers of comparatively slight projection, in which there may be seen a number of long narrow firing-slits and some small square windows, all of thirteenth-century character. No special arrangements seem to have been made for the defence of the entrance-doorway, which is centrally placed in the east curtain-wall and gives access to a landing-stage on the loch shore. Enough remains of the internal buildings to show that some at least were of stone, while to the south of the main enclosure there is a forewall having its own portcullis gateway. Lochindorb was a stronghold of the Comyns, lords of Badenoch, and was captured and occupied by Edward I in the autumn of 1303, and recaptured and strengthened by his son a few years later. Rothesay, too, has played its part in Scottish history; here in 1230, as Haakon Haakonsson's Saga relates, the Norse army 'made a hard assault' and, in spite of the boiling pitch poured upon them from the battlements, succeeded in hewing their way through the wall 'because the stone was soft'. The castle provides a good illustration of the employment of water defences, being entirely surrounded by a moat which has an average width of about 60 ft. The enclosure is remarkable for its almost circular plan, reminiscent of a shell keep, and this makes it impossible for the four symmetrically placed towers to provide adequate flanking fire. As it stands today Rothesay is very much a product of the later thirteenth century, and it is still an open question how much, if any, of it goes back to the time of the great Norse siege; the rectangular forework that masks the original gatehouse, however, is an addition of the first half of the sixteenth century.

Not a few of the great castles of enclosure were provided with a keep or donjon, even although this sometimes involved no more than making one of the towers of enceinte rather larger and stronger than its fellows so that it could accommodate the lord and his immediate retinue in conditions of maximum security. Inverlochy Castle, Inverness-shire, is an excellent example of an arrangement of this kind. The plan is nearly symmetrical and comprises a quadrangular courtyard, measuring about 90 ft. by 101 ft., strengthened at each angle by a massive circular tower; there are opposed entrance-doorways in the north and south curtains, the former being a water-gate. The north-west angle-tower is planned as a keep, its residential accommodation including the usual medieval form of sanitary provision, namely a garderobe with a mural discharge-chute; there was also at least one fireplace. Other points of interest at Inverlochy are the long narrow firing-slits and the splayed base-plinths of the towers, and the concentric ditch and outer bank, these last going some way towards providing an all-round defence in depth; all are typical late thirteenth-century features. Another, and perhaps rather earlier, West Highland castle incorporating a keep is Dunstaffnage, Argyll, where, probably on account of the nature of the site, the towers are of such shallow projection that the general lay-out has a good deal in common with that of certain contemporary simple castles of enclosure such as Mingary and Castle Tioram. In eastern Scotland the most notable representative of this group is Dirleton, East Lothian, where, although the flanking towers have been very largely removed to make way for later buildings, the thirteenth-century donjon remains almost intact and preserves its residential character.

Quite the most impressive of the great enclosure-castles, however, are those which have both keeps and well-developed gatehouses, and the two most notable examples, Bothwell, Lanarkshire, and Kildrummy, Aberdeenshire, are among the noblest monuments of medieval military architecture in Scotland. The ambitious scale upon which Bothwell was conceived by its builder, Walter de Moravia, in about the third quarter of the thirteenth century is at once apparent from its plan. Here provision was made not only for an exceptionally large enclosure, measuring up to 230 ft. by 215 ft., and strengthened by angle-towers and a double-towered gatehouse, but also for a massive circular donjon (5) so designed that it could be isolated from the remainder of the castle. Although foundations were laid out, the gatehouse and much of the enclosure were never completed and the comparatively small courtyard seen today is for the most part of later medieval date. The keep, too, is incomplete for it was partially dismantled by its owner in or after 1337 lest it should again house an English garrison. More than 30 years earlier it had withstood Edward I and his army for three weeks, before yielding to assault by mine, catapult and siege-tower. The walls rise to a height of nearly 90 ft. and measure about 15 ft. in thickness, all the facework being composed of excellent ashlar masonry. The entrance-doorway at first-floor level is contained within a projecting spur approached by means of a timber drawbridge spanning a wet moat. Additional protection for the doorway was provided by a portcullis, and there was also a projecting timber gallery at the wall-head from which missiles could be directed upon assailants attempting a passage of the moat. Within the donjon the principal apartment, probably the lord's private hall, occupied the first floor; there were two upper floors as well as a basement for stores equipped with its own draw-well.

The plan of Kildrummy (8) on Donside, which assumed its present form at about the turn of the thirteenth and fourteenth centuries, is similar to that of Bothwell, although the Aberdeenshire castle was conceived on a slightly smaller scale. The enclosure incorporates a circular keep, angle-towers and a gatehouse, while within the north-east angle there is a group of three buildings comprising hall, kitchens and chapel. Certain features of the design recall the contemporary Edwardian castles of North Wales, and in particular, it has been shown that the plan of the Kildrummy gatehouse corresponds closely to that at Harlech, Merionethshire. Quite probably one of Edward I's master-masons gave professional advice on this project to the proprietor of Kildrummy, the

2 Mote of Urr, Kirkcudbrightshire. Twelfth century

3 Hermitage Castle, Roxburghshire. Fourteenth and fifteenth centuries

4 Castle Tioram, Inverness-shire. Thirteenth century and later

5   Bothwell Castle, Lanarkshire. Late thirteenth century

6   Caerlaverock Castle, Dumfriesshire.
Thirteenth century and later

7   Tantallon Castle, East Lothian. Fourteenth century and later

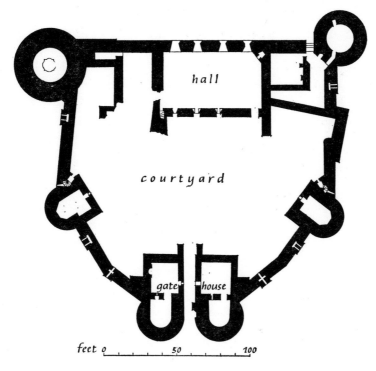

8 Kildrummy Castle, Aberdeenshire

Earl of Mar, but if so this is one of the rare occasions when the design and construction of a Scottish castle of the period can be associated with a particular individual, for the relevant financial records from which such information might be gleaned have all perished. Had Edward I succeeded in effectively conquering the country, however, he might well have erected a series of strategically placed (and well-documented) fortresses of the first rank as he did in Wales—it is known, for instance, that preparations were made for the construction of three new castles on the Firth of Forth in 1304–6 although nothing came of the project—and that he failed to do so is perhaps almost as great an architectural loss for Scotland in the twentieth century as it was a military gain in the early fourteenth century.

The double-towered entrance gateways of Bothwell and Kildrummy are a reminder that the gatehouse developed steadily in importance throughout the thirteenth century and that, particularly in England and Wales, massive heavily fortified gatehouses incorporating many of the characteristics of keeps were being erected in Edwardian times. Two of the great Scottish castles of enclosure, Caerlaverock, Dumfriesshire, and Tantallon, East Lothian, effectively illustrate this development, for neither has a separate keep or donjon, while both have powerful and largely self-contained gatehouses containing residential accommodation. Caerlaverock is admirably described by Walter of Exeter, who was present at Edward I's siege of the castle in 1300, not long after its completion. 'In shape it was like a shield,' he writes, 'for it had but three sides round it, with a tower at each corner, but one of them was a double one, so high, so long and so wide, that the gate was underneath it, well made and strong, with a draw-bridge and a sufficiency of other defences. And it had good walls, and good ditches filled right up to the brim with Water.' The castle has been slighted and rebuilt on more than one occasion since Walter of Exeter's day, but his description still holds good, for later builders followed the pattern laid down by the original designer. The distinctive triangular plan presents a visual impression of great strength (6) when the castle is approached from the north, the only quarter from which it can be reached on firm ground. Nor is the impression an illusory one for, even in its original form, uncomplicated by the later forework, the gatehouse must have been a formidable obstacle. The main entrance-doorway, defended by a portcullis, was approached by means of a timber bridge crossing the moat, which here measured some 40 ft. in width. Recent excavations have revealed extensive remains of this bridge, some portion of which was presumably removable in time of siege, as well as of three other wooden bridges that successively replaced the original one. When the forework was added to the gatehouse in the fourteenth century an additional counterpoise-drawbridge was incorporated in the defences. The ground-floor of the gatehouse was occupied by guardrooms, but the upper floors, although now much rebuilt, appear always to have contained residential accommodation and there are traces of a spacious vaulted hall on the first floor. These upper storeys, originally approached by means of a timber stair rising from within the courtyard, were in all probability the residence of the lord or his custodian, who was so placed that he could conveniently observe the domestic life of the castle in times of peace and retain personal control of arrangements for defence in conditions of insecurity.

The plan of Tantallon, probably erected by the first Earl of Douglas about the middle of the fourteenth century, is that of a great castle of enclosure adapted to a promontory site impregnable from assault on all sides save one. Across the exposed neck of the promontory there was constructed a massive curtain-wall some 12 ft. in thickness and 50 ft. in height having a central gatehouse and terminal flanking towers (7); a wide rock-cut ditch was drawn across the front of the curtain. The remainder of the enclosure was defined, rather than defended, by lesser curtain-walls interspersed with ranges of buildings grouped around a courtyard. The gatehouse itself shows extensive signs of alterations and rebuilding, and in its original form differed considerably in detail from the typical double-towered structures of the early Edwardian period of which Caer-laverock provides an example. At Tantallon the twin towers flanking the entrance passage were rectangular in form in their lower storeys, but were corbelled out at second-floor level into circular turrets, these turrets being linked at third-floor level by an oversailing bridge which commanded the entrance passage beneath. The provision of residential accommodation on the upper floors of the building, however, reveals the basic similarity of function of the two gatehouses, and provides some justification for applying to each of them the term of keep-gatehouse.

Hall-Houses

The castles of enclosure of the late twelfth, thirteenth and early fourteenth centuries were the residences of the highest ranks of society, for only the king and the most powerful of his subjects possessed the material resources necessary for the erection of buildings of such size and splendour. But when it is asked what the residences of the lesser barons and small landholders of the same period were like, it has to be admitted that remarkably few structures assignable to this class of proprietor appear to survive in Scotland.

Before attempting any solution of this problem the surviving buildings themselves must be described. All are compact, largely self-contained structures of modest size. They are usually known as 'hall-houses' or, more accurately, as 'upper-hall houses', and they comprise an undercroft together with a spacious upper living-apartment, or hall, which frequently rises to an open timber roof. The emphasis thus given to the hall was not, of course, peculiar to the type of building now under discussion, but was a fundamental factor of all medieval domestic planning and, just as the larger castles and palaces were provided with separate 'great halls' designed for occasions of state (p. 48), so towards the other end of the social scale the farmhouse had a 'ha'', which might be virtually the only family living-room, combining the functions of kitchen, eating-room and bedroom.

The three best-preserved examples of Scottish hall-houses, although widely scattered geographically, are very closely related in terms of plan form, and may all be ascribed to the same period. The most elaborate of them, Morton Castle, Dumfriesshire, occupies a promontory site, across whose exposed southern flank the hall-house is so placed as to leave a small triangular-shaped area of ground to the north free for the erection of subsidiary buildings. Although the site is naturally strong, no special provision for defence appears to have been made except at the main entrance, which is guarded by an imposing gatehouse situated at the west end of the main hall-range. The gatehouse has been partially dismantled, but enough of it remains to indicate that in the original arrangement the vaulted entrance-passage lay between D-shaped towers and was controlled by a drawbridge, a portcullis, and by outer and inner doors. The main body of the hall range is two-storeyed, the lower floor comprising an unvaulted undercroft lit by a series of small windows in the south wall and provided with a fireplace and a number of stone slop-sinks; this is evidently a kitchen with associated service-quarters. The first-floor hall, entered through a moulded doorway reached by means of a timber forestair rising against the north wall, measures more than 90 ft. in length and about 30 ft. in width. It was lit, principally, by large mullioned windows on the south and east sides, was provided with one, if not two fireplaces, and originally rose to an open timber roof; additional residential accommodation, directly accessible from the hall, was available on the upper floors both of the gatehouse and of the round tower at the south-east angle. On the evidence of its architectural detail Morton can be ascribed to the turn of the thirteenth and fourteenth centuries.

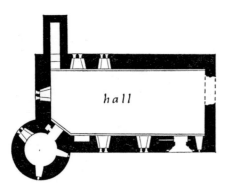

9 Rait Castle, Nairnshire

Rait Castle, Nairnshire (9, 11), probably erected by Sir Gervase de Rait or by his younger brother, Sir Andrew, about the first decade of the four-teenth century, presents a simplified version of the same plan carried out with somewhat less refine-ment of detail. There is no gatehouse, and the hall-house seems to have been freestanding with-in a walled and partly ditched enclosure. Again the undercroft is unvaulted and lacks direct communication with the hall above, which was formerly reached from a timber forestair. The arched doorway, secured by a portcullis and sliding draw-bar, gives access into what was evidently a screens passage situated at the lower end of an open-roofed hall, of which the main body measures 40 ft. in length and 20 ft. in width. Additional living-space of a more private nature is more limited than at Morton, being confined to a single room in an adjacent angle-tower, but there is direct sanitary provision for the hall. The undercroft has no fireplace, and there is some evidence to suggest that the kitchen was housed in a timber outbuilding abutting the east gable-wall.

The last of the trio, Tulliallan Castle, Fife, is in many ways the most remarkable. In size and general character it has much in common with Morton and Rait, but there is an interesting variant of plan in that, although the main hall occupies its usual position on the first floor, an additional series of dwelling-rooms is housed in the vaulted undercroft, which also contains the principal entrance-doorway. This doorway, defended by a drawbridge, portcullis, and sliding draw-bars, gives access to the foot of the main staircase, and thus to the hall above, and also to the western division of the undercroft. This appears to be a storage chamber or ante-room, and communicates with a small projecting wing at the north-west angle of the main block. The eastern portion of the undercroft is a handsome apartment, provided with a good fireplace and stepped window-seats, and it is roofed with a quadripartite ribbed vault which incorporates a central pier having a moulded base and capital; a doorway at the north-east corner now gives access to a prison, but it is not certain that this is an original arrangement. It is likewise uncertain whether or not the room communicated with the adjacent storage-chamber, but it undoubtedly had its own entrance-doorway, guarded by a portcullis and machicolation. The upper floor of the castle has been very much remodelled and little can now be said about the original arrangements within the first-floor hall which, if it occupied the full extent of the main block, must have measured fully 60 ft. in length.

The three hall-houses just described were all erected towards the end of one of the great building periods of Scottish architecture and share many of the qualities of the larger castles, cathedrals, and abbeys of the same era. Other examples, such as the Bishop's Palace, Kirkwall, in Orkney, and the earlier portion of Skipness Castle, Argyll (*12*), can be ascribed to the late twelfth and early thirteenth centuries, while the basic plan-form persisted here and there throughout late medieval times until its notable development in the laird's house of the late sixteenth and seventeenth centuries (p. 71).

Turning now to the problem raised by the paucity of surviving Scottish hall-houses, it is perhaps worth looking southwards to see what sort of building the small English landowner of the thirteenth and early fourteenth centuries was living in. The indications are that, while some members of this class resided in stone-built manor houses, the majority lived in buildings of timber or half-timber construction. A number of the 'fortified manor-houses' incorporate first-floor halls, and some bear a close resemblance to their Scottish counterparts; others have ground-floor halls, as presumably did the majority of the timber houses. When it is further recalled that there is ample documentary and archaeological evidence to show that many of the subsidiary internal buildings of even the most important Scottish castles such as Edinburgh and Stirling, were customarily built of timber, clay or wattle-and-daub, it may reasonably be suggested that the stone hall-houses that now survive in Scotland are simply the most elegant and substantial examples of what was once a much larger group of broadly similar buildings constructed of less durable materials. No traces of such structures have so far been discovered, and it is idle to speculate about their appearance until an opportunity has been taken to examine a recorded site by archaeological excavation. It is perhaps worth remembering, however, that occasional references to timber halls occur in contemporary documents. The *Exchequer Rolls*, for instance, contain a good deal of information about a 'new hall' of timber construction which was erected for Alexander III in Caithness in 1263, while the 'great hall' of Reginald More at Kinnaird, Stirlingshire, whose east gable is mentioned as a boundary mark in a Newbattle Abbey charter of 1329, may well have been constructed of similar materials.

One class of medieval earthwork also deserves mention here on account of its probable association with the landed proprietor of fairly modest means. This is the 'moated homestead', a rectilinear or rounded enclosure surrounded by a ditch, which was probably intended less as a defence against assault than as a barrier against animals, and as a drainage channel. It is assumed, partly on English analogies, that domestic buildings of timber or half-timber construction originally stood within the enclosure, and that a stout fence or stockade ran round the inner lip of the ditch. Examples of moated homesteads have been recorded in most lowland areas of Scotland as far north as the Cromarty Firth, but none has yet been excavated. Two neighbouring homesteads in Stirlingshire, the Peel of Gartfarren and the Peel of Garchell can be associated with landowners who swore fealty to Edward I in 1296, and one of them has yielded a fragment of pottery which suggests that it may still have been occupied about a century later. Another example in the same county, the Peel of Gargunnock, is described in a fifteenth-century account of the deeds of William Wallace as containing 'within a dyk, bathe closs, chawmer and hall'. This description could well embrace a building of the hall-house type, and the association of hall and moated homestead recalls the fact that Tulliallan itself is enclosed by a broad though somewhat irregular ditch. All three sites preserve the designation 'peel', a term ultimately derived from the Latin *palus*, a stake, and here no doubt used in reference to the timber palisades with which the homesteads were originally surrounded.

To sum up then it may be suggested that a number of the smaller Scottish landholders of the early Middle Ages lived in buildings of the hall-house type, which were constructed either of stone or timber, and which sometimes stood within moated enclosures. Others, however, probably continued to occupy the motte-and-bailey castles of their predecessors—the excavations at the Mote of Urr have yielded considerable quantities of thirteenth- and fourteenth-century pottery—while a few, even at this period, resided in a quite different type of stone building to which attention must now be drawn, namely the tower-house.

Tower-Houses

Although nobody seems yet to have calculated just how many tower-houses were built in Scotland, it is safe to say that the surviving buildings of this class easily outnumber the combined total of all other types of Scottish castle. From the remote island of Unst in Shetland to the banks of Tweed, and from Barra to Kinnaird Head, there is not a county that lacks its complement of tower-houses. Nor do they range less widely in time, for there are surviving examples of towers erected as early as the twelfth century and as late as the middle of the seventeenth century, although the majority belong to the later fourteenth, fifteenth, and sixteenth centuries. But, although no other country except Ireland displayed the same overwhelming predilection for the tower-house in later medieval times, it is worth remembering that buildings of the same essential form occur here and there in almost every country of western Europe over a very wide range of time. It is therefore unnecessary, and perhaps misleading, to argue about the origins of the Scottish tower-house, and to discuss the rival merits of those much-favoured (though perhaps somewhat overworked) prototypes, the broch and the Norman keep. The tower-house is, in fact, one of the simplest and most basic types of fortified residence, and as such its widespread occurrence throughout the medieval western world need occasion no surprise.

What does require some explanation, however, is the enormous popularity of the tower-house in Scotland among the upper ranks of society in later medieval times, almost to the exclusion of other types of residence, and the fact that the tower retained its pre-eminence in the Scottish architectural scene until well on into the seventeenth century. Its popularity was perhaps due primarily to the fact that, in a society which was economically straitened and politically unstable, the tower-house struck just the right balance between the claims of domestic comfort and those of defence. A self-contained residence, it incorporated all the essential ingredients of the normal medieval house in a remarkably compact form and offered a considerable degree of security in return for a comparatively modest outlay. Moreover, the plan-form was flexible enough to permit almost endless permutations of scale and detail, and allowed designer and patron to exercise their ingenuity or caprice to the full. Thus the tower-house was a suitable residence for all ranks of the landowning class, from the King himself, who as late as the second quarter of the sixteenth century thought fit to erect at the Palace of Holyrood 'ane greit towre to him self to rest into', to the modest Border laird whose tower stood within a farmyard. In addition, the architectural and aesthetic qualities of the tower-house admirably expressed the social status of its occupant, the tall vertical profile and solid stone construction contrasting sharply with the low flimsily built dwellings of the peasantry. That, once established as the standard type of baron's and gentleman's residence, the tower continued to flourish for so long was due largely to the fact that the basic social and economic factors that had originally ensured its popularity remained more or less constant right up to the time of the Union of the Crowns. Scotland was still a comparatively poor country in 1603, and conditions of insecurity were still widespread, particularly in the Borders and in the Highlands; in these circumstances it is scarcely surprising that Scottish designers and their patrons, with some few exceptions, were conservative in outlook, choosing rather to devote their energies to a further and vigorous development of a well-tried vernacular tradition than to seek inspiration from direct or indirect acquaintance with the architecture of the Classical Renaissance.

Much the same amount of accommodation was provided in a tower-house as in a hall-house, but it was disposed vertically rather than horizontally, one apartment being placed above another to a height of several storeys; communication between the various rooms was usually obtained by means of a turnpike stair placed in one corner of the building, acting as a vertical corridor. The defensive qualities of the tower were entirely passive, reliance being placed upon the limitation of the ground area to a minimum, and upon the construction of thick outer walls, bound together horizontally by one or more barrel-vaults, and pierced by few openings; the entrance itself was often protected by a yett, an outer door comprising a heavy wrought-iron grating of distinctive construction. In the earlier towers only the open parapet, often projected outwards upon stone corbels, allowed the defenders any opportunity for aggressive action, although with the introduction of firearms a variety of gun-loops was often provided. But although the tower-house, unlike the great castles of enclosure, was never designed to withstand a full-scale siege, it usually presented a very formidable obstacle to all but the most determined attacker. A sixteenth-century report on Cardoness Castle, Kirkcudbright-shire, estimated that an assault 'Witht two hundreitht men at a suddane' would be necessary, while in 1523 Cessford Castle, Roxburghshire, successfully resisted an attack by an English army equipped with a battery of 11 cannon and with scaling ladders. Some additional protection was often obtained by the erection of an outer courtyard or barmkin, which might be enclosed either by a ditch and palisade or, more usually, by a stone wall; within the barmkin subsidiary buildings and offices clustered round the tower in much the same way as in a motte-and-bailey castle.

The fragmentary remains of what may fairly be claimed as the earliest surviving Scottish tower-house stand upon the island of Wyre in Orkney, where there may be seen the lowest and only remaining portion of a small stone tower measuring about 26 ft. square over walls some 5 ft. in thickness. Little can be said about the original appearance of the building except that it was strongly constructed of undressed flag-stones bound in excellent lime-mortar, and incorporated a first-floor entrance and an unvaulted basement. It is traditionally known as Cobbie Row's Castle, a name that almost certainly derives from the mid-twelfth-century Norse lord of Wyre, Kolbein Hruga, 'a very mighty man', who as the *Orkneyinga Saga* relates 'built him a good stone castle there'. There is no reason to doubt that the existing structure is of twelfth-century date but, in common with one or two similar buildings in the far north and perhaps also with the small unvaulted tower of Kisimul on the island of Barra, it stands a little apart from the great majority of Scottish tower-houses, partly on account of its early date and partly because of its Norse origin.

The main stream of development begins with a small group of late thirteenth- and fourteenth-century towers. These are characterised by their simplicity of plan and by the massiveness of their construction; most are divided vertically into two or three main compartments by barrel-vaults, the uppermost vault supporting a heavy low-pitched roof composed of stone slabs. These main structural divisions are further subdivided by timber floors, the lowermost compartment always being devoted to storage and offices, while the one above contains the lord's hall, to which direct external access is usually provided by means of a forestair.

10 Drum Castle, Aberdeenshire

Drum Castle, Aberdeenshire, a thirteenth- or early fourteenth-century tower of the Irvine family, admirably illustrates most of these features. The building is of simple rectangular form with slightly rounded corners (*10*), and the walls measure up to 12 ft. in thickness. The only original entrance-doorway is at first-floor level, giving ready access to the lord's hall, and at the same time communicating by

11 Rait Castle, Nairnshire. Late thirteenth or early fourteenth century

12 Skipness Castle, Argyll. Late thirteenth or early fourteenth century

13 Threave Castle, Kirkcudbrightshire. Fourteenth century

14 Claypotts Castle, Angus. 1569–88

15 Borthwick Castle, Midlothian. *c.* 1430

16 Noltland Castle, Orkney. Sixteenth century

means of a mural stair with the basement, whose function as a storage apartment is emphasised by the provision of a well. There is evidence of a small entresol-apartment, perhaps the lord's solar, situated immediately above the hall, while the upper of the three main barrel-vaulted divisions contains another two floors, one at least of which has always extended over the full length of the building.

Another well-preserved early tower, Threave, Kirkcudbrightshire(*13*), shows some interesting variations of the standard pattern. The entrance-doorway, placed only a few feet above ground-level, leads into the entresol floor of the basement compartment, from which access to the first-floor hall is obtained by means of a turnpike stair. The entresol floor itself is a kitchen, an apartment apparently lacking in many tower-houses (including Drum) in which, presumably, the cooking was usually done in an out-building. Threave has no barrel-vaults above first-floor level, the two upper storeys having had joisted floors, while the flat timber roof was carried upon massive struts slotted into the side walls—a most unusual form of construction. There is also evidence for a projecting timber gallery or bretasche at wallhead level from which missiles could be discharged upon assailants below, a feature found also at Kisimul. A stronghold of the Douglases, Threave was probably erected by Archibald the Grim, third Earl of that ill-fated line, so-called 'because of his terrible countenance in weirfair', who died within its walls on Christmas Eve 1400.

The earliest tower-houses were four-square or oblong on plan, but it was not long before the advantages of adding one or more wings to the main block came to be appreciated. The resulting variations of plan, and particularly the two main types known as the L-plan and the Z-plan, are sometimes represented primarily as defensive measures, based on the principles that governed the use of flanking towers in the great castles of enclosure. But this is to misunderstand the nature of the balance between defence and amenity in the development of the tower-house, to which attention has already been drawn for, although the tactical advantages presented by each type of plan were often worked into the general pattern of design, there is little doubt that the main reason for their adoption lay in their contribution to improved standards of domestic comfort and efficiency.

One of the best and earliest examples of the L-plan is Neidpath Castle, Peeblesshire, erected by one of the Hays of Yester towards the end of the fourteenth century. It has many of the features of the simple rectangular towers of the period, but the provision of an additional sub-sidiary chamber in the wing at each level makes for a much greater flexibility of plan. Thus, on

17 Neidpath Castle, Peeblesshire

the first floor (*17*) the hall occupies the full extent of the main block, having at one end a dais, and at the other a screens passage which leads directly into an adjacent kitchen in the wing. A similar grouping in the basement leaves the whole of the main block free for storage, the wing being occupied by a pit-prison accessible only from an entresol floor. Arrangements of this sort were adopted in many of the larger L-plan towers such as Merchiston, Edinburgh, and Almond Castle, Stirlingshire, though in the smaller ones (*19*) the wing often housed the staircase, as at Greenknowe, Berwickshire (1581).

The Z-plan, in which two towers were placed at diagonally opposite corners of the main block, went a stage further in solving accommodation problems. It was adopted at Huntly, Aberdeenshire, as early as 1452, but did not become popular until the second half of the following century, when the tower-house was entering the final stage of its evolution towards a purely domestic residence. The best known example is

Claypotts, Angus (*14, 18*), built between 1569 and 1588, where the accommodation includes three storerooms and a kitchen on the ground floor, one large apartment in the main block on each of the three upper floors, and no less than eight other smaller rooms in the towers. The Z-plan also offered certain obvious tactical advantages and, as the use of firearms had by this time become general, many tower-houses of this class, like Claypotts itself, incorporate gun-ports so placed as to provide both direct and enfilade fire; notable examples include Terpersie, Aberdeenshire, and Noltland in Orkney (*16*).

18 Claypotts Castle, Angus

Another way in which the defensive possibilities of the Z- and L-plans were frequently exploited was in the siting of the entrance-doorway close to one of the re-entrant angles between main block and tower so that it could be overlooked from two sides, but it is worth remarking that a number of the earlier and stronger tower-houses, such as Neidpath, and Auchindoun, Banffshire, do not in fact make use of this device.

The L- and Z-forms, though the most frequent, were far from being the only variations of plan adopted by designers, and the more exotic deviations from standard practice include, at one end of the scale, the double-L plan of Borthwick, Midlothian (*15*), noblest of all Scottish tower-houses and, at the other, the equally unique circular plan of Orchardton, Kirkcudbrightshire (*21*), a building of such modest demeanour that the lord of Borthwick might perhaps have been pardoned for mistaking it for a dovecot. Other notably individualistic plans include Mochrum, Wigtownshire, where two independent towers of different periods stand within 15 ft. of each other, James V's Tower at Holyroodhouse, Edinburgh (1528–32), which was originally freestanding with circular angle-turrets at all four corners of the main block, and Thirlestane, Berwickshire, an elongated version of the Holyroodhouse plan in which the long sides are punctuated by a remarkable series of engaged half-round towers.

But, despite competition from such a variety of plan-forms, the simple oblong tower of primitive aspect never lost its popularity. Examples of every degree and period can be quoted, but there is space here to mention one only of the later tower-houses of this class, Coxton, Morayshire. With its stout walls, its ascending sequence of barrel-vaults and its first-floor entrance-doorway, this small, compact tower might be taken at first glance as a building of the fifteenth century. That its erection can be ascribed (on the evidence of an inscription) to the year 1644 clearly indicates that the simple four-square tower-house could meet the basic living requirements of a mid seventeenth-century Morayshire laird as successfully as it had met those of his predecessors.

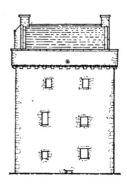

19 Drumcoltran Tower, Kirkcudbrightshire

Another way both of improving the service facilities of the tower-house and of obtaining more accommodation was to erect additional ranges of buildings inside the courtyard or barmkin in which the tower usually stood. These courtyard buildings, insofar as they were residential in character, were usually constructed some little time after the tower itself, new building operations often being undertaken in response to some improvement in the family fortunes. Their presence inevitably detracted from the tower's defensive potentiality, for its resistance to assault depended upon its isolation from other buildings. Nevertheless, the practice was widespread from quite an early period and was sometimes carried out on such a large scale as to change completely the character of the original tower and barmkin, converting it into a courtyard castle of a type that is described later on in this chapter.

Two well-known Midlothian castles clearly illustrate this development. The original L-shaped tower at Craigmillar was either free-standing or, more probably, stood within a palisaded enclosure. During the fifteenth century an enclosing wall of stone with corner towers was constructed, while against the north, south, and west walls of the courtyard thus formed there were erected buildings of stone or timber. In the sixteenth century a three-storeyed east range was added, containing kitchens and cellarage on the ground floor and living quarters above, while in 1661 the west range was reconstructed to provide a more up-to-date series of principal apartments. By its integration into this much larger complex of buildings, however, the tower lost its defensive qualities, openings being pierced through its walls to give convenient access to adjacent rooms on different sides. A similar process, attended by the same results, occurred at Crichton Castle, so that today only an archaeologist can decide where the original fourteenth-century tower ends and the courtyard buildings begin. Among the smaller towers Aldie, Kinross-shire, now attractively restored, may be mentioned as an almost perfect example of this progressive development in miniature, buildings of four different periods ranging clockwise round a court which is only about seven feet square.

The tower-houses of the Border counties deserve some special consideration. They are, in the first place, unusually thick upon the ground; Peeblesshire, by no means a large county, at one time contained at least 50 towers, and more than twice this number must have existed in Roxburghshire. Moreover, the great majority of the surviving examples are of quite modest size and most appear to be of sixteenth- or early seventeenth-century date. Their abundance at this period was evidently due in part to the exceptionally disturbed conditions of Border life, and some were probably erected in response to direct official encouragement, for an Act of 1535 laid down that each £100 landholder should 'big ane sufficient barmkyn—of Stane and lyme contenand thre score futis of the square ane Eln thick and vi Elnys heicht—with ane touer in the samin—gif he thinkis It expedient'; the goods and cattle of the laird and his tenants were to be brought into the barmkin 'in trublous tyme'. This measure was intended as a safeguard against invasion from England, but feud and foray persisted long after hostilities between the two countries had officially ceased, and even the smallest of Border lairds seems to have continued to find it essential to have some sort of tower-house. Something, too, may have been due to local peculiarities of tenure, for it is noticeable that when the Crown introduced perpetual heritable tenures in Ettrick Forest during the early sixteenth century instead of the short leases that had formerly been customary, the tenants at once began to build more substantial residences, most of which were of tower-house type.

Although barmkins without towers were envisaged in the Act of 1535, few if any survive, but good examples of barmkins of about the stipulated size having associated tower-houses may be seen at Buckholm, Roxburghshire, and also at Hills, Kirkcudbrightshire (23), which was erected by Edward Maxwell some time after 1528. Here the tower rises to a height of four storeys and an attic, and is rectangular on plan, measuring about 23 ft. by 30 ft. over all. The barmkin, which measures about 65 ft. by 55 ft. internally, has been partially rebuilt within recent years, but preserves an original and unusually complete gatehouse. The idea that the majority of Border tower-houses were deliberately sited so as to form a defensive chain of intercommunicating strong-points cannot be maintained, for each was erected where it might best serve the individual interests of its owner. Nevertheless, at least one surviving tower, Repentance, Dumfriesshire, is known to have been regarded primarily as a watch-tower, and the Border Laws indicate that it was fitted with a warning-bell and a beacon, which was to be 'keeped, and never faill burning, so long as the *Englishmen* remain in *Scotland*'.

Other specialised types of Border tower-house in which the balance seems to have been weighted almost entirely in favour of defence at the expense of amenity are represented by the terms 'peel' (or pele) and 'bastel-house', although due to a confusion both of contemporary and of later terminology it is now almost impossible to discover the distinguishing characteristics of either of these two classes of building. Something has already been said about the derivation and early use of the word peel (p. 36), but by the sixteenth century the term was being used to describe not only a defensive enclosure of earth and timber, but also a small tower-like building of stone, clay or timber (p. 23) which might or might not stand within such an enclosure. Recognisable examples of these lesser tower-houses, all of them stone built, are not uncommon in Northumberland and Cumberland, but in Scotland they have so far been identified only in the parish of Southdean, Roxburghshire, notably at Mervinslaw and Slacks. All are unvaulted, being built of rubble masonry laid in clay mortar; the absence of stone-built fireplaces and the inadequate lighting suggest that they were regarded as temporary refuges rather than as permanent residences. Bastels and bastel-houses are even more difficult to identify, but on some occasions at least the term seems to have been applied to those communal places of retreat with which many Border burghs and townships are known to have been equipped. Part of what is reputed to be a bastel-house of this type is incorporated within the fabric of the County Hotel, Peebles, but another supposed example, Queen Mary's House, Jedburgh (p. 186), is, in its present form, more reminiscent of a private town-house than of a strongpoint.

In conclusion mention must be made of what W. D. Simpson has termed the 'Indian Summer' of the Scottish Baronial style, the period about the turn of the sixteenth and seventeenth centuries that saw a last vigorous flowering of this essentially vernacular tradition. The most notable tower-houses of this era show no novelties of plan, but their elevational treatment is richly varied, and their upperworks exhibit an imaginative and profuse display of ornamental detail drawn primarily from native, and more occasionally from foreign, sources. Local schools of design can sometimes be distinguished, particularly in Aberdeenshire and the north-east, where one or two prominent families of master-masons were able to develop recognisable stylistic mannerisms.

Most of these features are well illustrated at Amisfield, Dumfriesshire, where the bold development of the wallhead, with its corbelled angle-turrets and curious dormer-windows, and the remarkable vertical progression of the south-east stair-tower (in which the skilful use of corbelling permits no less than three abrupt changes of plan-form within the ascent), evidently represent a conscious striving after effect. Amisfield was erected for John Charteris of Amisfield in 1600 by a designer who had previously worked at Elshieshields in the same county. By universal agreement, however, the Baronial style culminates in a small group of north-eastern castles of which the most notable are Midmar, Crathes (22), Fraser and Craigievar. All are associated with a local family of master-masons named Bell, and all were completed between about 1575 and 1626. The latest of them, Craigievar (24), is the most outstanding, for no later alterations mar the perfect balance of the elevations or disturb the homogeneity of the original interior decoration. Here, perhaps more readily than anywhere else in a country whose finest buildings are now often mere empty shells of studiously preserved masonry, it is possible to see a castle as its original occupants saw it, and to understand that pride of possession so well expressed by Sir Richard Maitland when he wrote of his own tower of Lennoxlove:

> *Thy tour and fortres, lairge and lang,*
> *Thy neighbours does excell;*
> *And for thy wallis thick and strang,*
> *Thou graitly beirs the bell.*
> *Thy groundis deep, and topis hie,*
> *Uprising in the air,*
> *Thy vaultis pleasing are to sie,*
> *They are so greit and fair.*

Courtyard Castles and Palaces

Although most later medieval Scottish castles were tower-houses, a few of the greatest landholders continued to build substantial castles of enclosure whose general form was directly derived from their thirteenth- and early fourteenth-century predecessors. By this time, however, the specifically military functions of the castle were beginning to decline throughout western Europe, and these courtyard castles of the later Middle Ages, like their counterparts in other countries, exhibit no new principles of fortification, emphasis being increasingly laid upon the provision of higher standards of domestic accommodation.

Mugdock, Stirlingshire, erected by one of the Grahams of Montrose some time in the fourteenth century, is a case in point. The portcullis gateway, the high wall of enceinte and the angle-towers are all in certain respects reminiscent of the great thirteenth-century castles of enclosure, yet the differences between Mugdock and a fortress such as Inverlochy are much more evident than the apparent similarities. Mugdock is, in fact, almost entirely inward-looking and its defensive qualities are about as passive as those of a tower-house. The rectangular corner-towers, strong though they are, are turned inwards into the courtyard instead of projecting into the field, so that the main responsibility for defence is placed upon the unusually high curtain-wall which, in the absence of firing-slits, must have been defended from the parapet-walk alone. Within the castle little now remains of the principal domestic buildings apart from what may have been a lofty hall on the west side of the courtyard.

The same lack of aggression is apparent in the design of Doune, Perthshire (20), although careful planning and the immense solidity of the fabric combine to make the castle a most formidable defensive stronghold. Erected as a principal residence of Murdoch, Duke of Albany, Regent of Scotland from 1419 to 1424, the castle was intended to be a structure of unusual size and splendour, comprising four ranges of buildings grouped round a large open court. In the event, however, only the north range and part of the west range were completed, the accommodation thus provided evidently meeting the needs both of the original owner and of his successors. The north range incorporates two distinct component parts, of which the eastern includes, on the ground floor, the main gateway and a long entrance-passage flanked by guardrooms and, on the upper floors, a series of well-appointed private apartments from which partial control could be exercised over the entrance below. This upper portion in fact constitutes a secure and self-contained residence for the lord of the castle similar in character to the keep-gatehouses of Caerlaverock and Tantallon. The main feature of the western portion of the range is the great

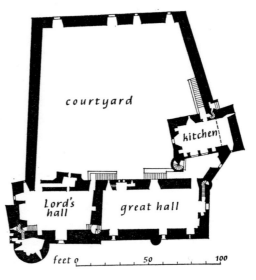

20 Doune Castle, Perthshire

hall with its central fireplace (one of the few Scottish examples), and open timber roof; this communicates with the kitchen and service rooms in the west range. Apart from the special arrangements made for safeguarding the entrance, Doune, like Mugdock, relies for its defence chiefly upon its high curtain-wall, which is provided with a continuous parapet-walk, and with corbelled rounds at the angles. The design may therefore be regarded as a transitional one, the keep-gatehouse looking back to the thirteenth-century donjon, and ultimately to the motte tower, and the complete integration of the defensive and domestic arrangements into a regular courtyard-plan anticipating the development of later courtyard-houses and palaces.

The next stage in this development, namely the virtual exclusion of defensive features in return for a more spacious and convenient lay-out of the residential accommodation, is most clearly seen in the royal castles and palaces of the fifteenth and sixteenth centuries. At Linlithgow, West Lothian, a start was made in the fifteenth century to rebuild an earlier royal castle on more up-to-date lines, and by the reign of James V (1513–42) the structure had assumed the quadrangular form that it preserves today. Although described by a seventeenth-century traveller as a 'very fair palace, built castlewise', Linlithgow, despite its sprinkling of gun-ports, its corbelled parapets and its guarded entrance-doorways, is in fact an almost exclusively domestic building. Externally its true character is made clear by the large regularly disposed window-openings, while within there is a well-organised system of communication by means of stairs, corridors and mural lobbies.

The finest of the State Apartments at Linlithgow is the 'Lion Chalmer' or Great Hall, which, with its adjacent service-rooms and underlying kitchens and cellarage, occupies the greater part of the east quarter of the Palace. A similar pattern can be traced at Edinburgh Castle, where a great hall was erected along the south side of the courtyard now known as Crown Square at about the turn of the fifteenth and sixteenth centuries. In the earlier castles of enclosure the great hall, in common with such buildings as chapels, kitchens and storerooms, usually stood by itself at some suitable point within the bailey, and its full integration into a courtyard lay-out at Doune and Linlithgow before the middle of the fifteenth century marks a further stage in that gradual drawing together of the component parts of the medieval castle into a coherent whole which was to culminate in the compact and symmetrical plans of the Renaissance.

Not all late medieval great halls were so readily accommodated, however, and two of the most important examples, situated within the royal castles of Stirling and Falkland respectively, were originally freestanding buildings, although both were subsequently absorbed into rather loose courtyard-plans. The great hall at Stirling (25), built about the same time as the one at Edinburgh Castle, is the finest achievement of late Gothic domestic architecture in Scotland. Before its mutilation at the end of the eighteenth century travellers compared it to Richard II's hall at Westminster, while to Defoe it was 'the noblest I ever saw in Europe'; even today, after a century and a half's use as a military barracks, the building retains traces of its former splendour. The plan was fairly orthodox, the hall itself being set over a vaulted basement, and having at one end a dais and at the other an entrance-doorway and screens; less usual features, however, included an open gallery running along the west façade, and a stair tower on the east side which gave access to a private balcony overlooking the body of the hall. The building measures 126 ft. by 36 ft. internally and the original hammer-beam roof was more than lofty enough to permit the remarkable model boat that figured in the festivities of Prince Henry's christening-banquet of 1594 to be freely 'sailed' round the hall, even though this nautical prodigy measured 40 ft. 'from her Bottom to her highest Flag'. The dais was lit by large bay-windows ceiled with rib-vaults, the details of the bay designs, like the contemporary roof-corbels of the Edinburgh hall, beginning to reflect the influence of the Renaissance. At Falkland, Fife, the great hall stood on the north side of the Palace, but only the foundations now remain to indicate its general resemblance in plan and proportion to the Stirling hall.

The activities of the designers of the Royal Works were intensified during the 14 years of the effective reign of James V (1528–42), a period which saw a sustained programme of royal building on a scale unparalleled in Scottish architectural history. The first stage of this programme, the erection of the Great Tower of Holyroodhouse in 1528–32 has already been mentioned (p. 42), while the second stage, namely the completion of the principal quadrangle of the Palace and its integration with the Great Tower, need not be described in detail here because none of the buildings of this period,

21 Orchardton Tower, Kirkcudbrightshire. Fifteenth century
22 Crathes Castle, Kincardineshire. Late sixteenth century

23 Hills Tower, Kirkcudbrightshire. Sixteenth century and 1721

24 Craigievar Castle, Aberdeenshire. Early seventeenth century

25 (*Below*) Great Hall, Stirling Castle. Late fifteenth
and early sixteenth centuries

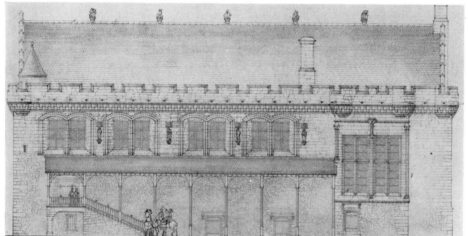

26 Falkland Palace, Fife. 1537–41

apart from the Tower itself, survived the seventeenth-century reconstruction of Holyroodhouse.

With the renewal of the Franco-Scottish alliance in 1537 through the king's marriage policies, however, the activities of the Royal Works were at once subjected to influences from a new quarter. Indeed, as Lesley tells us, not only were 'mony new ingynis and devysis, alsweill of bigging paleices—first begun and used in Scotland—eftir the fassione quhilk thay had sene in France', but direct steps were taken by the court to ensure the appointment of selected French master-craftsmen to high office under the Scottish Crown. Encouraged by royal patronage the new arrivals were not slow in making their presence felt. Extensive building operations were undertaken in 1537–41 at Falkland, where the courtyard façades of the east and south ranges of the Palace (26), in which the bays are defined by buttresses modelled as classical columns and incorporate medallion busts, are clearly of French inspiration. This work can be attributed to Nicholas Roy and Moses Martin, two French master-masons whose names appear in the building accounts; it contrasts sharply with the design of the Palace gatehouse which, as its appearance suggests, was completed by a master-mason who had previously worked at Holyroodhouse.

From Falkland the designers and craftsmen of the Royal Works moved to Stirling, where a self-contained building of courtyard plan was completed within the castle precincts before James V's death in 1542. In contrast to the arrangements at Falkland, where most of the emphasis is placed upon the courtyard façades, the Palace of Stirling is a completely outward-looking building, the inner elevations being treated very simply, but the external ones with considerable elaboration. Yet the symmetrical division of the external elevations (30) into series of boldly recessed bays, each containing a sculptured figure set upon an ornamental baluster-shaft, is no less French in inspiration, even although some of the sculptures themselves are derived from German engravings. Within, there is a fine suite of State Apartments at first-floor level, although little now remains of their original fittings apart from some handsome chimney-pieces and a number of wooden medallions (the 'Stirling Heads'), which were formerly incorporated in a remarkable compartmented ceiling in the King's Presence Chamber.

The façades of the royal palaces of Falkland and Stirling were among the earliest attempts at coherent Renaissance design in Britain, yet they had no successors and exerted no general influence. For the rest of the sixteenth century Scottish architecture remained for the most part obstinately Scottish, classical motifs penetrating only as ingredients of an essentially vernacular style of decoration, where they were often used so incongruously, and with such scant regard for the rules of scale and proportion, as to make it quite clear that the craftsmen's knowledge of source-material was obtained at second or third hand. Indeed the few later sixteenth-century buildings whose designs do in fact reflect foreign influences are chiefly of interest as individual curiosities. Thus the plan of Drochil, Peeblesshire (*c.* 1578), clearly derives from France, and that of Barnes, East Lothian (*c.* 1594), from Elizabethan England, while the remarkable court-yard façade at Crichton Castle (*c.* 1581–92) is evidently the *jeu d'esprit* of a wealthy aristocrat seeking to recreate the sophisticated environment of his Italian exile, albeit on a bleak Midlothian hillside.

During the second half of the sixteenth century the role of the Crown as principal initiator of important new building projects increasingly passed to the greater land-holders and men of state, a movement which was consolidated by the departure of the Court for Whitehall in 1603. Many members of this class were content to live in tower-houses, but others built substantial mansions of courtyard type. One of the most interest-ing of these, and one which shows the lengths to which native conservatism could go, is Boyne Castle, Banffshire, erected by one of the Ogilvies of Dunlugas towards the end of the sixteenth century. With its high wall of enceinte, massive circular angle-towers, and strong gatehouse, Boyne might well be taken at first glance for a great thirteenth-century castle of enclosure, but the symmetrical grouping of the courtyard buildings, now largely ruinous, and the distinctive character of the gun-ports, are more accurate indicators of its true date. Tolquhon, Aberdeenshire (1584–9), bears a considerable resemblance to Boyne, though in this case the courtyard design is not entirely homo-geneous as it incorporates at one corner the fabric of an earlier tower-house. There are two salient towers only, and these are placed at diagonally opposite corners of the courtyard so that the gun-ports of each tower command two sides of the main building, as in certain tower-houses of Z-plan. The accommodation is generous, all the principal rooms being placed, as was still customary, on the first floor; it includes a hall with an adjacent withdrawing-room, and a long gallery, a feature which is not uncommon in the larger Scottish mansions of the period, being found at Holyroodhouse as early as 1535–6.

Perhaps the most remarkable courtyard building of the period is the Earl's Palace, Kirkwall (*28*), erected soon after 1600 by Patrick Stewart, Earl of Orkney, whose father had built a house of the same type at Birsay, also in Orkney, a generation earlier. The accommodation of the Palace includes a group of three principal apartments arranged *en suite* on the first floor, the largest of these being a fine hall lit by oriel and bay windows and heated by two fireplaces, one of which has a width of no less than 18 ft. Access to these rooms is obtained by means of a stair composed of straight flights alternating with landings, a type which was now beginning to supersede the turnpike stair. But the most curious feature of the building is its carved decoration, which is evidently derived from a very wide variety of sources; both French late-Gothic and Elizabethan elements can be recognised, but the overall effect remains characteristically Scottish. A similar combination of elements occurs contemporaneously in the show-front of the Castle or Palace of Huntly, Aberdeenshire. Typologically, Huntly is a hall-house, and its desig-nation as a 'palace' illustrates the distinctive later medieval Scottish application of this term to include almost any stately domestic building which, in contrast to the all-prevalent tower-house, is primarily horizontal rather than vertical in aspect—not that native usage was ever quite undiscriminating enough to justify Captain Burt's criticism of a certain Scottish writer that he 'calls almost all their houses palaces'.

The Union of the Crowns saw Scottish architecture still largely untouched by the fundamental principles of classical design, and this conservative independence of out-look remained acceptable both to designers and to their patrons until well after the Restoration. Uninfluenced by developments in plan-form that were taking place in neighbouring countries, most large houses went on being built on the well-tried court-yard model—although increasing attention was paid to symmetry of plan and elevation. Considerations of security could now safely be disregarded, but certain traditional features of design that had originally had some defensive significance, such as the placing of the principal apartments over a vaulted undercroft, persisted for a remarkably long time. One noticeable characteristic of the years immediately following 1603 was a change in fashions of decoration, the Scottish Baronial manner being replaced by a new, but equally distinctive, style whose ultimate origins can be traced to pattern books published in Germany and the Low Countries, but which reached Scotland in the developed form that had been evolved in Elizabethan England. This Anglo-Flemish ornament, with its elaborate cartouches and grotesques, and intricately patterned strap-work, was used both for external and for internal decoration, some of the earliest examples being the work of incoming English craftsmen; it is found first in Fife and the Lothians, but soon spread to other parts of the country, becoming one of the most characteristic features of Scottish Renaissance architecture of the first half of the seventeenth century.

One of the last great houses to be built before the introduction of this new style of ornament, but one which nevertheless incorporated many novel features, was Abbey House, Culross, erected for Edward Bruce, Lord Kinloss, in 1608. It was evidently intended that the building should be of quadrangular plan with square angle-pavilions, but only two sides of the structure were completed in the early seventeenth century, and of these only a much reduced fragment of the south range remains today. The surviving portion is of special interest, however, in that the ground floor appears always to have been unvaulted, while the entire range seems to have been divided longitudinally by a spine wall to house two sets of rooms within its width instead of one, a refinement of planning hitherto rare in Scotland. Both main façades of the south range originally incorporated two ranges of symmetrically disposed windows, those on the first floor having pilastered jambs and moulded triangular pediments with thistle finials; the horizontal character of the elevations was further emphasised by a continuous string-course at first-floor level and by a pronounced eaves-cornice. The immediate sources of this design are not clear, but while many of the individual components that appear in Lord Kinloss's house can be found in earlier Scottish work, there is no doubt that the overall conception was very much in advance of its time, as befitted a patron who was a prominent figure at the Jacobean court and a member of the English Privy Council.

But while earlier buildings of comparable individuality had exerted little or no general influence, many of the elements found in the design of Abbey House soon re-appear elsewhere. Thus, the practice of placing two sets of rooms side by side within the width of a building was continued in the King's Lodging, Edinburgh Castle, in 1615–17 and in the rebuilt north quarter of Linlithgow Palace in 1618–21, both erected under the direction of William Wallace, the King's Master-Mason. Clearly, an arrangement of this kind made for a more compact plan than the traditional method of placing rooms end to end, while the dividing wall could conveniently be utilised to house the chimney flues, allowing the stacks to be grouped together for decorative effect, as at Linlithgow. The design of the Abbey House elevations also reappears both at Edinburgh and at Linlithgow, although by this time the ornamental detail, much of it designed and executed by Wallace himself, has become thoroughly Anglo-Flemish in character. In addition, it is noticeable that the north range at Linlithgow is unvaulted and that the ground floor is given over to living accommodation.

These were the only two considerable royal building projects of the first half of the seventeenth century, a period which saw the architectural activities of the Crown quite overshadowed by those of private individuals and corporations. A year or two earlier, probably in 1613, the reconstruction of the palace of Pinkie, Midlothian, had been begun by Alexander Seton, Earl of Dunfermline, who was Chancellor of Scotland and one of Lord Kinloss's fellow-members of the English Privy Council. The Seton family were among the greatest builders of their day and the Earl had already enlarged and extensively remodelled his Aberdeenshire castle of Fyvie in an ambitious interpretation of the local Baronial style. At Pinkie, however, he wholeheartedly adopted new fashions, perhaps employing as his master-mason William Wallace, who was evidently a key figure in the popularisation of the Anglo-Flemish style, and as much a devisor of buildings as a skilled carver. As at Fyvie a full courtyard scheme was envisaged but never brought to completion, work being concentrated upon two main ranges of buildings. These exhibit no novelties of plan, although the east range incorporates a stately long gallery on the upper floor; but the new style of decoration is very much in evidence, while the tall regularly disposed chimneys of the east front, and the remarkable bay window at the south-east angle, suggest direct English influence.

The best known building of the period, and one that well illustrates the mixed origins of the Scottish Renaissance style, is Heriot's Hospital, Edinburgh, begun in 1628. The main features of the symmetrical courtyard-plan (27) probably derive, as Sir John Summerson has suggested, from an Italian pattern-book, but their conversion into three-dimensional form must be credited to the successive master-masons, William Wallace, William Ayton, and John Mylne, younger. In general the elevations follow the lines laid down at Abbey House, Culross, and at Linlithgow, but the mock-castellated superstructureof the corner pavilions looks back to the Baronial style (the turrets mirror those at Pinkie and the King's Lodging, Edinburgh Castle), while the Gothic windows of the chapel reflect the even more conservative outlook of post-Reformation Scottish church architecture. The boldly carved ornamental detail is entirely Anglo-Flemish in character.

Curiously enough the same plan had been utilised ten years previously by the designer, perhaps Wallace himself, who prepared a scheme for remodelling Drumlanrig Castle, Dumfriesshire, for Sir William Douglas, later first Earl of Queensberry.

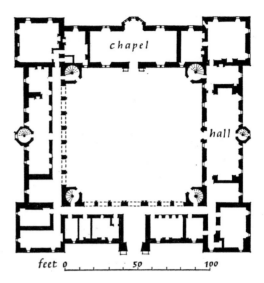

27 Heriot's Hospital, Edinburgh

The project seems to have gone no further at this stage, but in 1679–90 it was revived by the 1st Duke, who, evidently believing that what was good enough for his grandfather was good enough for him, proceeded not only to make use of the first Earl's plans, but to execute them in what must have been a consciously archaic manner. The result is a building almost identical to Heriot's Hospital in plan and massing, to which the Duke's architect, in an attempt at professional face-saving, has added an exuberant Caroline show-front (29). This has an arcaded lower storey above which the applied pilasters of a giant Corinthian order rise through two ranges of pedimented windows to an entablature and crowning balustrade; the projecting centre-piece, containing the entrance porch, is approached by a handsome double stair and surmounted by a clock-tower capped with a ducal coronet. The entire front is further enriched by a lavish display of carved ornamental detail. The architect in question, on the evidence now available, appears to have been James Smith, a versatile designer then just beginning a career whose significance will be discussed more fully in another chapter (p. 101). The show-front derives directly from Sir William Bruce's slightly earlier west façade at Holyroodhouse, and indirectly from France, but the handling of the classical elements, though bolder and more imaginative than Bruce's, betrays a complete lack of understanding of their underlying principles. Yet critical analysis cannot altogether resolve the design of Drumlanrig into a mere assemblage of unrelated parts, for the overall effect is one of immense dignity and splendour, a unique alliance of the Castellated and Renaissance styles in which Scottish Baronial is unexpectedly translated into Baroque.

Apart from Viscount Tarbat's contemporary but much less pretentious mansion at

Royston, Midlothian (now known as Caroline Park), Drumlanrig was about the last of the great courtyard-houses stemming directly from the castles of the later Middle Ages, for with Bruce's reconstruction of Holyroodhouse in 1671–80, classical architecture had at last come of age in Scotland and the days of the independent native school were already numbered.

Artillery Fortifications

The manufacture of gunpowder appears to have been introduced into Europe at the beginning of the fourteenth century, and within a comparatively short period the use of cannon in warfare became quite widespread. Weapons of this type may first have been used against the Scots during Edward II's invasion of 1327, and were probably again employed at the siege of Stirling Castle some ten years later. The earliest guns were small breech-loading pieces, but by the end of the fourteenth century much larger cannon were being manufactured, including massive siege-weapons known as bombards, which were capable of discharging heavy stone shot. So far as Scotland was concerned, the considerable expense of such ordnance made it very much a monopoly of the Crown, and the royal army appears to have been equipped with several of these pieces by the middle of the fifteenth century, the most celebrated of them being Mons Meg itself, now preserved at Edinburgh Castle, which weighs 5 tons and was capable of projecting a stone shot of more than 500 lb. for a distance of nearly 3000 yd. Nonetheless, early artillery was far from being the invincible weapon that it is sometimes made out to have been cumbersome, expensive, unreliable, and inaccurate, it was long before it won universal acceptance or exercised any considerable influence upon military architecture.

At first, provision for the defensive use of firearms was primarily a matter of the adaptation of existing methods of fortification. Thus the customary archers' firing-slits in curtain-walls and towers began to be replaced by apertures designed to house small cannon or hand-guns—though the precise manner in which these weapons were mounted is not always apparent. In Britain the earliest gun-ports were of the 'inverted key-hole' type, comprising long narrow slits rising from circular holes some 6 in. in diameter. Such gun-ports began to appear in England during the last decades of the fourteenth century, and are first found in Scotland during the following century, usually in buildings that incorporate no other features specifically related to the use of firearms; good examples can be seen at Craigmillar, Threave and Mugdock. During the sixteenth century horizontal wide-mouthed gun-ports came into fashion, to be joined as the century progressed by numerous other varieties, some evidently designed to accommodate hack-buts, hand-guns, or pistols, and others, to judge from their dispositions, intended solely for display or decoration. Many castles and houses of the period incorporate such gun-loops, but few have any comprehensively designed scheme of defence; one of the most notable exhibitions of strength occurs at Noltland Castle,

Orkney, where the many tiers of horizontal gun-ports give the building something of the appearance of a naval man-of-war (*16*).

Likewise the threat from besieging artillery could to some extent be met by adaptation and improvisation. Heavy cannon had a lower trajectory and greater penetrating power than the traditional siege-engine, and the high walls and towers of thirteenth- and fourteenth-century castles could become an unnecessary embarrassment to later defenders. Efforts were therefore made to increase the thickness of defensive walls and, in some cases, to reduce their height. During the construction of the Half Moon Battery at Edinburgh Castle in 1574, for example, the fourteenth-century tower known as David's Tower was reduced in height, partially packed with rubble, and then completely engulfed within the new work, where it remained undiscovered until 1912. At Tantallon, where a siege by a royal army equipped with heavy cannon had been successfully resisted in 1528, instructions were afterwards given to fill up all apertures in the main curtain-wall with masonry to render the castle even more secure for the future. This work can still be seen today, as may also the traces of outer ditches and ramparts on the landward side of the Castle, evidently forming part of a scheme of artillery defence.

Measures of the same sort appear in more coherent form in the few buildings designed specifically with the new arm in mind. The earliest of these appears to be the royal castle of Ravenscraig, Fife, where a promontory site is straddled by a curtain-wall and terminal D-shaped towers, all of unusually massive construction. The towers and the lower parts of the curtain are equipped with inverted key-hole gun-ports of early form, while the upper portion of the curtain carries a later artillery-platform whose embrasures house wide-mouthed ports of sixteenth-century type. The main residential accommodation is contained within the western tower, which retains a remarkable sloping wall-head evidently intended to deflect the full impact of an assailant's shot.

Ravenscraig was followed half a century later by the Forework at Stirling Castle (*30*), which was approaching completion under the direction of two masons of the Royal Works, John Lockhart and John Yorkstoun, in 1508. It comprises a central gatehouse, a curtain-wall incorporating two D-shaped towers, and two terminal rectangular towers, the Prince's Tower on the west balancing the Elphinstone Tower on the east. The curtain measures up to 12 ft. in thickness and may originally have carried an artillery-platform like those at Ravenscraig. Most of the gun-ports in the Forework are of dumb-bell shape, having circular holes at the top of the vertical slit as well as at the bottom; loops of this type occur also at Threave, but it is difficult to see what advantages they offered over the key-hole variety, apart perhaps from facilitating the dispersal of powder smoke.

Cadzow Castle, Lanarkshire, has also been claimed as an early Scottish example of artillery fortification, though a close inspection of the existing remains suggests, to this writer at least, that their present appearance reflects the activity of a romanticising landscape gardener rather than of a military engineer. But if 'ennobled Cadyow's Gothic towers' turn out to be Gothick after all, the same can hardly be said of the neighbouring castle of Craignethan, an equal favourite of Sir Walter Scott, and his model for Tillietudlem in *Old Mortality*. The existing arrangements at Craignethan appear to be largely the creation of Sir James Hamilton of Finnart, one of James V's courtiers, whose career as an administrator in the Royal Works had given him the opportunity to cultivate an interest in architecture and to gain a close familiarity with building practice. The site itself is inherently vulnerable to artillery assault from the high bank that overlooks it from the west, but every effort was made to minimise the effects of these natural disadvantages. The principal residential building, a tower-house of novel design, is of unusually squat proportions, and is protected on all sides by a curtain-wall having rectangular corner and intermediate towers. The curtain on the exposed western side of this inner court was demolished in 1579, but there is evidence to show that it had an overall thickness of no less than 16 ft.; no doubt it was provided with gun-ports, as are the surviving curtain-walls and towers. Separating the west curtain from an outer courtyard there is a broad flat-bottomed ditch within which recent excavations have revealed the remains of a loopholed traverse and of a caponier (*31*) (a covered passage designed to rake the ditch with cross fire). Considerable interest attaches to this discovery, for if, as seems probable, the lay-out of the west curtain and ditch formed part of Hamilton's reconstruction of the Castle in 1532–40, the Craignethan caponier has the distinction of being the earliest known example of its kind in Britain.

These early artillery works, like their counterparts in other countries, involved no radical departure from medieval methods of fortification, but the invention of a new style of angular bastion in Italy during the fourth decade of the sixteenth century soon led to revolutionary developments in military practice. Such bastions, specifically designed to mount artillery, usually took the form of solid, straight-sided earthen platforms, having external revetments of timber, brick, or masonry. They were connected to the main curtain by flanking walls, but the exact angle of projection—and thus the overall size and shape of the bastion—was capable of almost infinite variation in the designer's search for a scientifically complete defensive system in which all exposed surfaces were protected by adequate flanking fire, a search that was to continue to exercise the minds of military engineers for almost four centuries.

No considerable examples of such artillery fortifications of the pre-Cromwellian period now survive in Scotland, although it was the threat of a Scottish invasion that led to the construction of the important early Elizabethan defences of Berwick-upon-Tweed. North of the Border there may be seen the remains of one or two temporary works such as the 'French Camp' at Dunglass, East Lothian, constructed during the English occupation of Haddington in 1548–9, while the recently discovered Petworth drawing makes it clear that Leith was elaborately, if unsuccessfully, fortified to meet the English siege of 1560. The Cromwellian occupation itself produced four major citadel-forts

28 Earl's Palace, Kirkwall, Orkney.
Early seventeenth century

29 (*Below*) Drumlanrig Castle,
Dumfriesshire. 1679–90

30 Forework and Palace, Stirling Castle. *c.* 1500–10 and 1540–2

31 Caponier and ditch, Craignethan
Castle, Lanarkshire. *c.* 1530–40

32 (*Below*) Ruthven Barracks,
Invernessshire. *c.* 1720

33 Fort George, Inverness-shire. *c.* 1745–63

sited respectively at Inverness, Perth, Leith and Ayr, but very little remains of any of these works today, although in most cases their designs are known from contemporary drawings. The slightly later fort at Lerwick, Shetland, which was erected to protect Bressay Sound during the Dutch war of 1665-7, remains reasonably intact, however, having been partially reconstructed at the end of the eighteenth century, when it was renamed Fort Charlotte. The internal buildings have disappeared, but the massive curtain-wall and corner bastions survive, the roughly pentagonal enclosure covering an area of more than two acres.

But far more government money was to be expended in North Britain to maintain law and order within the Highlands than was ever to be required to meet the threat of foreign invasion. Already at the end of Charles II's reign there had been a project for strengthening the defences of Stirling by the erection of a powerful artillery-fort at the north end of Stirling Bridge. Although this came to nothing, a new fort, named Fort William, was constructed at Inverlochy in 1690, while in 1708-14 the outer defences of Stirling Castle were extended and remodelled, and in the period between the rebellions of 1715 and 1745 a comprehensive programme for the pacification of the Highlands was carried out using the same methods that had enabled the Roman armies to subjugate Lowland Scotland 1500 years previously. Roads and bridges were built where they had never been built before, garrison posts were established at strategic points, the defences of existing castles were improved, and two new major forts, Fort Augustus and Fort George, were erected on the line of the Great Glen.

The most interesting of the garrison posts is the group comprising Inversnaid in Stirlingshire, and Kiliwhimen, Ruthven and Bernera in Inverness-shire. Suitable sites for these works were agreed upon by the Board of Ordnance in 1717 and building began in the following year under the direction of James Smith (p. 101), and was continued by his successors Andrews Jelfe and J. L. Romer, Inversnaid being completed early in 1720 a little in advance of the other three barracks. The designs of all four works were based upon a common plan in which a pair of barrack blocks faced each other across a square courtyard enclosed on its two remaining sides by vaulted rampart-walks. Two tower bastions projected from diagonally opposite corners of the enclosure to provide flanking fire, while direct fire could be maintained from loop-holes in the ramparts and in the rear walls of the barrack blocks. Kiliwhimen and Bernera were slightly larger than Inversnaid and Ruthven, and their barrack blocks were designed as double tenements. Little now remains at Inversnaid and less at Kiliwhimen, but the other two barracks are comparatively well preserved, Ruthven (32), in upper Speyside, standing upon a particularly fine site formerly occupied by the castle of the medieval lords of Badenoch.

Fort Augustus and Fort George were conceived upon an altogether more massive scale, the first as the permanent administrative headquarters of all the Highland garrisons, and the second as a key fortress guarding the head of the Great Glen and the opening of the Moray Firth. Fort Augustus, completed between 1729 and 1742, proved surprisingly vulnerable, falling to a Jacobite army in 1746 after receiving a direct hit upon a powder magazine. It was at once slighted, but was afterwards repaired, and reoccupied until the time of the Crimean War; the remains have since been absorbed within the Benedictine monastery of the same name. Fort George, at Ardersier Point, was begun soon after the Forty-five and was completed by about 1763 under the direction of Colonel William Skinner, Chief Engineer in North Britain. The plan is adapted to the converging promontory-site (33), the main weight of the defence being concentrated upon the landward side, where the principal curtain-wall and angle bastions are strengthened by a broad ditch and a ravelin; the works occupy an area of some 16 acres and the plain, well-proportioned, Georgian barrack blocks contain accommodation for about 2000 men. Unlike Fort Augustus, Fort George has enjoyed a singularly uneventful history and remains today much as Skinner left it, its excellent state of preservation and well-documented record of construction making it one of the most interesting examples of Hanoverian artillery fortification in Britain.

Sites or Buildings Specially Worth Visiting

The use of italics signifies that a structure is, at the time of writing, the subject of a long-standing arrangment giving either regular or occasional public access. Buildings marked by an asterisk may usually be visited by appointment.

Motte-and-Bailey Castles

Aberdeenshire	Doune of Invernochty
	Bass of Inverurie
	Peel of Lumphanan
Dumfriesshire	Auldton Motte, Moffat
Kirkcudbrightshire	Mote of Urr
Lanarkshire	Carnwath Motte
	Coulter Motte Hill
Morayshire	*Duffus Castle*
Stirlingshire	Sir John de Graham's Castle, Fintry
Roxburghshire	*Hawick Motte*
Wigtownshire	*Druchtag Motehill*, Mochrum

Simple Castles of Enclosure

Argyll	*Castle Sween*, Knapdale
	Mingary Castle, Ardnamurchan
	Skipness Castle, Kintyre
Ayrshire	*Loch Doon Castle*
Inverness-shire	Castle Roy, Nethybridge
	Castle Tioram, Moidart

Great Castles of Enclosure

Aberdeenshire	*Kildrummy Castle*
Argyll	*Dunstaffnage Castle*, Oban
Bute	*Rothesay Castle*
Dumfriesshire	*Caerlaverock Castle*
East Lothian	*Dirleton Castle*
	Tantallon Castle
Inverness-shire	*Inverlochy Castle*, Fort William
Lanarkshire	*Bothwell Castle*
Morayshire	Lochindorb Castle, Grantown

Hall-Houses

Dumfriesshire	Morton Castle, Thornhill
Fife	Tulliallan Castle, Kincardine-on-Forth
Nairnshire	Rait Castle, Nairn

Tower-Houses

Aberdeenshire	Craigievar Castle
	*Drum Castle
	Huntly Castle
Angus	*Affleck Castle*, Monikie
	Claypotts Castle, Broughty Ferry
	Glamis Castle
Argyll	Carrick Castle
Berwickshire	*Greenknowe Tower*, Gordon
	*Thirlestane Castle, Lauder
Clackmannanshire	*Castle Campbell*, Dollar
	Sauchie Tower, Alloa
Dumfriesshire	Amisfield Tower
	Comlongon Castle, Ruthwell
	Gilnockie or Hollows Tower, Canonbie
Fife	*Scotstarvet Tower*
Kincardineshire	*Crathes Castle*
Kinross-shire	*Aldie Castle, Rumbling Bridge
	Lochleven Castle
Kirkcudbrightshire	*Orchardton Tower*, Castle Douglas
	Threave Castle, Castle Douglas
Inverness-shire	*Kisimul Castle*, Barra
Lanarkshire	*Craignethan Castle*, Lanark
Midlothian	Borthwick Castle
	Craigmillar Castle, Edinburgh
	Crichton Castle
	Holyroodhouse, Edinburgh
	Liberton Tower, Edinburgh
Morayshire	*Duffus Castle*
	Spynie Palace
Peeblesshire	Barns Tower
	Neidpath Castle, Peebles

Roxburghshire	*Hermitage Castle*, Newcastleton
	Smailholm Tower
Selkirkshire	Newark Castle, Philiphaugh
	Oakwood Tower, Selkirk
Stirlingshire	*Bardowie Castle

Courtyard Castles and Palaces

Aberdeenshire	*Huntly Castle*
	Tolquhoun Castle, Tarves
Ayrshire	*Rowallan Castle*, Kilmarnock
Banffshire	Boyne Castle, Portsoy
Dumfriesshire	*Caerlaverock Castle*
Fife	*Falkland Palace*
	St Andrew's Castle
Midlothian	*Caroline Park, Edinburgh
	Crichton Castle
	Edinburgh Castle
	Heriot's Hospital, Edinburgh
	Holyroodhouse, Edinburgh
	Pinkie House, Musselburgh
Orkney	*Earl's Palace*, Kirkwall
Peeblesshire	Drochil Castle, Romanno Bridge
Perthshire	*Doune Castle*
Stirlingshire	Mugdock Castle, Strathblane
	Stirling Castle
West Lothian	*Linlithgow Palace*

Artillery Fortifications

Dunbartonshire	*Dumbarton Castle*
Fife	*Ravenscraig Castle*, Dysart
Inverness-shire	Bernera Garrison, Glenelg
	Fort George, Ardersier
	Ruthven Garrison, Kingussie
Lanarkshire	*Craignethan Castle*, Lanark
Midlothian	*Edinburgh Castle*
Orkney	*Noltland Castle*, Westray
Shetland	*Fort Charlotte*, Lerwick
Stirlingshire	*Stirling Castle*

II LAIRDS' HOUSES

While the castles and tower-houses of the Middle Ages and the great country mansions of the later Stuart and Georgian eras are familiar to all students of Scottish architecture, very little attention has been given to the type of building that forms the subject of the present chapter. The houses comprising this group may be defined broadly as the residences of lesser landholders of the later sixteenth, seventeenth and early eighteenth centuries—a category that embraces both the lower ranks of the baronial class and the 'bonnet lairds' who figure so prominently in records of Scottish domestic life of that period. The causes that led to the emergence of so numerous a class of small landholders at this time are by no means clear, but many families seem to have owed their origin to the introduction of feu-farm tenures by the great landowners, and in particular by the Crown and the Church, at the end of the Middle Ages. This involved the replacement of the customary short leases by heritable tenures that gave tenants security of occupation, and thus encouraged them to improve and develop their holdings and to build themselves substantial dwelling houses of stone and lime. The secularisation of ecclesiastical property at the Reformation led ultimately to a further distribution of land among the gentry, but small estates seem always to have been more numerous than large ones, and the traditional picture of the assets of a Lowland laird—'a pickle land, a mickle debt, a doocot and a lawsuit'—finds a good deal of support in the pages of contemporary writers. With the beginning of the agrarian revolution about the middle of the eighteenth century, however, and the coming of a new generation of planting, farming and improving landowners, the days of the small laird were numbered, and their estates were gradually absorbed by more substantial proprietors, their dwellings, as often as not, becoming farmhouses.

Lairds' houses do not conform to a standard architectural pattern throughout the period now under review—indeed, it will be suggested that a well-defined process of evolution can be observed. They also vary a good deal in size, in accordance with the means of the builder, and likewise in distribution, the houses of Highland lairds and tacksmen generally following a separate and more primitive building tradition until the eighteenth century (p. 237). But certain common factors are apparent, notably a conservatism and informality that betoken the work of local craftsmen and designers, and stand in sharp contrast to the more academic essays of master-masons and architects of national reputation. The typical laird's house of the earlier part of the period is nowhere better portrayed than in John Galt's description of the mansion of Auldbiggins, that venerable residence of Laird Malachi Mailing, with its 'multiform aggregate of corners, and gables, and chimneys', its shapeless offices, and its conspicuously informal garden in which 'the luxuriant grass walks were never mowed but just before haytime, and every stock of kail and cabbage stood in its garmentry of curled blades, like a newmade Glasgow bailie's wife on the first Sunday after Michaelmas'.

The Legacy of the Tower-House

The laird's house of the seventeenth century evolved directly from the late medieval tower-house, but the development was so gradual as to make nonsense of any attempt at neat classification. Individual buildings erected during the period of transition, that is to say from about the time of the Reformation to the Civil War, combine castellated and domestic features in very variable proportions and contemporary writers themselves display little common agreement in their use of such terms as castle, house, tower and fortalice. Moreover, the tower-house had from the first been a dual-purpose building balancing the claims of security against those of amenity, and the ultimate tipping of the scales towards domesticity was no more than the logical conclusion of a process that had begun in medieval times. It has already been pointed out that the simple tower-house of traditional form continued to be regarded as a suitable form of gentleman's residence until well into the seventeenth century (p. 43), but if any confirmation of this statement is required it can readily be found in the remarks of English and other foreign travellers of the period. Sir William Brereton, riding through West Lothian in 1636, 'observed gentlemen's houses built all castle-wise', while as late as 1689 Thomas Morer, writing of the Lowlands in general, noted that 'the houses of their quality are high and strong, and appear more like castles than houses', though he did add that 'now they begin to have better buildings, and to be very modish both in the fabrick and furniture of their dwellings'. But while it is clearly a mistake to think of buildings such as Coxton Tower as anachronisms, it is equally important to realise that not all post-Reformation tower-houses were of such conservative design.

Outwardly, at least, the most noticeable development was a gradual withering away of specifically defensive features. Gun-loops, for instance, tended to be provided more sparingly, and their arrangement frequently suggests that they were designed more for display than for hostile use. Buildings such as Glenbuchat, Aberdeenshire (1590), which incorporates a comprehensive series of enfilading loops, had few successors, the protection of the entrance-doorway by one or two flanking loops, as at Newton, Perthshire, and Pitreavie, Fife, evidently being considered an adequate measure of defence. Killochan Castle, Ayrshire (1586), like its near relation Castle of Park, Wigtownshire (1590), has a bare minimum of gun-loops, but in addition there is corbelled machicolation overlooking the main entrance-doorway. This feature, too, was becoming uncommon, although there are good examples at Elcho Castle, Perthshire (34), and Old Leckie, Stirlingshire, at which latter building double machicolation, yett, and gun-loop guard the entrance, while all other parts are left quite undefended. One of the latest instances in which effective use is made of this form of defence is at Tullibole, Kinross-shire (1608), where an aggressively crenellated box-machicolation belies the inscription on the doorway beneath it: 'The Lord is onlie my defence'.

It is invariably at the entrance-doorway that defensive precautions persisted longest, and the wrought-iron yett itself remained a standard fitting until about the time of the Civil War, despite periodical attempts at official discouragement such as the Privy Council decree of 1606 (optimistically) entitled 'Irone Yettis in the bordouris ordanit to be removit and turnit in plew Irnis'. At Muchalls, Kincardineshire, an interesting transitional building erected by the Burnetts of Leys between 1619 and 1627, the house itself is almost entirely domestic in character, but the courtyard is defensible—although perhaps less a serious than a mock fortification. The entrance-gateway is flanked by elaborately moulded gun-loops and was formerly surmounted by a parapet-walk and crenellated open rounds.

No less significant were the developments that were taking place at the wall-head. One of the chief defensive provisions of the earlier towers was the open parapet-walk, which was often corbelled out over the wall-face beneath and equipped with angle-turrets; the main roof usually rose within the parapet-walk, its heavy outer covering of stone flags being partially protected by the battlements. In the post-Reformation tower-house, however, there was an increasing tendency for the open parapet to disappear, and for the roof, now invariably a construction of slate and timber, to be extended in an unbroken sweep from apex to external wall-face, as at Killochan, where there is an enclosed parapet on one side. An intermediate stage in this process is well illustrated at the two Fife castles of Fordell (1580) and Earlshall (1546–1617), where in each case the pitched roof of the main block is continuous to the eaves, but open battlements crown an angle-turret. Elcho (34) and Balmanno, Perthshire, show a similar development, while at Gogar House, Midlothian (1626), a further step has been taken, the parapet being transformed into an elegant classical balustrade.

Angle-turrets, too, were going out of fashion. The primitive open rounds of the early towers had been succeeded by the picturesque conical-roofed 'studies' of the Scottish Baronial style, but even before the end of the sixteenth century some buildings were being constructed with straightforward gabled roofs. Torwoodhead Castle, Stirlingshire (1566), provides an early instance of this form, while the slightly later castle of Tilqu-hilly, Kincardineshire, has interesting vestigial angle-turrets formed by the squaring up of the rounded external angles a little below eaves level. Another good example of transitional wall-head development (if it is not a result of reconstruction) occurs at Craigston, Aberdeenshire, erected by John Urquhart, the 'Tutor of Cromartie', in 1604–7; here the angle-turrets are represented by enriched corbel-courses and the open parapet by an ornamental balcony and mock crenellation. This evident reluctance to abandon the traditional postures of defence was probably due more to social than to architectural factors, for the castle had always been recognised as a symbol of rank and authority. Sir Robert Kerr tried to make this point to the Earl of Lothian when he wrote to him about proposed improvements at Ancrum House, Roxburghshire, in 1636: 'By any meanes do not take away the battlement, as some gave me counsale to do—for that is the grace of the house, and makes it looke lyk a castle, and hence so nobleste, as the other would make it looke lyke a peele.' But most, at least, of Kerr's contemporaries were more ready to take the advice contained in a later section of the same letter: 'you must make all things of bewty and ornament and vse—I love to see a house not straitted or minsed, but to have aneugh of roome in a large noble manner'.

It was, of course, only natural that as the requirements of defence grew less pressing more attention should be given to display and embellishment. This development is particularly noticeable in the Aberdeenshire tower-houses of the Scottish Baronial school (p. 45), but it is not confined to any one region or style. The quasi-classical decoration of the dormer-window pediments at Castle Menzies, Perthshire, the bold Elizabethan pierced work at Hill House, Dunfermline (35), and the elaborate Anglo-Flemish ornament of Winton House, East Lothian, are all inspired by a common motive. Boldly carved armorial panels and commemorative inscriptions became an extremely popular means of adornment at this period. At Castle Menzies, erected by James Menzies in 1577, the initials and coat of arms of the laird and his wife, Barbara Stewart, appear over the entrance-doorway, while further initials and a pious text are carved on a dormer window. Similar examples can be quoted from every part of the country, from Muness in Shetland (1598), whose builder was evidently a man of some poetic sensibility:

> List ze to knaw yis bulding quha began
> Laurence the Bruce he was that worthy man
> Quha ernestly his airis and ofspring prayis
> To help and not to hurt this vark aluayis

—to Killochan, Ayrshire, whose laird favoured a more matter-of-fact approach: 'This work was begyn the 1 of Marche 1586 be Ihone Cathcart of Carltovn and Helene Wallace his spous.'

The taste for embellishment went beyond a concern for the external appearance of a building, for a general increase in the size of window openings, and the more frequent use of glass, opened up more opportunities in the field of interior decoration. The subject is not one that can be considered comprehensively here, but something should perhaps be said about the style of interior painted decoration that is such a characteristic feature of Scottish buildings of this period. As a number of surviving fragments of medieval paintings in castles and churches bear witness, decorative painting itself was no novelty. Its enduring popularity was probably due partly to its comparative cheapness, and partly to the fact that it could be used either in conjunction with other decorative materials, such as carved woodwork and wrought-iron work, or by itself, applied to canvas hangings, wall plaster and timber boards.

34 Elcho Castle, Perthshire. Late sixteenth century

35 Hill House, Dunfermline, Fife. 1623

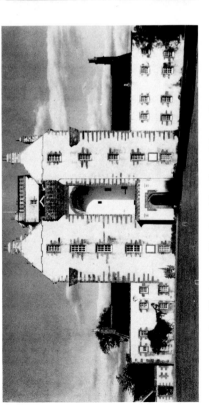

36 Craigston Castle, Aberdeenshire. 1604–7

37 Lochryan, Wigtownshire. 1701

38 Innes House, Morayshire. *William Ayton*, 1640–53
39 Glamis Castle, Angus. Seventeenth century and earlier

40 Old Hamilton House, Prestonpans, East Lothian. 1628

It was in the decoration of walls and ceilings (*46*) that the painters of the post-Reformation period chiefly excelled. Drawing upon a rich vocabulary of medieval and Renaissance ornament culled from imported pattern-books and from the armorial and genealogical associations of their patrons, native craftsmen developed a distinctive style of interior decoration which persisted until English fashions in panelling and modelled plasterwork gradually asserted themselves in the years after the Union of the Crowns. This type of decoration is, of course, found in churches, palaces and town mansions, as well as in lairds' houses, but many good examples are contained in structures of this latter class, the most outstanding being the painted ceilings at Northfield, East Lothian, and at Earlshall. The former are of open-beam construction and, because they lay concealed beneath later plasterwork until recent years, the colours retain all their original freshness and brilliance. The gallery ceiling at Earlshall (1620) is close-boarded and the design, executed in black-and-white, draws upon themes from heraldry and natural history; the upper portion of the walls, also boarded, is painted as an arcaded frieze.

Important as changes of attitude in matters of defence and of embellishment may have been, the most significant developments in the transition from tower-house to laird's house were those relating to plan-form. The tower-house is, by definition, a structure occupying a very limited surface area in relation to its height, that is to say it is essentially a tall narrow building in which rooms are placed one above the other. There was, therefore, a definite limit to the amount of dwelling space that could be provided and, although problems brought about by steadily rising standards of accommodation had to some extent been met by the introduction of the L- and Z-plans, by the later sixteenth century a point had been reached beyond which further expansion could take place only by means of a fundamental change of plan-form.

Thus it came about that proprietors who, unable to aspire to a full-scale courtyard lay-out, nevertheless felt unduly restricted within an orthodox tower-house, found that an acceptable compromise could be achieved by limited longitudinal expansion—a solution which in some respects represented a return to the hall-house form that had been popular during the thirteenth and fourteenth centuries (p. 33). Melgund Castle, Angus (*41*), provides an early instance of this development. Probably erected soon after the middle of the sixteenth century, the building comprises a four-storeyed tower-house of L-plan, from whose east wall there extends a contemporary domestic range of two storeys. The vaulted basement of the

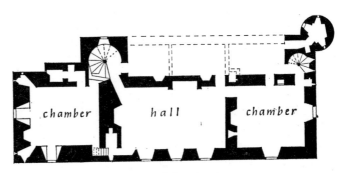

41 Melgund Castle, Angus

extension contains a kitchen and storerooms, while above there is a spacious hall and a withdrawing-room; communication between the two parts of the castle is maintained by means of a corridor provided with a turnpike staircase at each end. At Melgund, and likewise at Carnasserie, Argyll, where there is a similar arrangement but on a slightly smaller scale, tower-house and domestic range retain their separate identities and are roofed at different levels, but once the advantages of this type of plan came to be more generally appreciated such distinction of parts was usually abandoned. Torwoodhead Castle, built by Sir Alexander Forestar of Garden in 1566, is an early example of this form. The main block is planned as a single architectural unit and incorporates a vaulted basement, a principal floor and an attic, while a projecting stair-tower rises two storeys higher.

The same tendency towards horizontal expansion can be observed in the later tower-houses of Z-plan. At Glenbuchat the main block, while still containing only a single apartment at principal-floor level, is noticeably long in proportion to its breadth, while at Castle Menzies, Fordell and Earlshall a further extension of the main block permits two principal apartments to be placed *en suite*. At Elcho (*34*) additional complications are introduced by multiplying the number of projecting towers to provide a greater number of private rooms and better circulation, but what is probably the most striking example of an elongated Z-plan design occurs at Muness, where the main block measures 74 ft. in length by about 26 ft. in width over all—a dimensional ratio of almost three to one. The ground floor is vaulted and contains a range of three store-cellars, while at first-floor level a central hall of generous dimensions is flanked by two private apartments each of which communicates with a smaller room in one of the angle-towers; a similar arrangement obtains on the second floor.

Comparatively few lairds required, or could afford, larger buildings than these, but in such cases longitudinal expansion could be carried a stage further to produce a part-courtyard lay-out, most structures of this class being sufficiently removed in appearance from an orthodox tower-house as no longer to warrant the application of this term. This development can be seen at Newark Castle, Renfrewshire, and at Barra Castle, Aberdeenshire, although in both these cases the existing Jacobean lay-out seems to have been achieved by the reconstruction and extension of older buildings. At Muchalls, however, the house was planned as a whole; it extends round three sides of an open court, the vaulted ground-floor providing ample service-accommodation, and the upper floors containing a series of well-appointed living-rooms, some of them enriched with modelled plasterwork such as was then becoming fashionable.

A slightly less ambitious but much neater variant of the same theme could be contrived by limiting and regularising the size and projection of the courtyard wings to form a symmetrical double-L- (or half-H-) plan. Craigston (*36*) provides a uniquely compact example of such an arrangement, the two wings being so close together that the space between them can be spanned at eaves level by an arched balcony. More typical, however, are Pitreavie and Castle Stewart, Inverness-shire; in the former the outer walls of the wings are direct extensions of the gable walls of the main block, while in the latter the wings are set further apart in the manner of angle-towers. Moreover, in each case the symmetry of the plan is plainly reflected in the elevations—an indication that master-masons were at last beginning to grasp some of the basic principles of Renaissance design. Baberton, Midlothian, follows the same form as Pitreavie, and in both buildings extruded circular stair-towers rise within the inner re-entrant angles of main block and wing. The house was erected in 1622–3 by James Murray of Kilbaberton, Master of Works to the Crown, who, as a former master-wright and an acknowledged 'architect' (a term rarely used at this period), may have been personally responsible for its design. This type of plan continued to be employed until the end of the seventeenth century, a late and exceptionally attractive instance being Gallery, Angus, a plain harled building which probably dates from the year 1680. Neither Baberton nor Gallery retains any defensive features, but both are tall narrow buildings of single-room width, their strong vertical expression still clearly betraying the influence of the tower-house.

The double-L-plan could be combined with the T-plan, as in the late seventeenth-century house of Philipstoun, West Lothian, or developed into a full H-plan by extending the flanking wings from both sides of the main block instead of from one side only. Neither variant became common, but the latter form was employed to particularly good effect in a small group of lairds' houses of the later Stuart period. The most impressive of these is Bannockburn House, Stirlingshire, a symmetrically planned four-storeyed building in which two staircases serve a series of well-appointed public and private rooms; the lay-out is unusually formal for a house of this class and suggests the hand of a professional architect rather than of a master-craftsman. The external detail is of Scottish Renaissance character, by then somewhat old-fashioned, but the decorative plasterwork of the interiors is in the latest Restoration style and is comparable in quality and workmanship to that of the State Apartments at the Palace of Holyroodhouse.

Of even more distinctive appearance is Lochryan, Wigtownshire, built by Colonel Agnew of Croach in 1701. Here the main block is less elongated than at Bannockburn and houses the single main staircase at its rear. The most remarkable feature of the design is the treatment of the elevations, for the main block rises through the hipped roofs of the wings and presents a lofty battlemented parapet to the main approach (37)—a delightful *jeu d'esprit* which can be regarded either as a last assertion of the tower-house form or as an anticipation of romanticism. Considering the remote situation of the house, the interior decoration is unexpectedly sophisticated, a number of rooms being furnished with painted pine panelling and elegant bolection-moulded fireplaces of stone or marble. The last house of this group to be considered is Kincraig, Fife, where the H- and T-plans are combined, the fifth limb being formed by an old-fashioned turn-pike staircase that projects from the centre of the rear elevation of the main block. The building must have been erected at the very end of the seventeenth century and although the plan itself is distinctly conservative, the halting classicism of the elevations evidently represents an attempt by a local master-mason to employ the new architectural vocabulary that was then being introduced by Sir William Bruce and his circle (p. 93).

Conservatism of plan-form is even more marked in the case of the L-plan, whose chief advantages had been exploited by tower-house designers as early as the fourteenth century but which remained in common use until the time of the Union. Among lairds' houses that still retain one or two defensive features, Castle of Park (1590) shows the L-plan in its simplest form, all the principal apartments being contained within the main block, and the wing being no more than a stair-tower. At Gilbertfield, Lanarkshire, however, erected some 20 years later, the wing extends beyond the stair and houses additional rooms at each level, bringing the number of living apartments up to a total of eight.

An economical method of increasing the amount of accommodation available in a house of limited size was to extrude the staircase, the most convenient position for it to occupy being the re-entrant angle formed between main block and wing, where it could provide direct access to rooms in both portions of the building. This expedient had occasionally been adopted in the late medieval tower-house, but it did not become common until after the Reformation. The staircase could be formed in a number of different ways. During the second half of the sixteenth century it was not uncommon for the lower part of the stair to be enclosed within the wing and for the upper portion alone to be extruded by means of corbelling. This device is seen in its most rudimentary form at Castle of Park itself, where the garret stair takes this form, while at Brackie Castle, Angus (1581), Old Jerviston House, Lanarkshire, and at Killochan (1586) the process is carried a stage further. At Brackie and Jerviston a broad turnpike-stair rises within the wing to the first floor, while the remaining levels are reached by means of a much narrower stair corbelled out in the re-entrant angle. The arrangements at Killochan are similar, but the lower portion of the stair is of the scale-and-platt variety (that is to say composed of short straight flights and landings) providing an unusually dignified approach to the hall, while the square tower that houses the continuation incorporates an entrance porch at ground-floor level; the upper floors are served by additional subsidiary stairs.

Such an arrangement enabled the upper levels of the wing to be given over to living accommodation, but it was also possible to free the lower levels of the wing for the same purpose by extruding the whole of the staircase within a tower rising from ground level. This lay-out occurs at Randerston, Fife, and Innerpeffray, Perthshire, both of which date from about the turn of the sixteenth and seventeenth centuries, while at Balmanno a further refinement is introduced by making the staircase-tower itself residential above second-floor level and thrusting out the uppermost portion of the stair between tower and main block.

One of the most interesting structures of this class, and one of the last lairds' houses to incorporate specifically defensive features, is Leslie Castle, Aberdeenshire. At first glance the building might be taken for a late sixteenth-century tower-house, complete with vaulted basement, angle-turrets, iron-grilled windows and a generous array of wide-mouthed gun-ports. Yet the egg-and-dart ornament of the corbel-courses, the plain gable-copings and the tall diagonally mounted chimneys clearly point to a later period, and there is no reason to distrust the evidence of an inscription which records

42 Leslie Castle, Aberdeenshire

that the building was founded in 1661. The plan is of L-form (42) with the customary extruded stair-tower, the stair itself being of scale-and-platt construction with a hollow square newel. Above the service quarters there are three residential floors, some of the rooms containing close garderobes (the usual sanitary provision at that time) and built-in cupboards. The erection of this businesslike little castle in a remote corner of Aberdeenshire brings the history of the fortified house in Scotland to an end, for, as Lord Strathmore wrote of his own stronghold of Huntly a few years later, 'such houses truly are worn quyt out of fashione, as feuds are, which is a great happiness'.

The typical L-plan laird's house of the mid and late seventeenth century is a plain three- or four-storeyed building having an extruded stair-tower, which contains the main entrance-doorway at ground level. The tower is commonly of octagonal or circular form, but may also be square, while the stair itself is usually of turnpike construction. Such buildings occur in fairly large numbers throughout the lowland area of the country. Two houses erected on the outskirts of Edinburgh shortly before the Civil War,

43 Pilrig House, Edinburgh

Peffermill and Pilrig (43), provide good examples of the circular stair-tower, while the octagonal form can be seen at Crichton House, Midlothian, and Auchenbowie, Stirlingshire, and the square form at Kersie Mains, in the same county. Of similar design, but more refined execution, are Hill House, Dunfermline (35) and Innes House, Morayshire. The former, erected by William Monteith of Randieford in 1623, is ashlar fronted and displays moulded string-courses, carved window-pediments, and a remarkable pierce-lettered parapet. Innes (1640–53) is one of the most substantial houses of its class, the main block and the wing incorporating four storeys, and the square staircase-tower rising one floor higher (38). The treatment of the elevations resembles that at Hill House, but the detail is better carved and of more pronounced Scottish Renaissance character. Most lairds' houses of this type were built by local master-masons whose names are not recorded, but the Inneses of that Ilk could afford to look further afield for a designer and contemporary documentation shows that in this case William Ayton, the Edinburgh master-mason who had superintended the construction of much of Heriot's Hospital (p. 54), was paid £26 13s. 4d. Scots 'for drawing the form of the House on paper'. There seems little doubt that Ayton carved much of the ornamental detail himself, an illustration of the way in which the distinctive architectural fashions that had been developed in the great houses of Fife and the Lothians might be carried into the provinces.

The L-plan could be adapted to buildings of widely differing size without changing

44 Ford House, Midlothian

its basic form, a point that is clearly brought out when Innes is compared with Ford House, Midlothian (1680). The general lay-out of both houses is much the same, but the ground area of Ford is only half that of Innes, and there are only two storeys and an attic as against four full storeys. Despite its modest size Ford is one of the most attractive examples of its kind, the douce harled walls and wayward roof-line giving it an informal quality wholly appropriate to its purpose and situation (44).

The simple L-plan with internal staircase was not altogether lost sight of after the beginning of the seventeenth century. Barscobe House, Kirkcudbrightshire, erected by William Maclellan of Bombie in 1648, follows the pattern of Castle of Park, but is more thoroughly domesticated. The building is quite small, the wing being no more than a stair-tower; the accommodation comprises two storeys and an attic, the upper floor being lit by dormers. Bishop Graham's house at Breckness, Orkney (1633), is more akin to Gilbertfield in that the wing contains a series of living-rooms as well as the staircase. The lower flight of the stair is straight, however, and rises from an entrance-doorway placed, not within the re-entrant angle, but at the centre of the opposite wall of the main block.

Although the fortified private residence became obsolete after the Restoration, the ghost of the tower-house lived on in the vertical profile and medieval lay-out of the L-plan laird's house until the time of the Union. Smailholm House, Roxburghshire, erected (or perhaps thoroughly reconstructed) in the year 1707 itself, is an appropriate example with which to conclude this section. Three storeys and a garret in height, and of simple L-plan with the entrance-doorway in the re-entrant angle, Smailholm differs in no essential from its countless forebears, only the handsome oak stair that rises within the wing striking a contemporary note.

Another lay-out popular in the seventeenth century was the T-plan, a form that was arrived at by throwing out a staircase wing midway along one side of an elongated tower-house. Crosbie Castle, Ayrshire, affords a good illustration of this class of building. It rises to a height of three storeys and an attic and the main block is long enough to contain two or more rooms at each level. The central position of the staircase makes for exceptionally good circulation, convenient access being provided to apartments at both ends of the house. As in certain buildings of L-plan, the upper portion of the wing was often given over to living accommodation, the stair itself being corbelled out in one of the re-entrant angles. This arrangement can be seen at Tullibole (1608) and Old Leckie. In both houses the main stair rises to the first floor only, the ascent being continued by means of a corbelled turnpike, but at Leckie the lower portion of the original stair has been replaced by an eighteenth-century forestair. In addition to the main staircase each building has a subsidiary stair. At Tullibole the principal stair-tower is not central, being placed about two-thirds of the way along one of the long walls, while the sub-sidiary stair is diagonally placed on the opposite side of the house. At Leckie the additional stair was probably intended to be a service stair; it rises from the ground floor to the second floor as a projection within the remaining re-entrant angle of the principal staircase-tower and the main block. One of the most attractive of the smaller houses of this class is Williamstoun, Perthshire. In this case the stair-tower is round at base, where it houses the stair, but rectangular above, where it contains a small attic living-room; corbelling is employed both to vary the plan-form of the tower and to extrude the upper portion of the stair. In all these buildings the main entrance-doorway is placed at the foot of the stair-tower, thus providing ready access to the principal apartments at first- and second-floor levels without the necessity of traversing the service area on the ground floor. Few houses of this type can show as well-preserved an

internal lay-out as Pilmuir, East Lothian (1624) (45), where the upper floors contain a fine series of living-rooms, many of which retain their original pine panelling and modelled plasterwork.

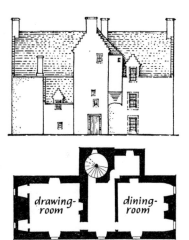

45 Pilmuir, East Lothian

One noticeable feature in the later evolution of the tower-house is the increasing extent to which the external elevations of a building came to be regarded as coherent units of design rather than mere assemblages of parts. At first this meant no more than making a half-hearted attempt to introduce some measure of regularity into the disposition of doorway and window openings. At Castle Menzies (1577), for example, the windows of each range are of fairly uniform size and shape, but the spacing is haphazard, the dormer windows in particular having little vertical corre-spondence with the first- and second-floor openings. At the somewhat later castle of Newark, Renfrewshire, however, there is a marked sym-metry in the design both of the front and of the rear elevations, and the same is true of Duntarvie, West Lothian, where the entrance-doorway is more or less centrally placed in the main frontage. When the plan itself was of symmetrical form a more comprehensive uniformity of treatment could be achieved, and the double-L-plan houses of Pitreavie and Castle Stewart have already been mentioned in this context. At Sir Hugh Paterson's house of Bannockburn, where the H-plan was employed, the front and rear elevations may originally have been almost identical, an arrangement that would have won the admiration of at least one of the laird's noble contemporaries—the Earl of Strathmore—who at about this time was struggling to bring the great medieval castle of Glamis (*39*) up to date, and 'did covet extremely to order my building so as the frontispiece might have a resemblance on both syds'.

A device commonly employed to give unity to the various constituent parts of an elevation (and one obviously deriving from the Renaissance vocabulary) was the continuous horizontal string-course. It appears in a rudimentary fashion at Duntarvie, where a single string-course extends across the central portion of the main front at first-floor level embracing an armorial-panel recess above the entrance-doorway, and in a more developed form at Pitreavie and Peffermill. At Innes (1640–53), however, moulded string-courses return round the principal frontage at each storey (*38*), binding main block, wing and stair-tower together and at the same time countering the strong vertical thrust of the building by horizontal subdivision.

Conservatism of plan-form inevitably made for conservatism of interior design, but a gradual improvement in standards of accommodation can be observed during the period under review. Since nearly all houses were of only single-room width it was usual for apartments to open directly into one another, as in medieval times, but short corridors were occasionally introduced. Something has already been said about the various types of staircase that were in use, the general tendency being for stairs to become wider and more spacious, and for the scale-and-platt stair to replace the traditional turnpike or wheel stair. One of the earliest dated examples of a scale-and-platt stair occurs at Killochan (1586), while at Duntarvie and Breckness, and perhaps also at Outters Hill, Midlothian, the stair seems to have risen in a series of straight flights. Larger buildings, such as Tullibole, sometimes had subsidiary stairs designed either for service purposes or to give individual access to private apartments.

Most of the earlier towers had been bound together by massive barrel-vaults at two or more levels, a device which made for great structural stability and at the same time afforded some protection against the risk of fire. As the defensive role of the tower-house receded, however, walls were reduced in thickness and vaults were used more sparingly, the lowermost storey alone being barrel-vaulted in most of the later towers. In post-Reformation times this precaution, too, was occasionally dispensed with, as at Leckie and Newton where the ground floor is partly vaulted and partly joisted, and many seventeenth-century lairds' houses such as Tullibole, Barscobe, Innes and Kersie Mains, were wholly unvaulted. Whether vaulted or unvaulted, however, the ground floor was invariably used, as in times past, for storage and service purposes, the principal living-rooms being placed at first- and second-floor levels and, so far as larger houses are

46 Painted Ceiling, Delgatie Castle, Aberdeenshire. 1597

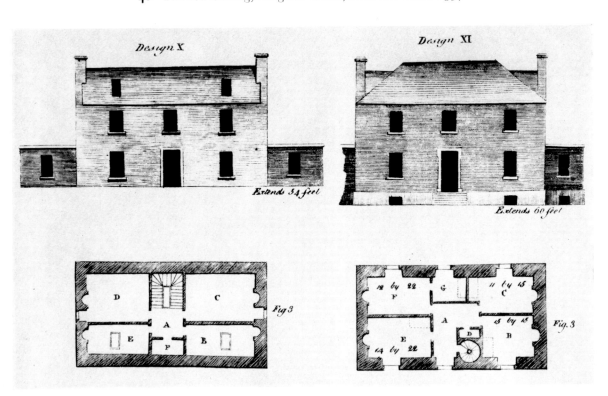

47 Designs for houses from *Rudiments of Architecture* (published 1773)

49 Forebank, Kincardineshire. 1757

51 Old Allangrange, Ross and Cromarty. 1760

48 Old Auchentroig, Stirlingshire. 1702

50 Catter House, Dunbartonshire. 1767

concerned, this arrangement persisted until the general introduction of the sunk basement in Georgian times. One of the few exceptions to the general rule occurs at Old
Hamilton House, Prestonpans (1628) (*40*), where a part courtyard lay-out provides
sufficient ground-floor superficial area to accommodate both living and service rooms.
In smaller houses, however, where service requirements were more modest, one of the
principal rooms was occasionally placed alongside the kitchen on the ground floor. This
seems to have been the arrangement at Crosbie, and likewise in the L-plan house of
Orchardhead, Stirlingshire (1678), but the practice did not become a general one until
the beginning of the eighteenth century.

Lairds' Houses of the Eighteenth Century

During the years immediately preceding the Act of Union a new type of medium-sized
domestic residence, which owed nothing to the tower-house, began to appear in
Scotland. The typical house of this class is a plain, rectangular, gable-roofed block of
two main storeys and an attic having a symmetrical plan in which a single large room is
placed on either side of a central staircase on each floor. More accommodation is sometimes obtained by the addition of a basement, and by increasing the width of the
building so that two rooms, instead of one, can be placed on each side of the stair. The
symmetry of the plan is clearly reflected in the elevations, particularly in the main front,
where the windows are almost always regularly disposed about a central entrance-
doorway at principal-floor level. In smaller houses kitchen and parlour usually occupy
the ground floor, with perhaps one other living-room and bedrooms above, but where
there is a service basement as many as three or four principal rooms may be grouped on
the two main floors.

The antecedents and origins of this type of house are not altogether clear. It has
already been pointed out that a degree of symmetry, both of plan and of elevation, can
be observed in certain lairds' houses of the seventeenth century. Clonbeith, Ayrshire
(1607), for instance, has a regular three-window front with a central entrance-doorway,
and there is a similar uniformity of window spacing in the main elevations of many
slightly later houses such as Kersie Mains and Pilmuir. On the upper floor of Spedlin's
Tower, Dumfriesshire, which was remodelled in the early seventeenth century, the
rooms are regularly disposed on each side of a central corridor, while Dalnair Manse,
Stirlingshire (1682), anticipates all the essential elements of the typical laird's house of
the following century with the exception of the central staircase. In general, however,
the contrast between the conservatism and retrospection of the pre-Union laird's house
and the advanced standards of design displayed in its Georgian successor is so marked
as to be explicable only in terms of a minor revolution in architectural styles.

But although very much of a novelty in Scotland in 1707, the small symmetrically
planned rectangular block had already become a standard house-plan of the lesser

English gentry, and the growth of intercourse between the two countries following upon the Union no doubt helped to promote its adoption in North Britain. English architectural fashions may, in fact, have penetrated into quite remote parts of the country as early as the period of the Cromwellian occupation, when the Ordnance Department engineers are known to have erected a number of important fortifications and barracks at strategic centres as far apart as Ayr and Inverness (p. 61). Certainly the houses that stood within this latter fortress, described by Richard Franck as 'built very low, but uniform', must have been greatly superior to the dwellings of local Highland lairds and tacksmen. Nor, in the years after the Restoration, can the architectural achievements of Sir William Bruce and his circle (p. 93) have failed to exercise a widespread influence, the new-fashioned classical mansions of the wealthy inevitably serving as models for the small laird and his master-builder. Illustrated pattern-books, too, helped to popularise the vocabulary of classical architecture. Most of these were of English origin, but there were also one or two native productions of varying degrees of originality. John Reid's *The Scots Gard'ner*, first published in 1683, illustrates a symmetrically planned house comprising a basement, two main storeys and an attic, describing it as 'little, yet very commodious & Cheap'. In point of fact the standard of accommodation provided is that of a small mansion, but many of the plates in George Jameson's *Thirty-three designs with the Orders of Architecture according to Palladio* (1765) and in the *Rudiments of Architecture: or, the Young Workman's Instructor* (1773) illustrate less commodious houses (47).

Whatever its antecedents, the small symmetrically designed house quickly found favour in all parts of the country, becoming the standard form of residence not only of the lowland laird and Highland tacksman, but also of the parish minister, of the merchant and master-craftsman in the provincial burgh and, ultimately, of the prosperous farmer. So far as the laird's house itself is concerned buildings of this type began to make their appearance about the last decade of the seventeenth century, most of the earlier examples being of the simplest design and of very modest dimensions. These were evidently the residences of the lowest ranks of the landowning class, a group which is known to have been particularly numerous at this period.

52 Old Auchentroig, Stirlingshire

Old Mains of Rattray, Perthshire, must have been one of the very first of these houses to have been erected. It rises to a height of two storeys and an attic and has a three-window front with a central entrance-doorway whose lintel bears a coat of arms, the name of the builder, David Crichton, and the date 1694—all the carving now being in a very decayed condition. The only other decorative features of the exterior are the skewputs, which are carved as human heads. The interior of Old Mains of Rattray has been much altered, but Old Auchentroig, Stirlingshire (48, 52), a house of very similar character built only eight years later, survives almost in its original condition. Here the lintel of the entrance-doorway bears the initials of the laird and his wife, together with the date of erection, while the MacLachlan coat of arms appears on a separate panel. The whole building measures only 37 ft. by 19 ft. over all. One of the two ground-floor apartments is the parlour and the other the kitchen, this latter room, like its counterpart at Rattray, still retaining an original fireplace-opening of spacious dimensions. The entrance-doorway has been provided with a sliding draw-bar, a sensible enough precaution at that time in a locality on the fringes of the Highlands, and one that appears to have been justified by subsequent events, Rob Roy himself being credited with an attack upon the house in 1710.

There are a number of other examples of this type of house in Stirlingshire. Borrowmeadow and Dalquhairn, which both date from the first half of the eighteenth century, are slightly larger than Auchentroig and have five-window fronts. Despite its semi-ruinous condition, Dalquhairn is a structure of considerable interest, the lay-out of the courtyard buildings, which incorporate cartsheds, stable, byre and other offices, showing quite clearly that the laird farmed at least part of his lands himself. The house itself, which appears to have been erected a little in advance of the courtyard buildings, bears the date 1711, together with the initials of James Shaw and his wife Isobel Mill. The plan is conventional except for the fact that the flues are contained within the two mid-partition walls, an arrangement more usually associated with a hipped than with a gabled roof. The stone wheel-stair is situated at the rear of the entrance hall, where there is also a back door, and the upper flight of the stair, leading to the attic, was evidently of timber. At Borrowmeadow, on the other hand, the entire stair is of timber, being of 'dog-leg' construction, with a moulded newel.

In general, houses varied little in appearance from one part of the country to another. Old Holylee, Peeblesshire (1734), the residence of a Border laird, bears a strong family resemblance to the Stirlingshire houses described above, and the same could be said of the great majority of comparable structures in Highland areas. One of the earliest cases of the penetration of this essentially lowland plan-type into the Highlands is Shierglas, near Blair Atholl, Perthshire, which was built for the Stewarts of Strathgarry in 1728; it has a three-window front, the date of erection appearing in its usual position above the doorway. Of similar plan, but of more individual character, are the two east-coast houses of Parleyhill, Fife, and Garlet, Clackmannanshire. The former stands on the northern outskirts of Culross, its curvilinear gables and distinctive oillet windows making it a familiar landmark to visitors to the near-by abbey church. Garlet (now threatened with demolition) appears to have been built a generation or so after Parleyhill, that is to say about the middle of the eighteenth century. Here the central portion of the main elevation is slightly advanced and rises to a gablet having plain copings and roll-moulded skewputs. The entrance-doorway has a lug-moulded architrave, above which a moulded cornice runs the full width of the central projection at first-floor level. More typical, but of interest in view of its comparatively late date, is Little Kilry (1767), on the Angus–Perthshire border, which is almost a facsimile of its neighbour, Old Mains of Rattray, erected some 70 years previously.

In most cases the builders of houses such as these must have been only too glad to pull down their previous dwellings, particularly when these were of a fairly primitive nature. The laird of Hills Castle, Kirkcudbrightshire, however, already the possessor of a fine late medieval tower-house (23), preferred to make the best of both worlds, and by placing his compact and symmetrically planned house of 1721 hard against one wall of the old tower cast himself in the dual role of castellan and country gentleman. A similar conjunction of styles occurs at Bonshaw, Dumfriesshire (53), and Auchanachy Castle, Aberdeenshire (54), but in this latter case the two main elements are so closely inter-locked that it is hard to say where the tower-house finishes and the new laird's house begins. The houses so far described could provide only a very limited range of accom-modation, most of them in fact containing no more than four main apartments together with a variable number of smaller rooms. More space could readily be found, however, by elongating the main block, an arrangement that enabled the main rooms to be either enlarged in size or increased in number. The late eighteenth-century house of Braes, Stirlingshire, provides a good example of this development. The traditional three-window front is retained, but the overall length extends to 56 ft., and this allows three main rooms to be provided on each of the two principal floors, while a fourth is contained behind the stair, which for once loses its central position. None of the rooms at Braes is particularly well lit, but Dunbarney, Perthshire, a house of about the same size, has a six-window front, while Brightmony, Nairnshire, an exceptionally long building, has an eight-window front. Brightmony can be dated to the year 1752 on the evidence of an inscribed skewput, but Dunbarney is probably a little older.

An alternative, but less common, method of obtaining more accommodation was by the adoption of a T-plan, the additional limb being utilised to house either the staircase or an extra room. Nether Ardgrain, Aberdeenshire, illustrates this arrangement, the projecting wing in this case being frontally placed and containing the entrance-doorway, which has a roll-moulded surround bearing the date 1731. At Old Ballikinrain, Stirling-shire, a house of about the same period, the wing is at the rear. The internal arrange-ments have been very much altered, but an early plan of the building shows that the stair formerly occupied a position immediately within the entrance-doorway, and that the wing contained a series of small rooms, the ground-floor one being a cellar. A similar arrangement exists at another Stirlingshire house, Seton Lodge, which appears to have been built by the Setons of Touch in about 1800 to serve either as a factor's house or, more probably, as a dower-house. This would explain the relatively sophisticated character of the main elevation, which incorporates a Tuscan entrance-porch set within a bowfront; the roof is hipped.

Larger versions of the standard type of laird's house, in which the main block was increased in width so as to accommodate two rooms on each side of the staircase, began to appear about the second quarter of the eighteenth century. One of the earliest and best-preserved examples is Glen, Kirkcudbrightshire, where the conventional five-window front is dignified by rusticated quoins and a moulded eaves-course; one of the rear quoins bears the inscription 'Founded Iune 22 1734 by I McD'. Like Glen, Mains of Glins, Stirlingshire (1743), has been a gable-roofed block of two main storeys and an attic with a symmetrical five-window front. In this case, however, the house was comparatively narrow, and the two rooms lying on each side of the stair were of very unequal size and the smaller ones had corner fireplaces. A fifth room was formed at the rear of the geometric stair, of which the lower flight was of stone and the upper of timber. Occasionally a satisfactory plan of this type could be contrived within the framework of an older building. Dunbarney, for instance, was doubled in width towards the end of the eighteenth century by the erection of a second range of apartments immediately behind the long narrow block of the original house.

In many cases these houses of double-room width were equipped with service basements, their standards of accommodation being equivalent to those of a small mansion. Forebank, Kincardineshire (49), and Gourdie, Perthshire, provide excellent illustrations of this type of arrangement. Each is a gable-roofed block comprising a basement, two main storeys and an attic, and each has a symmetrical internal lay-out about a central staircase. At Forebank (1757), where the stair is at the rear, the 'double-pile' nature of the plan is emphasised by the central corridor that traverses the long axis of the house at first-floor level, giving access to rooms in each corner of the building. The internal lay-out of Gourdie is conventional; there is a good geometric stair with twisted balusters, and the attic retains a well-preserved series of unusually elegant box-beds. The principal front shows rusticated quoins and a bracketed eaves-cornice, the Gibbsian entrance-doorway being approached by means of a bridge spanning the basement area.

Another notable pair of houses that have a number of features in common are Bankton, East Lothian, and Catter, Dunbartonshire, the former dating from about the second quarter of the eighteenth century and the latter from the year 1767. Both have symmetrical five-window fronts with central gablets, this latter detail being repeated at Bankton on the rear elevation as well. Catter (50) has a hipped roof with paired chimney-gablets and roll skewputs, while at Bankton paired chimneys are associated with a gabled roof having bold curvilinear copings and cable-moulded skewputs. The original internal lay-out of Bankton has been obliterated, but Catter has been little altered, the principal floor containing a single large room on each side of the staircase and the second floor four correspondingly smaller rooms with a fifth over the entrance-hall. There is a handsome, if somewhat old-fashioned, stone staircase of 'dog-leg' construction, lit from above by an oval cupola and from the rear by a window from whose internal sill a central stone column rises to support the upper landing.

Houses of similar design can be seen in most parts of the country. Bankton and Catter find a northern counterpart at Straloch, Aberdeenshire, while the tall gabled block of Orrock House, in the same neighbourhood, recalls Forebank and Gourdie. Arnprior, Stirlingshire, has a rather more square-cut plan and a three-window front, while Glenae, Dumfriesshire (55), provides a similar range of accommodation, but with more spacious rooms, thus requiring a five-window front. Glenae is one of the few documented houses of its class, the building contract showing that it was designed in 1789 by Thomas Boyd, a Dumfries architect who is known to have drawn up plans for alterations to Cally House, Kirkcudbrightshire (p. 118), in 1794. Two houses in the far north also deserve mention, Embo, Sutherland, as one of the most substantial buildings of its kind, and Old Allangrange, Ross and Cromarty, as one of the most individualistic. Embo comprises a basement and three main storeys—one more than Allangrange. Both are plain harled gable-roofed blocks, but at Allangrange the central bay of the otherwise unadorned main front (51) is emphasised by a boldly rusticated doorway-surround of red sandstone surmounted by a coat of arms and a pedimented window set out on carved brackets; above there is a stone panel bearing the date 1760 in Roman numerals.

The great majority of the houses described in the last four paragraphs are gable-roofed and all are gable-chimneyed. Hip-roofed houses having chimneys in the two mid partition-walls are much less common, although this was a standard arrangement in the larger country mansion. Two Ayrshire houses, Greenan and Drumburle, illustrate this form. Both have regular five-window fronts with central doorways, that at Greenan being enclosed within a pedimented Doric porch approached by a flight of steps; at Drumburle, where no basement exists, there is a simpler porch at ground-floor level. The internal lay-outs are similar to those of the gable-roofed buildings described above and both houses may probably be ascribed to the third quarter of the eighteenth century. Aquhorthies, Aberdeenshire, has a much less orthodox plan, a tall three-storeyed main block with a standard five-window front being set between hipped end-bays to produce a building of unusually elongated proportions; the original internal lay-out does not survive.

A few houses of this class are built on a T-plan, the most outstanding example being Lochlane, Perthshire, which is one of the earliest hip-roofed buildings of the type illustrated by Greenan and Drumburle. Lochlane (57) is small, but compact, and there is no basement storey; it has a four-window front, the pedimented entrance-doorway being wedged rather uncomfortably between the inner pair of windows. The attic storey is lit by dormers, a central window on the principal front being contained within a rudimentary gablet bearing the inscribed date 1710. The interior is exceptionally well-preserved, and the kitchen still retains its wide segmental-arched fireplace and stone-lined oven; the principal apartments at first-floor level have bolection-moulded fire-places and pine panelling. The timber stair is housed within the wing, which is centrally placed at the rear, while to judge from an early estate-plan that is preserved within the house there were originally single-storeyed wings or pavilions at the two front corners of the main block. Later T-plan houses include Whitelaw, East Lothian, and Pittrichie, Aberdeenshire (1818), which have wing staircases, and Craigivairn, Stirlingshire, and Bourtie, Aberdeenshire (1754), where the stairs are centrally placed within the main block and the wings contain living-rooms. All these are gable-roofed buildings with basement storeys.

Manses

The provision and upkeep of a suitable residence for the minister was a responsibility of the heritors, or local landowners, and the standard of accommodation provided varied a good deal from one parish to another. Literary evidence shows that many seventeenth- and early eighteenth-century manses, particularly those in the Highlands, were mean buildings of primitive construction, comparable to the small houses mentioned in Chapter VII. Eneas Sage's manse at Lochcarron, in Wester Ross, had walls of stone and turf, and living-rooms and cow-byre were housed beneath the same thatched roof, without any internal dividing wall. The more fortunate minister lived in a building of stone and lime similar in character to the residences of many of his heritors, and the few surviving pre-Union manses are all of this class. Thereafter the great majority of new parish manses were modelled upon one or other of the smaller versions of the symmetrically planned laird's house of the eighteenth century, buildings of this type continuing to be erected until well into the Victorian era.

Old Kilrenny Manse, Anstruther (56), is probably the oldest post-Reformation manse now extant. It was a more substantial structure than most of its kind for, as the minister, James Melville, recorded in his diary, the burgesses of Anstruther Easter helped the heritors to make an unusually generous provision for him. The building was begun in 1590 and completed within ten months at a cost of some £2300 Scots. Melville himself bent all his considerable energies to the task in hand and closely supervised the day-to-day progress of the building operations, afterwards reflecting, in sentiments that have been echoed by builders of all generations, that the house 'wald neuer haiff bein perfyted giff the bountifull hand of my God haid nocht maid me to tak the wark in hand myselff'. The manse is an L-plan building of three storeys, the lowermost one comprising a series of barrel-vaulted cellars; the lower portion of the turnpike stair is housed within the wing while the upper part is corbelled out in the re-entrant angle between wing and main block. The arrangement is thus closely comparable to that of Castle of Park, Wigtownshire, built in the same year.

Two seventeenth-century Stirlingshire manses are of interest in that they in some measure anticipate the characteristic small laird's house and manse of the post-Union period. Larbert Old Manse can be ascribed, on the evidence of an inscription, to the year 1635. It is a plain oblong block of two storeys and a garret divided vertically by a mid partition-wall; the arrangement on both main floors is the same, two rooms being placed on one side of the partition, and a single larger room on the other side. The ground floor is partly residential and comprises not only the kitchen and an under-stair cellar, but also the parlour and what may have been the minister's study. Dalnair (1682) is similar in character to Crosbie, Ayrshire. The ground floor contains a kitchen and a parlour separated by a central wall that opens from the staircase wing; the entrance-doorway is situated at the foot of the stair, which is of turnpike construction. The lay-out is thus very close to that of certain T-plan lairds' houses of the eighteenth century, while the more typical oblong house of the same period can be arrived at by omitting the wing and bringing the entrance-doorway and staircase into the central compartment of the building.

One of the best examples of a T-plan manse of the Georgian era is Kilbucho Old Manse, Peeblesshire, built in 1751. The accommodation comprises two main storeys and an attic, the ground floor containing kitchen, parlour and study, and the first floor three bedrooms, of which the central one incorporates a well-appointed box-bed. The projecting staircase wing is semicircular on plan, the stair itself being of timber. Symmetrically planned oblong manses, most of them plain two-storeyed structures with three-window fronts, can be seen throughout the country, their style of construction varying little from one generation to another. Standardisation is particularly well marked in the Highlands, where a very large number of new churches and manses were erected in late Georgian times. Donald Sage, the grandson of the above-mentioned minister of Lochcarron, relates that all the manses constructed in Sutherland and Easter Ross between 1760 and 1804 were of uniform design (the plans being supplied by James Boag of Dornoch), and gives a detailed description of his own birthplace, Kildonan Manse (1766), 'built after the unalterable model for manses in those days', with 'the usual number of chimneys, namely two, rising like asses' ears at either end, and ensuring the purpose for which they were designed as ill as usual'.

Better known, perhaps, are Thomas Telford's 'parliamentary manses', of which about 40 (together with a similar number of no less uniform churches) were constructed in the Highlands during the second quarter of the nineteenth century. Two standard plans, one for a two-storeyed T-plan building and the other for a more modest single-storeyed H-plan building, are reproduced in Telford's autobiography (1838), and many of these manses are still extant; both forms are well represented in Argyll where examples may be seen at Duror, Iona, Kilmeny, Kinlochspelvie, Lochgilphead, Portnahaven, Salen, Tobermory and Ulva.

Dovecots

In a land where food was often difficult to obtain and winter menus could show little variety pigeons made a welcome addition to the table, and most people of any conse-quence had their own dovecot. So many were erected, in fact, that in 1617 legislation

53 Bonshaw, Dumfriesshire.
Sixteenth century and later

54 Auchanachy Castle,
Aberdeenshire. Sixteenth
century and later

55 Glenae, Dumfriesshire.
Thomas Boyd, 1789

56 Old Kilrenny Manse,
Anstruther, Fife. 1590

57 Lochlane, Perthshire. 1710
58 Lower Polmaise Dovecot, Stirlingshire, showing potence and nesting-boxes.
Late eighteenth or early nineteenth century

59 Dirleton Castle Dovecot, East Lothian. Sixteenth century
60 Carloonian Dovecot, Inveraray, Argyll. *Roger Morris*, 1747–8

was introduced in an attempt to confine dovecot rights to the larger landed proprietors. Even so, there were estimated to be as many as 320 private dovecots, containing 36,000 pairs of breeding pigeons, in Fife alone at the end of the eighteenth century. The flocks fed indiscriminately, preying not only upon the crops of the proprietor, but also upon those of unprivileged tenants and of neighbouring lairds, and it is not surprising that severe penalties were laid down for those found destroying dovecots or shooting pigeons.

Most existing Scottish dovecots are small single-chambered buildings of stone construction. They are of very plain external appearance, the walls being pierced only by an entrance-doorway and, occasionally, by small ventilation-apertures. In most cases one or more continuous string-courses are set out a few feet above ground level— a device probably intended to prevent rats and other vermin from gaining access to the interior by climbing up the walls. Entry-holes for the pigeons are usually contrived within the roof, although rows of small openings in the upper walls sometimes serve this purpose. The whole of the interior, from a height of some two or three feet above floor level, is invariably lined with nesting boxes, to which access is obtained by means of a 'potence', or revolving ladder (58). The nesting boxes themselves are about 8 in. square and 12 in. or more in depth, and while the average dovecot may contain some 500 or 600 boxes, a number of the larger two-chambered structures, such as Johnstounburn, East Lothian, and Finhaven, Angus, may house 2000 or more.

The oldest surviving dovecots are of sixteenth-century date, most of them being circular on plan with gently tapering walls and flat domed roofs (59), which contain central entry-holes. One of the earliest dated examples of these 'bee-hive' dovecots stands in the grounds of Mertoun House, Berwickshire; it measures about 30 ft. in height and 18 ft. in overall diameter, and the lintel of the entrance-doorway bears the date 1576. The bee-hive dovecot was succeeded by the 'lectern' form, so called because of its rectangular plan and distinctive lean-to roof, which usually faces south; the pigeon-ports are nearly always placed midway down the roof, while the characteristic crow-stepped gables make excellent perches. This was easily the most popular type of dovecot during the seventeenth and early eighteenth centuries and numerous examples survive, the majority of them being found in the prosperous east-coast counties—notably Fife and the Lothians.

Before the agrarian improvements of the late eighteenth and early nineteenth centuries rendered it obsolete the Scottish dovecot passed through a third main phase of architectural development. This was characterised by the introduction of new plan-forms, such as the octagon and the cylinder, and by the employment of new materials of construction, particularly hand-made brick of local origin. Hitherto, architectural refinement had seldom been attempted—the boldly corbelled upperworks of Auchmacoy, Aberdeenshire (1638), provide one of the rare exceptions—but Georgian dovecots, especially those that stood within the landscaped policies of the larger country mansions, had to be ornamental as well as useful. Thus there appeared dovecots of every imaginable shape and style, some masquerading as garden pavilions, others as towers or temples, and others again so architecturally well-mannered as to need no disguise. Among the more elaborate dovecots of the period mention may be made of Huntington, East Lothian, Fothringham, Angus, and the Carloonian Doocot (Roger Morris, 1747–8) (*60*) at Inverary Castle, while attractive examples of plain octagonal dovecots, of brick and stone respectively, may be seen at Treesbank, Ayrshire (1771), and Denbie, Dumfriesshire (1775).

Buildings Specially Worth Visiting

Since most of the buildings described in this chapter are occupied as private dwelling-houses the following list includes only those which, at the time of writing, are the subjects of long-standing arrangements giving either regular or occasional public access. Buildings marked with an asterisk may usually by visited only by appointment.

Lairds' Houses

Aberdeenshire	*Auchanachy Castle, Cairnie
	*Barra Castle, Old Meldrum
	*Bourtie House, Old Meldrum
	*Craigston Castle, Turriff
	Glenbuchat Castle, Alford
Argyll	*Carnasserie Castle*, Kilmartin
Ayrshire	*Killochan Castle*, Girvan
East Lothian	*Old Hamilton House, Prestonpans
	*Northfield House, Prestonpans
	*Winton House, Pencaitland
Kincardineshire	*Muchalls Castle, Stonehaven
Kinross-shire	*Tulliebole Castle, Fossway
Lanarkshire	*Old Jerviston House, Motherwell
Midlothian	*Ford House, Pathhead
	*Gogar House, Edinburgh
Perthshire	*Elcho Castle*, Perth
Renfrewshire	*Newark Castle*, Port Glasgow
Shetland	*Scalloway Castle*
Sutherland	*Embo House, Dornoch
Wigtownshire	*Castle of Park*, Glenluce

Dovecots

Angus	*Tealing*
East Lothian	*Dirleton Castle*
	Tantallon Castle
Fife	*Aberdour Castle*
Midlothian	*Corstorphine*, Edinburgh
Nairnshire	*Boath*, Auldearn
Stirlingshire	*Westquarter*, Falkirk

III COUNTRY MANSIONS

Scottish Classicism (1660–1750)

The great courtyard-houses erected by the nobility in the years before the Civil War were the direct descendants of the castles of the Middle Ages and it would have needed more than the customary veneer of Renaissance ornament to disguise their feudal ancestry. They were designed, moreover, by master-craftsmen whose knowledge and skill had been acquired, as in medieval times, through practical experience rather than through study, and whose rule-of-thumb methods were attuned to the wishes of patrons who regarded houses simply as living-containers, and who would have been surprised to learn that they might also be works of art. When classical architecture in a fairly developed form eventually penetrated into Scotland after the Restoration, however, a more formal variety of country house began to make its appearance, and with it there emerged two new types of designer, the gentleman architect and the professional architect. Since the absence of the Court, the poverty of the burghs, and the unsettled condition of the Church allowed the erection of few public or ecclesiastical buildings of any importance, the country mansion became the principal vehicle for the introduction of classicism and continued, for the best part of a century, to provide the only real opportunity for Scottish architects to exercise their talents in their native land. Those who went to try their fortunes in the south—Colen Campbell to become the leading figure in the English Palladian movement and James Gibbs to establish a no less influential style of his own—built little in Scotland, where the architectural scene was dominated by the three men whose successive careers must now be considered.

The most important of the three, and the most interesting, was Sir William Bruce of Kinross (c. 1630–1710). No detailed study of Bruce's career has yet been made and almost nothing is known about the formative years of his life. The younger son of a Fife laird, Bruce is said to have owed his advancement to activities undertaken in the royalist cause in the years before the Restoration. Certainly he stood high in royal favour during the early years of Charles II's reign, receiving the lucrative office of Clerk to the Bills in 1660 and a baronetcy eight years later. Thereafter he combined what became an increasingly fitful political career with the life of a country gentleman, acquiring estates in Fife and Kinross, and serving on occasion as sheriff of his county and as a member for parliament. His loyalty to the house of Stewart evidently remained constant, for towards the end of his life he was imprisoned on more than one occasion for real or alleged Jacobite activities. Bruce's architectural pursuits thus engaged no more than part of his career, and it was only during the years 1671–8, when he held the office of Overseer of the Royal Works in Scotland, that he could be regarded as a professional architect.

For the remainder of the time he executed commissions in a much less formal manner, sometimes giving advice on architectural matters by correspondence, sometimes preparing designs for mason contractors, and only occasionally exercising a direct superintendence of building operations. No information has so far come to light as to the way in which Bruce acquired his architectural knowledge, but it is reasonable to suppose that an inherent interest in the subject was developed both by theoretical studies and by travel. Douglas's account of the family in the *Baronage of Scotland* (1798) implies that Bruce's political activities during the Interregnum took him to the Low Countries, and he is known to have visited France in 1663, and to have travelled in England on more than one occasion after the Restoration. Certainly it was to these two latter countries that his style was most heavily indebted, his country houses, in particular, closely following the pattern introduced into England by Hugh May and Roger Pratt about the time of the Restoration.

Bruce's earliest recorded works all took the form of alterations or enlargements of existing buildings. His own house of Balcaskie, Fife, was probably one of the first objects of his attention, for the estate was purchased as early as 1665 and sold less than 20 years later, when Bruce moved to Kinross. The main block of the house—a tall narrow building of about the beginning of the seventeenth century—was retained almost unchanged, apart from some interior redecoration, attention being concentrated on regularising the principal front, and creating a more dignified approach by means of a formal courtyard lay-out. Tower-like pavilions were erected at the outer angles of the main front linked by means of curved screen-walls to opposed two-storeyed office wings —a distinctly novel arrangement in early Restoration Scotland, but one that became extremely popular a little later on. To Bruce also must surely be attributed the creation of the terraced gardens at Balcaskie (now somewhat restored) and the associated vista of the East Lothian coast and Bass Rock, for very similar axial lay-outs occur at some of his later houses such as Kinross and Hopetoun.

At about the same time that work was going on at Balcaskie Bruce found himself engaged on a number of commissions for the second Earl (afterwards Duke) of Lauderdale, then the king's chief favourite and virtual ruler of Scotland, to whose patronage Bruce probably owed the considerable advance in his fortunes that took place during this period. The most important of the tasks entrusted to him by Lauderdale was the remodelling of Thirlestane Castle, Berwickshire, where work was in progress in the early 1670s. As at Balcaskie, only relatively superficial alterations were made to the existing building, the main effort again being directed towards the creation of a dignified entrance-approach. The narrow double-towered west elevation of the sixteenth-century castle (p. 42) was framed by pavilion-towers similar to those at Balcaskie (an extra storey seems to have been added at Lauderdale's own request), while a centrally recessed entrance-doorway, approached from a terraced forecourt, was formed at first-floor level. Further additions were contemplated, notably the formation of an outer courtyard, whose angle pavilions would have carried the progressive recession of the west front a stage further, and the erection of additional pavilions at the east end of the house and (flanking the long south elevation) of garden loggias modelled on those at Ham House, the Lauderdales' London residence; but despite the fact that they are depicted in Slezer's drawings, these features do not appear to have been carried out. The connections between Ham and Thirlestane extended into the sphere of interior decoration, for the Duke is known to have sent his Dutch joiners north to Berwickshire, while the English plasterers who worked at Thirlestane, Holyroodhouse and elsewhere, probably followed in their footsteps. The traffic was not entirely in one direction, however, for Bruce had himself been asked to supply designs for a gateway at Ham in 1671 (there was talk of the iron gates being made in Scotland), the year before Lauderdale's marriage to the Countess of Dysart brought the property under the Duke's direct control.

Well before the building programme at Thirlestane had been completed Lauderdale was making plans to remodel his second Scottish house, Brunstane, on the eastern outskirts of Edinburgh. Once again operations had to be conducted in a piecemeal fashion for, as Lauderdale explained in one of his letters, 'I will only patch what is already built—but will by no means build a fine house there'. In fact Bruce accepted Brunstane for what it was, namely a conventionally planned laird's house of Charles I's reign, and his additions harmonize with the original work. The pavilion-towers of Balcaskie and Thirlestane re-appear, however, and there is some rich interior decoration by Lauderdale's imported craftsmen.

Bruce was also to have been consulted about alterations to yet another of the Duke's northern residences, Lennoxlove Tower, and he may have been responsible for some of the contemporary work at Hatton House, Midlothian (now demolished), which belonged to Lauderdale's younger brother and successor, Charles Maitland. But the greatest opportunity afforded him as a result of Lauderdale's patronage was the remodelling of the palace of Holyroodhouse, Edinburgh, in his capacity as Surveyor of the Royal Works in 1671–8. As it stood at the Restoration the Palace was a loosely knit assemblage of various elements, of which the most important were the medieval nave of the Augustinian abbey church (p. 144), the great north-west tower of James V (p. 42), and, linking church and tower and extending southwards from them, the principal quadrangle, which contained domestic buildings and a chapel of sixteenth-century date. Bruce's proposals, in whose formulation the King's Master-Mason, Robert Mylne, evidently played an important part, revived Charles I's scheme for regularising the main west façade of the Palace by the erection of a second great tower to balance the existing one, and at the same time made provision for rebuilding the principal quadrangle to house a new series of State Apartments. The massive terminal tower-blocks of the west elevation left the architect little scope for manœuvre in this quarter, and Bruce did no more than to link the towers by a low balustrated range containing a central Doric portico. Although the main quadrangle-buildings are not much more ambitious, their pure if restrained classicism introduced a completely new idiom into Scottish architecture. All the main elevations are adorned at each storey with pilasters of the appropriate classical order, and the west elevation of the quadrangle breaks forward to rise to an enriched pediment. The design clearly represents the fruits of Bruce's travels to France, whence he may have returned bearing not only memories and sketches, but also, perhaps, current architectural treatises such as Le Muet's *Manière de bien bastir*, whose second edition (1647) includes at least one set of engravings incorporating all the main features seen at Holyroodhouse.

Relieved of his position as Surveyor upon the completion of the Palace in 1678 (it may be significant that his dismissal coincided with the waning of Lauderdale's political influence) Bruce resumed his role as gentleman architect, devoting most of his energies over the next 15 years to the erection of a mansion for his own use on his newly acquired estate of Kinross. Before settling himself to this congenial task, however, Bruce furnished designs for two Perthshire houses of which the first, for Thomas Moncreiffe of that Ilk, was completed in 1679. Although recently demolished following a disastrous fire, Moncreiffe House must be mentioned here since it appears to have been the first of Bruce's country houses to have been designed and executed as a complete and self-contained unit. A hip-roofed block, comprising a basement, two principal storeys and an attic, the house was nearly square on plan, being divided on its shorter axis into three main portions by two thick partition-walls containing the chimney flues (*61*)—an arrangement probably deriving from earlier English houses of the same type, such as Chevening, Kent. The principal staircase, a handsome scale-and-platt erection of timber, occupied the front of one of the outer divisions, while the central area housed the main apartments, the High Dining-Room at first-floor level and the gallery above it running the full width of the building. Externally the house was very plain, only the principal entrance-doorway (still preserved) showing any architectural elaboration; the most distinctive feature was the suppression of the attic, an arrangement which again echoed Chevening, and also foreshadowed Kinross. The second Perthshire house, Dunkeld, commissioned by the first Marquess of Atholl in 1676, was very similar in design to Moncreiffe, but took much longer to complete; it was demolished in about 1828.

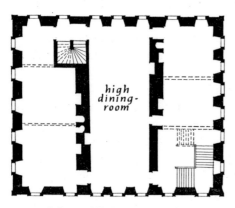

61 Moncreiffe House, Perthshire

Bruce was to return to the simple tripartite plan later on, and it subsequently became a standard lay-out for the smaller Georgian mansion, but for his own house at Kinross he employed a 'double-pile' plan such as Pratt had used at Coleshill, that is to say one in which an oblong block of double-room width was bisected on its long axis by a central corridor. At Kinross the main block comprises a slightly recessed central portion and flanking wings, and Bruce's academic approach can be seen both in the carefully proportioned inter-relationships of the principal elements, and in the forms of the individual apartments, one of these, the Saloon on the second floor, being a 'double-cube' room after the fashion introduced by Inigo Jones and John Webb at Wilton, in Wiltshire. The external elevations (*63*), like those of Moncreiffe, give prominence to the two principal storeys, but the attic is still further suppressed, its windows (those in the centre front formerly helping to light the Saloon) peeping out between the cornice and the overhanging eaves of the roof; all the exposed masonry is of beautifully dressed warm-coloured ashlar, and there is some spirited relief carving, much of it probably executed by the Dutch stone-carvers whose names appear in the building accounts, although the overall responsibility for the construction of the main fabric lay with Bruce's principal master-mason, Tobias Bauchop of Alloa. The lay-out of the gardens and policies echoes that of Balcaskie, although the vista of the Bass gives way to a no less pleasing prospect of the island ruins of Lochleven Castle.

Kinross was probably begun in 1686, but building evidently went on for a number of years, and by the time the house was completed Bruce was well advanced in age. His architectural interests were undiminished, however, and, although none of Bruce's later compositions could quite match the serene dignity of Kinross, a number of important works were executed during the last decade of his life. Craigiehall, West Lothian, completed for the second Earl of Annandale in 1699, can be ascribed to Bruce on the evidence of letters preserved in the Kinross papers. The plan is very much the same as that of Moncreiffe, except that the staircase occupies a central position, but the elevations are a good deal more sophisticated, the central bays of the two principal façades breaking forward to terminate in triangular pediments such as Bruce had introduced at Holyroodhouse.

As Craigiehall approached completion the foundations of another of Bruce's houses were being laid out on the neighbouring Forthside estate of young Charles Hope, afterwards first Earl of Hopetoun. Hopetoun House, erected between 1699 and 1702, was the grandest of all the architect's country mansions and it is, in many respects, unfortunate that in later years the Earl called in William Adam to re-cast the principal façade and forecourt. Bruce's house was a great three-storeyed rectangular block, the principal elevation having angle pavilions of the same height, linked by convex (instead of the more usual concave) screen-walls to terminal office-wings. The main block was almost square on plan, the internal arrangements focusing upon a central staircase lit from a cupola. French influence is apparent in the overall horizontal rustication of the principal façade and in the bold semicircular pediment of the garden front, while for the side elevations Bruce went back to his Craigiehall design with its distinctive

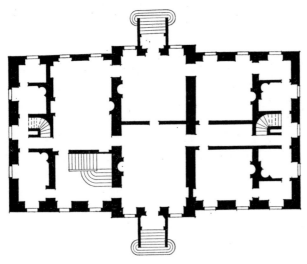

62 Mertoun House, Berwickshire

two-window pedimented centre-piece.

Lastly, among Bruce's surviving houses, there are Mertoun, Berwickshire, and Auchindinny, Midlothian. The former, erected for Sir William Scott of Harden in 1703, has a 'double-pile' plan (*62*) like that of Kinross, whence also are derived the ingeniously contrived mezzanine floors at each end of the house. The principal elevation, which is rusticated throughout, has a three-window pedimented frontispiece. Auchindinny, completed in about 1707, is a much more modest building, but one, nevertheless, of considerable interest inasmuch as it appears to be the progenitor of a long line of small mansions and lairds' houses of the Georgian era. The formal lay-out of the great Restoration mansion is here reproduced in miniature with a corresponding simplification of expression. The main element in the composition, a plain hip-roofed rubble block with a five-window front, has a conventional tripartite plan in which the principal rooms are regularly disposed about a central staircase. Denbie, Dumfriesshire (1706), is a small-scale version of Auchindinny and could be classed as a small laird's house but for the unusual refinement of its architectural detail; the windows of the main elevation have boldly rusticated architraves and are grouped so as to emphasise the centre, where there is a Doric entrance-doorway very similar in character to that at Moncreiffe. The name of the architect is unknown.

A number of other houses of the period have less direct associations with the name of Sir William Bruce. It is known that the Marquess of Queensberry intended to consult him about the remodelling of Drumlanrig Castle (p. 55), while Prestonfield, Midlothian, is said to have been rebuilt to his designs in 1687, its lavish interior decoration certainly showing some affinity with that of the Lauderdale houses. But the external appearance of the mansion, with its Jacobean quoins and Dutch gables, is traditional in character (perhaps because of the survival of earlier work), a contrast in styles which was repeated a few years later at Cammo House, in the same county. Another near-by house that was being remodelled at this time is Caroline Park, where there is some more rich Restoration plasterwork. But for its comparatively late date it would be tempting to ascribe the new south front of 1696 to Bruce, for the rusticated pilasters of the

63 Kinross House, Kinross-shire. *Sir William Bruce, c. 1686–91*

64 Design drawing for Melville House, Fife. 1697–1701

65 Chatelherault, Lanarkshire. *William Adam, c. 1732*

66 Mavisbank, Midlothian. *Sir John Clerk and William Adam, c. 1727*

67 Duff House, Banffshire. *William Adam, c. 1730–40*

68 Hopetoun House, West Lothian. *William, John and Robert Adam, c. 1723–54*

centrepiece, the angle pavilions and the high French roofs are all consistent with known work of his elsewhere. Of more general importance, however, is Raith House, Fife, which was completed between about 1693 and 1698 for Alexander, Lord Raith, the eldest son of the first Earl of Melville. Among the names mentioned in the building accounts is that of Mr James Smith, but, bearing in mind the part that Bruce appears to have played in the design of Melville House itself (p. 102), it is not improbable that he was also consulted in the case of Raith. Although now much altered, the house is of interest as the earliest known Scottish example of the combination of a pedimented frontispiece with a hip-roofed block of the type introduced at Moncreiffe, for Craigiehall was not completed until 1699.

Towards the end of Bruce's life a number of other gentlemen architects, including Sir John Clerk of Penicuik and John, sixth Earl of Mar, began to make their appearance, but the most important of Bruce's successors, James Smith, followed a strictly professional career. Born in 1646 or 1647 Smith was a craftsman by trade, and first comes on record in 1678 as one of the master-masons engaged upon the remodelling of Holyroodhouse. Thereafter promotion was rapid for, after becoming an Edinburgh burgess in 1679, on his marriage to a daughter of the King's Master-Mason, Robert Mylne, and acting as arbiter in a building dispute in the following year (when he is described as 'Mr James Smith, architectour, a man who hes the repute to be very well skilled in works of this nature'), Smith was in 1683 appointed Overseer of the Royal Works in Scotland— the post formerly held by Bruce. Smith's appointment to this office, which he continued to hold for no less than 35 years, was made upon the recommendation of the Marquess of Queensberry, for whom he seems then to have been working at Drumlanrig Castle (p. 55). Little need be said here about his official career, for there was not much royal building in Scotland at this period, Smith's most important contribution being his work in connection with the construction and repair of the various Highland garrisons and forts in the years after the Union (p. 61). The payment of a fairly generous official salary (latterly wrung from Queen Anne's government only with much dispute and delay), and the combined profits of certain business enterprises and of his work as an architect and building contractor, enabled Smith to purchase the small estate of Whitehill, near Musselburgh, and his establishment as a landed proprietor was marked by a grant of arms and by appointments as a Commissioner of Supply and Justice of the Peace. Although dismissed from his official position in 1719, he continued to engage in various business and professional activities and, busy to the last, was still pressing a lawsuit against the Earl of Leven (for payments due for work done at Melville House) at the age of 80, while at the same time laying out large sums of money to set up a steam pumping-engine in a local colliery that he had leased. He died in 1731, a reputed Roman Catholic, and the father, on his own testimony, of 32 children, one at least of whom appears to have been a practising mason.

Something has already been said about Drumlanrig and Raith, the two earliest country houses with which Smith's name can be associated, and a third, Hamilton Palace, has been completely demolished. Less important, perhaps, than any of these projects, but not without interest, was his work for Charles, fourth Earl of Traquair, at Traquair House, Peeblesshire, between 1695 and 1705. Smith seems to have been commissioned primarily to lay out a new forecourt and service wings, but he also produced a scheme for tidying up the long rambling front of the main block without abandoning its by then distinctly old-fashioned Baronial character. In fact, only the service wings were built, together with a handsome screen-wall and gateway and, at the rear of the house, two garden pavilions of the type favoured by Bruce.

While work was going on at Traquair, Smith was engaged upon a much more considerable project in Fife, where he completed a new mansion (64) for the Earl of Melville between 1697 and 1701. Following an explicit statement to this effect by Colen Campbell in the second volume of *Vitruvius Britannicus* (1717), it has been generally accepted that Smith (who is described as the 'most experienc'd Architect of that Kingdom') was the designer of Melville House, and contemporary documents leave no room to doubt that he acted as building contractor and superintendent of works. On the other hand, a letter in the Leven and Melville muniments, written by Sir William Bruce to the Earl of Melville in April 1697—only two months before the building contract was signed—makes it clear that Bruce himself was at that time preparing a design for the Earl's consideration, Smith's name being mentioned only in the capacity of executive contractor. Smith's own admission some years later that 'before the Earl fixed himself upon a Draught He had severall Draughts from diverse Architects Sir William Bruce and others' does little to resolve the problem, but whoever its author, or authors, may have been, the design clearly shows the influence of contemporary architectural fashions on the other side of the Border. Melville has a formal courtyard lay-out, with garden pavilions and service wings very similar in character to those at Traquair, while the main dwelling-house—a taller but more compact version of the type of English country mansion represented by Belton, Lincolnshire—is a four-storeyed H-plan block of which the central axis alone is of double-room width. This portion houses the handsome scale-and-platt oak staircase and, at first-floor level, a fine panelled Saloon of similar proportions to the one at Kinross; the remainder of the principal apartments are similarly well appointed, the overall standard of accommodation going some way to justify Smith's own claim that 'there is not a more Convenient Dwelling house nor any better built in North Brittain'.

As the main block of Melville House approached completion in the autumn of 1701 Smith embarked upon a no less ambitious scheme for the Duchess of Buccleuch at Dalkeith House, Midlothian. Here, as at Drumlanrig and Traquair, it was a question of remodelling an existing house rather than of designing an entirely new one, for Dalkeith was already quite a large building, its straggling courtyard-plan having evolved as the result of successive enlargements of a fifteenth-century tower-house. Smith handled the problem with characteristic ingenuity, masking the older work as best he could on the rear and side elevations, but providing a completely new front of considerable dignity on the east side of the house. The main elements are skilfully grouped, the receding planes of the pavilions and flanking wings directing attention to the central block, where giant Corinthian pilasters rise through all four storeys to support a full entablature and raking pediment. The centrepiece, which strongly recalls its vanished predecessor at Hamilton, is of ashlar, with a rusticated basement and moulded windows, but the main wall-surfaces are of rubble and may originally have been harled. The interiors are even more splendid than those at Melville. The great staircase, lit by two tall windows inserted in the medieval curtain-wall, is approached through a marble arcade, the lower portion of the stair-well being panelled in the same material. The principal apartments, arranged *en suite*, are richly panelled in oak and contain several notable chimney-pieces, a number of them carved by Grinling Gibbons.

About this time Smith seems to have built a small country mansion for his own use on his recently acquired estate of Whitehill, afterwards re-named New Hailes. So much, at least, may be inferred from a chance remark of Lord Hailes (reported by Ramsay of Ochtertyre) to the effect that 'the place (of New Hailes) was first made by a Mr Smith, a Popish architect, employed in fitting up King James's chapel at the Abbey (Holyrood-house), who planted the oldest trees'. New Hailes is now quite a substantial house, having been remodelled and enlarged during the second quarter of the eighteenth century and only the central portion, a plain hip-roofed block of very modest dimensions, is likely to go back to Smith's time. The design follows that of Raith; the accommodation comprises a basement, two main storeys and an attic, and the rooms are disposed on each side of an open-well staircase, whose simple wrought-iron balustrade contrasts sharply with the exuberant rococo decoration that was afterwards introduced through-out the rest of the house.

The last major building project with which Smith is known to have been concerned was the design and commencement of Yester House, East Lothian. The architectural development of the house has not yet been worked out in detail, but the existing building may have been begun shortly after the accession of the fourth Marquess of Tweeddale in 1715. When Macky visited Yester eight years later the shell of the building had been completed, together with the basement and principal-floor apartments, but the upper storey was still unfloored and the Marquess and his mother were living in the pavilions 'till the Body of the House is finished'. In fact the building did not assume its present appearance until much later, most of the interior decoration having been executed by William Adam and his son Robert, who subsequently remodelled the principal façade. The original design owed a good deal to two of Bruce's houses, the external treatment following that of the east front of Hopetoun, and the 'double-pile' plan looking back to Mertoun, and beyond it to Kinross. All the elevations appear to have been treated uniformly and the two principal storeys are given equal prominence; the masonry is of ashlar throughout with pronounced horizontal rustication in the French manner. Of the two original pavilion-wings, which may have been linked to the main block by curved screen-walls, only one now remains.

By this time Smith was more than 70 years of age and it is not surprising to find him receiving the collaboration of a younger colleague, Alexander Macgill, whose name appears in *Vitruvius Scoticus* as joint-architect of Yester. Macgill was the son of the minister of a country parish in Angus and, like Smith himself, began his career as a mason, being apprenticed to Alexander Nisbett of Edinburgh in 1697. His association with Smith goes back at least to 1709–10, when the two architects co-operated in drawing up a scheme (apparently unexecuted) for the enlargement of Cullen House, Banffshire, while nearly 20 years later his name appears again as one of the witnesses of an agreement concerning Smith's pumping-engine (p. 101).

Macgill also executed commissions on his own account, however, the most important of his recorded works being the enlargement of Greyfriars Church, Edinburgh (1722), and the erection of Newbattle Church, Midlothian (p. 165), and of two major country houses, Blair Drummond, Perthshire (1715–17; demolished) and Donibristle House and Chapel, Fife. He also advised Lord Milton about building projects at Brunstane, Midlothian (1730) and Whim, Peeblesshire (p. 241), as well as being responsible for several minor buildings in Edinburgh, where he seems to have held the post of burgh architect from 1720 until his death 14 years later. The only one of these buildings that calls for mention here is Donibristle House, which appears to have been erected in the early 1720s. The original design, illustrated in *Vitruvius Scoticus*, comprised a main block with detached L-plan service-wings flanking a forecourt. The main block itself, a plain three-storeyed building whose H-plan was a compressed version of that of Melville House, has been completely destroyed, but the unusually spacious service-wings remain, together with a fine terraced staircase and screen-walls at the forecourt entry, the gateway itself incorporating a remarkable wrought-iron overthrow arch.

The smaller mansions of this period followed the pattern introduced by Sir William Bruce about the turn of the century. Drylaw House, Edinburgh, for instance, erected by George Loch of Drylaw in 1718, has a strong family resemblance to Auchindinny, Midlothian (p. 98). The accommodation comprises a sunk basement, two principal storeys and an attic, the main floors containing two apartments on each side of a central staircase. The exterior is quite plain, with harled rubble walls and few mouldings; the fenestration is symmetrical and the hipped roof has bell-cast eaves. Tullibody House, Clackmannanshire (recently demolished), was another good example of a house of this type, the plan in this case being attributed to James Gibbs's patron, the Earl of Mar, while the near-by mansion of Brucefield (*c.* 1724) happily survives to illustrate the same theme. Here the absence of a partially sunk basement gives the main block of the house (originally, it would seem, a self-contained unit) an unusually lofty appearance, the principal floor having formerly been approached by means of a central forestair. There

69 Touch House, Stirlingshire.
c. 1750 and earlier

70 Airds House, Argyll. 1738

71 Dumfries House, Ayrshire. *John* and *Robert Adam,* 1754–60

72   Culloden House, Inverness-
shire. *c.* 1788

73   Gask House, Perthshire.
Richard Crichton, 1801

74   Montgomerie, Ayrshire.
John Paterson, 1804

75   Cairness House, Aberdeenshire. *James Playfair*, 1791–7

is a conventional tripartite plan, the chimney flues being gathered into the two main transverse partitions, but the staircase, a scale-and-platt construction about a solid stone newel, is not placed in the central division of the house, as is customary, but at the front of one of the outer divisions.

The last member of the trio of Scottish architects whose careers span the period between the Restoration and the Forty-five is William Adam, Senior, who had already established himself as the leading figure in his profession by the time of James Smith's death in 1731. The son of a Kirkcaldy builder and architect, Adam was born in 1689 and, according to tradition, served his architectural apprenticeship under Sir William Bruce. Enterprising and ambitious, and possessing a shrewd head for business as well as original artistic ability, his rapid rise to distinction would scarcely have been possible had he not also been able to win the support and attachment of patrons such as the Clerks of Penicuik and the Hopes of Hopetoun, in whose service his architectural career was commenced. In 1728 Adam was elected a burgess of Edinburgh for services rendered to the burgh, and in the same year he obtained the first of his numerous public appointments, of which the most important were to be those of Surveyor of the King's Works and Master-Mason to the Board of Ordnance. At the same time his business interests were expanding, projects for brick and coal works, salt-pans, mills, canals and aqueducts all receiving careful attention, and the profits thus derived being invested in the purchase of a small estate in Kinross-shire. Most of Adam's architectural commissions were for country mansions, of which some 20 were actually built to his designs (a similar number of designs remaining unexecuted), but he was also responsible for some important urban buildings including Gordon's College, Aberdeen (p. 202), the Old Royal Infirmary, Edinburgh, and Dundee Town House (both now demolished). Many of these designs were engraved with a view to publication, but this project was still unrealised at the time of Adam's death in 1748, and it was only in 1810 that an enlarged and corrected edition of engravings appeared under the somewhat grandiose title of *Vitruvius Scoticus*. A more important legacy, however, was the family business itself, in which the eldest of Adam's four sons, John, had already begun to play an active part, for it was from this closely knit circle that the 'promising young men' (as the writer of one of their father's obituary notices termed them) were ultimately to go out to carry the name of Adam throughout western Europe and into the New World.

William Adam was the last major Scottish architect whose work was fundamentally different in character from that of contemporary designers on the other side of the Border. Yet most of the ingredients of Adam's architectural style were derived from English sources, chiefly, it would seem, from Vanbrugh and Gibbs, whose work he could have studied either at first hand or through the medium of published architectural treatises— the name 'Mr William Adams, Architect' appears among the subscribers to the first edition of Gibbs's *Book of Architecture* (1728). For the severities of the English neo-Palladian school, on the other hand, Adam seems to have had little taste, although the achievements of its leading exponents, such as Colen Campbell and Lord Burlington, were certainly familiar to him and he often utilised individual Palladian motifs; nor did he show much regard for the restrained classicism of Sir William Bruce and James Smith. Indeed, as Mr John Fleming has recently pointed out, Adam's own inclinations, although readily suppressible when they came into conflict with those of his patrons, were themselves directed towards the attainment of immediate dramatic impact, an effect which he frequently sought to obtain by the free employment of a richly diverse vocabulary of surface decoration. When this concern for first impressions led him to neglect the more basic architectural qualities of unity and proportion the results were often bizarre; some of Adam's work, on the other hand, achieved real dignity and grandeur, none was dull, and all of it displayed a robustness and directness of expression that were entirely appropriate in the intellectual climate of North Britain.

Nothing is yet known about the first decade or so of Adam's professional career, his earliest recorded architectural activities dating from the mid 1720s, when he was some 35 years of age. When Sir John Clerk of Penicuik called him in to assist in the construction of a small country house at Mavisbank, Midlothian, however, Adam already had a reputation as a skilful architect, and one whose opinions deserved the respect even of a knowledgeable and discerning patron. Nevertheless, Adam's role was in this case a subordinate one, for the main features of the design seem to have been of Sir John's own invention, while the original conception went back to Sir John Clerk, first of Penicuik, who had prepared plans for a house in this vicinity in 1696–8. As finally completed in about 1727 Mavisbank (66) was as much of a novelty as Moncreiffe had been half a century earlier and little less influential; a free translation of a Palladian villa, elegant in appearance and compact of plan, Sir John's house set a new architectural fashion for Scottish country mansions of the middle rank. Indeed, before Mavisbank was finished Adam had already begun to build a second house of the same type for Lord Somerville at Drum, on the southern outskirts of Edinburgh. Here, away from the restraining influence of Sir John Clerk, the architect made much bolder use of surface decoration, crowding the principal façade with a rich assortment of Palladian and Gibbsian elements and allowing his stuccoer, Samuel Calderwood, free play within. The general lay-out of main block, screens and pavilions echoes that of Mavisbank, and a number of rooms likewise attain the correct Palladian proportions (a square, a square and a half, a square and a third, and so on), but the plan (76) is more ambitious, incorporating some quite spacious apartments and an elegant oval staircase.

The second of the two patrons chiefly instrumental in setting Adam upon a successful career as a country-house architect was Charles, first Earl of Hopetoun, who as early as 1721 had begun to make plans to enlarge the mansion that Sir William Bruce had built for him some 20 years earlier (p. 97). By entrusting this project to Adam he gave the Kirkcaldy architect an unrivalled opportunity for building in the grand manner for, as the Earl's ideas gradually took shape it became clear that he intended to create a house

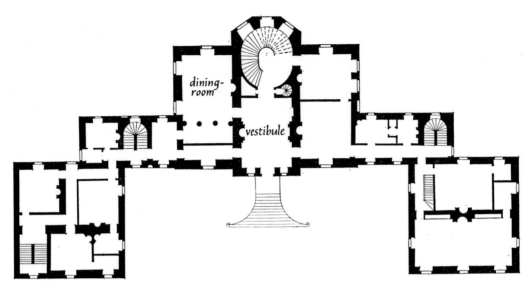

76 Drum House, Edinburgh

of a size and splendour hitherto unknown in Scotland. The outline of the scheme seems to have been decided upon by about 1723. The whole of the rear portion of Bruce's house was to be left intact, but the remainder was to be remodelled and extended in length to form the central feature of an impressive show-front linked by concave screen-walls to terminal pavilions (*68*). Adam's design for the principal elevation (published in *Vitruvius Scoticus*) was probably indebted in varying degrees both to Wren and to Van-brugh, the ponderous attic-storey, uninterrupted even by the pediment of the great tetrastyle portico that was intended to provide a centrepiece, looking back to Hampton Court, and the giant order of Corinthian pilasters and the emphatic round-headed windows with grotesque key-stones no less strongly recalling Castle Howard. Work progressed much more slowly than had been anticipated, both patron and architect dying while the mansion was still incomplete. In 1750, however, the second Earl of Hopetoun made a determined effort to bring the project to a speedy conclusion, turning for advice to the two elder Adam brothers, John and Robert, who were now managing the family business. Certain alterations were made to the original design, the most drastic of these being the omission of the central portico. This removed the focus of the whole composition, accentuated the massiveness of the main block, and threatened dullness—an effect which was skilfully countered by the introduction of a new note of lightness in a modified design for the pavilions.

William Adam's second opportunity to build a country mansion of the first rank came in 1730, when William Duff (later Baron Braco and Earl of Fife), a wealthy Whig landowner, commissioned him to design and erect a suitably imposing house on his

Banffshire estates. Notwithstanding its present shorn and semi-derelict condition (it has recently been officially safeguarded from further decay), Duff House, Banff, is the most arresting of all Adam's surviving major works; a medieval castle in Baroque dress, its rich texture and towering bulk convey a memorable impression of seignorial pomp (67).

The general lay-out was conventional enough, a main block being connected by quadrant screen-walls to two-storeyed pavilions (77), but the actual form of the main block itself is of considerable interest. It is nearly square on plan, measuring about 100 ft. by 80 ft. over all, and rising to a height of four storeys; the angles are defined by square towers of bold projection which are carried up rather higher than the main attic-storeys to terminate in domed roofs and turreted chimneys. This type of plan, with its undertones of military feudalism, had already made more than one appearance in early eighteenth-century Britain, being most closely linked with the name of Sir John Vanbrugh, whose unconventional interest in old castles had borne fruit not only in the erection of his miniature 'Bastille' at Greenwich, but also in a sketch design for a neo-medieval mansion for the Duke of Argyll at Inveraray (p. 125). Indeed the names of Vanbrugh and Adam appear in association with each other at Floors Castle, Kelso, where a great oblong four-storeyed block with square angle-towers was erected for the Duke of Roxburgh in about 1718. Its design is traditionally ascribed to Vanbrugh, but Adam takes the credit for it in the pages of *Vitruvius Scoticus*, and is certainly known to have been superintending building operations there in 1723. Floors has been very much altered during the course of the nineteenth century and a good deal of doubt exists as to its original appearance, but it is not unlikely that it helped to inspire Duff House— although it is perhaps worth pointing out that James Gibbs, too, made use of at least one plan very similar in form and in overall dimensions (though not in vertical projection) to that of Duff, and illustrated it in one of the plates in his *Book of Architecture*. When Bishop Pococke visited Duff in 1760 he remarked that certain features of the exterior were 'in the style of Lord Carlisle's house at Castle Howard in Yorkshire', but there seems little doubt that Adam's own Hopetoun drawings provided a more immediate source of inspiration for the design of the elevations. Thus the pediment set against a high attic-storey, the round-headed windows, and the giant fluted Corinthian pilasters all reappear at Duff, as does the great double approach-stair that was projected at Hopetoun but never completed.

Although building may have begun as early as 1730, progress was slow—the main block was not roofed until 1739—and costs high, a state of affairs that seems to have been due largely to the fact that the hewn freestone and dressings employed in the construction were shipped ready worked from quarries or building-yards on the Firth of Forth. In consequence, the cordial relationships between architect and patron that Adam usually maintained with such success broke down completely, Lord Braco becoming increasingly convinced that he was being overcharged. The resulting lawsuit, while doing little harm to Adam's reputation for fair dealing and soundness of method,

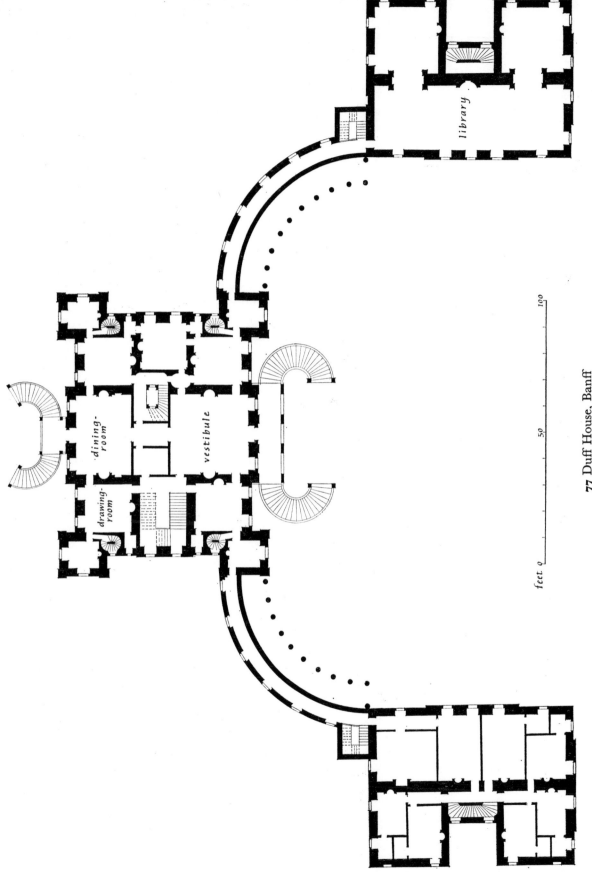

library

dining-room

vestibule

drawing-room

feet 0   50   100

77 Duff House, Banff

brought an end to any hope of the completion of Duff House, for although the main block itself was ultimately made habitable, no immediate attempt was made to erect the associated screen-walls and pavilions.

Adam built a number of other country houses, but none as grand as Hopetoun and Duff and few as expressive as Mavisbank or Drum. One of the most original is Dun House, Angus, for which plans were prepared as early as 1723, although the house was not actually built—and then to a revised design—until nearly ten years later. Here, too, the influence of Vanbrugh is apparent, although the clumsy handling of the window treatment in the 'triumphal arch' entrance-portico shows that the pupil was not always worthy of his master. Arniston, Midlothian, begun in the 1730s but not completed until after Adam's death, is another ambitious composition, the richness of the north elevation (now partially obscured by an ill-proportioned Victorian porch) preparing the eye for baroque splendours within. Some houses, on the other hand, display considerable restraint. Haddo, Aberdeenshire, completed for the second Earl of Aberdeen in 1732, is a conventional but dignified design which relies for its effect upon a basic soundness of rhythm and proportion, for external surface-decoration, even had it been considered desirable, was largely precluded by the intractable nature of the local granite building stone. The tall double-pile block of Pollok House, Glasgow (probably designed in 1737, but not erected until 1747–52), likewise displays an external aspect of considerable severity—though the ornate plasterwork of the interior reflects a very different mood—while at Craigdarroch, Dumfriesshire (1729), notwithstanding the similarity of the plan to that of Mavisbank, the design of the elevations shows a reticence that borders on plainness. Tinwald, Dumfriesshire, and Lawers, Perthshire, both ascribed by Mr John Fleming to the late 1730s, are also comparatively plain buildings of fairly modest size (though the latter has been subsequently enlarged by Richard Crichton), but neither has the charm of Gray House, Angus, where the principal elevation, derived, perhaps, from a design published in Gibbs's *Book of Architecture*, is diversified by square ogee-roofed angle-towers which connect the wings to the main block.

Lastly, in this brief review of William Adam's major surviving works, some mention must be made of the remarkable garden building of Chatelherault, erected for the fifth Duke of Hamilton in the High Parks of Hamilton Palace (p. 102) in or about the year 1732. In *Vitruvius Scoticus* the structure is somewhat implausibly termed a 'Dogg Kennell', but present observation and the accounts of earlier writers make it clear that it was intended to serve primarily as a garden retreat and hunting-lodge and, visually, as a striking frontispiece to the large walled flower-garden that lay immediately to the south of it. Façade architecture in the grand manner seems always to have held a strong appeal for William Adam, and on this occasion he handled a characteristic mixture of Palladian and Gibbsian motifs with more than usual versatility and freedom to produce a composition of great boldness and originality (65). The building comprises a central gateway and screen-wall flanked by double pavilions, the façade itself, which extends to a length of nearly 300 ft., being executed in beautifully worked pink-sandstone ashlar masonry. The distant view is, designedly, the most effective, the tall pedimented towers of the pavilions rising above the deeply scalloped parapet of the screen-wall in dramatic silhouette. Internally, interest is concentrated upon the western pavilion, which formerly contained a suite of three lavishly appointed apartments, one of them a banqueting-room; two of these were gutted by fire about 20 years ago, but the third (now itself threatened with destruction by current proposals to demolish the entire work) still retains rococo decoration of exceptionally high quality, the plasterwork in all probability having been executed by the Edinburgh stuccoer Thomas Clayton, who is known also to have worked under Adam at Drum in 1740, and who subsequently undertook the re-decoration of the principal apartments at Blair Castle, Perthshire.

Little is known as yet about the work of other architects of the period, but the best of them seem to have produced compositions similar in character to the more restrained examples of Adam's own design. Two of the most distinguished of these are Gilmerton, East Lothian, and Touch, Stirlingshire (69), the latter having been skilfully contrived within the framework of a much earlier building; both contain notable interiors, the elegantly decorated music-room at Gilmerton—perhaps an afterthought—being somewhat remotely housed within a two-storeyed wing at the rear. Archerfield, in the same county, displays an individuality strongly akin to that seen in Adam's own work, the principal elevation showing an ornate semi-octagonal central bay flanked by rows of emphatic Gibbsian windows. The house seems to have been built for William Nisbet of Dirleton in the early 1730s, but Robert Adam completely remodelled the interior (now gutted for storage purposes) in about 1790. Inveresk Manor House, Midlothian, with its plain rubble walls, coarse detail, and old-fashioned ogee-roofed pavilions, is a good example of the less sophisticated country house of the period, while the charming little mansion of Airds (1738) (70), on the Appin coast, is content to follow the pattern introduced a generation earlier at Raith (p. 101). More remarkable, however, is the makeshift classicism of the House of Hedderwick, Angus, a rambling seventeenth-century building which was partially reconstructed in 1740 to incorporate a new principal front complete with egg-and-dart moulded doorways and windows and a central relief figure-composition, all modelled in that most un-Scottish of all external cladding materials, stucco.

British Neo-classicism and the Romantic Movement (1750–1840)

Notwithstanding the efforts of the architects whose careers have just been considered, there was no more than a sprinkling of post-Restoration country mansions in Scotland in 1750, the majority of the nobility and gentry still residing, either of choice or necessity, in their ancestral castles and towers. Looking back at this period from the late Georgian comforts of his modest mansion at Ochtertyre, John Ramsay could declare that 'a very mean style of architecture, both in public and private buildings, prevailed in Scotland between the Restoration and the Union', and go on to describe, almost as if it were a subject of antiquarian curiosity, a mode of domestic life already quite remote from the customs of his own day. For during the second half of the eighteenth century a general rise in prosperity had led to a great upsurge of building activity which, continuing almost uninterrupted into the Victorian era, had stamped a large part of the Scottish landscape with its now familiar chequer of abandoned castles and well-appointed country seats.

This increased volume of building inevitably created more opportunities for native architects and, although the most able men still tended to go south to establish professional reputations, most of them now returned, either permanently or upon occasion, to build in Scotland, while at the same time it became more common for leading English architects to take on work north of the Border. Thus, Scottish architecture, at least at its upper levels, rapidly lost the distinctive national identity that it had retained for so long and, although the continued use of local building-materials still for a time allowed superficial regional mannerisms to persist, henceforward all major technical and stylistic developments were closely related to the progress of British architecture as a whole.

Scottish country mansions of the period may be divided for convenience into two main categories, those of the first group comprising houses executed in the classical style, and those of the second the various types of Georgian Gothic and Picturesque buildings. Such distinctions, of course, mean little in terms of architectural authorship, for as the stylistic boundaries of late eighteenth-century neo-classicism broadened architects acquired more comprehensive vocabularies and became equally proficient in several styles.

Classical Houses

Considering first the classical houses, the work of the Adam brothers serves to link the early and mid-Georgian eras. Something has already been said about the completion of Hopetoun House by John and Robert Adam in the 1750s (p. 109) and it was to Lord Hopetoun that Robert was chiefly indebted for the opportunity to tour Italy in 1754–8 —a visit that was to exercise a formative influence upon the subsequent evolution of the 'Adam style'. The Earl seems also to have been responsible for securing John and Robert Adam a commission to build a fair-sized country house for Lord Dumfries in Ayrshire, for which the contracts were signed shortly before Robert embarked upon his Italian tour. As one of the first major building projects associated with the name of Robert Adam, Dumfries House (71) is a structure of considerable interest, and its

78 Strathcathro, Angus. *Archibald Simpson*, 1827–30
79 Glendoick, Perthshire. *c.* 1750–60

80 Inveraray Castle, Argyll. *Roger Morris*, 1745–61, and later

81   Culzean Castle, Ayrshire. *Robert Adam,* 1771–92

restrained Palladian design (though the interior plasterwork is lively enough) is very different in character both from the work of William Adam, Senior, and from the later work of Robert and James Adam. Whether the two elder Adam brothers were also consulted by Lord Dumfries's neighbour, Alexander Boswell, Lord Auchinleck, about the erection of Auchinleck House is doubtful. Certainly these two Ayrshire houses have a good deal in common, more particularly with regard to the manner of their execution, though the round-headed key-stoned windows and over-panels of the subordinate elevations of Auchinleck are more reminiscent of some of William Adam's houses, notably of Arniston. Auchinleck has, perhaps, a further claim to notice in that it won the critical approval of Dr Johnson, who passed a few days within its walls in 1773, though the visitor felt bound to add that he was 'less delighted with the elegance of the modern mansion, than with the sullen dignity of the old castle'. The same architects may also have had a hand in the design of Paxton House, Berwickshire, where the Doric restraint of the exterior strongly recalls Dumfries, while the rococo plasterwork within is very similar in character to that both at Dumfries and at Hopetoun. At Paxton, however, the rococo work is confined to one or two rooms, the remainder being decorated in the more advanced style introduced by Robert and James Adam in the 1760s.

John Adam built at least two other houses of some interest, Hawkhill, on the north-eastern outskirts of Edinburgh (for Lord Alemoor), and Moffat House, Dumfriesshire (for the Earl of Hopetoun in 1762). The former is an ingeniously planned villa of quite modest size, while the latter, although conventional enough in plan, achieves distinction by virtue of the unusually lofty proportions of the main block and the beautifully contrasted textures of the principal building materials. The assured elegance of Robert Adam's later classical style is exemplarily expressed at Newliston, West Lothian (for Thomas Hogg, 1789–92) (*82*), and, in a heavier key, at Dunbar House, East Lothian

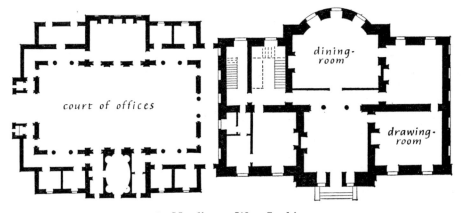

82 Newliston, West Lothian

(remodelled for the Earl of Lauderdale in 1790–2; now the Castle Park Barracks), where the rear elevation forms a handsome terminal feature to the burgh high street, while the principal façade presents an imposing, if rather gloomy, Ionic portico seawards.

The Adam brothers' chief rival, Sir William Chambers (1723–96), was responsible for only one Scottish mansion, Duddingston, Midlothian, although he also designed two town houses in St Andrews Square, Edinburgh. Duddingston, built for the Earl of Abercorn in 1763–8, has an unusual lay-out (*83*) in which the basement is eliminated; the whole of the two-storeyed main block is reserved for dwelling-rooms while the service accommodation is grouped within an adjacent courtyard-building. The house incorporates a fine double staircase of generous proportions, and the interior decoration of the principal apartments bears witness to the architect's customary fastidiousness of taste.

During the course of a long and successful career as an architect and engineer Robert Mylne (1734–1811), the descendant of a long line of famous Scottish master-masons (p. 95, 163), is known to have prepared designs for several country houses in North Britain. Two of the earliest appear to have been Galloway House, Wigtownshire (for Lord Garlies, later seventh Earl of Galloway, *c.* 1759–63), and Cally House, Kirkcudbrightshire (for James Murray of Broughton, *c.* 1763–5). Much the same plan was employed in each case—the main block having a broad pedimented frontispiece and a projecting central bow at the rear—and both houses have subsequently been much altered and enlarged. Cally is now the more interesting building of the two, being especially notable for its boldly contrasted external colour-scheme in which white Creetown granite masonry (the mansion is said to have been the first granite-built house in the south of Scotland) is employed in conjunction with dressings of dark red sandstone.

Among houses designed by other architects, Charleton, Fife (for John Thomson of Charleton, 1759; designer unknown), and Culloden House, Inverness-shire (probably for Arthur Forbes, seventh of Culloden, *c.* 1788; designer unknown) (*72*), are illustrative of a fairly large group of Georgian houses in which academic and vernacular features occur in combination with one another while, in contrast, the chaste splendours of Penicuik House, Midlothian (*c.* 1761; gutted by fire 1899), reflect a more single-minded devotion to the canons of English Palladianism than does any Scottish building of William Adam's day. The house appears to have been designed by Sir James Clerk, third of Penicuik, with some professional assistance from John Baxter. Like his father (p. 108) Sir James was a keen student of antiquity as well as an enthusiastic amateur architect, and within the adjacent court of offices at Penicuik (entered through a portico bearing a handsome Gibbsian steeple) he incorporated a full-sized representation of the famous Classical shrine known as Arthur's Oon (oven), which had been one of the principal monuments of Roman Scotland until its destruction in 1743.

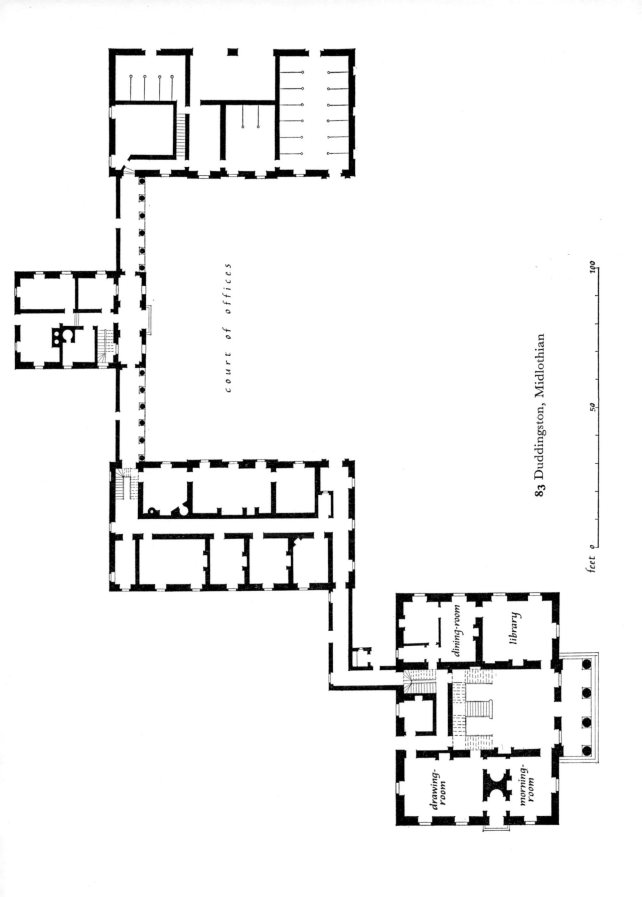

court of offices

dining-room

library

drawing-room

morning-room

83 Duddingston, Midlothian

feet 0   50   100

Although the castellated and Gothic styles enjoyed a particular vogue in Scotland during the late Georgian era, a considerable number of major classical houses were erected during the same period. Richard Crichton of Edinburgh (1771–1817), for example, best remembered for his Gothic abbey at Abercairny, Perthshire (p. 128), also designed Gask House (73), in the same county (for Laurence Oliphant of Gask, 1801), a restrained composition in the later manner of Robert Adam, and the more advanced Balbirnie, Fife (for General Robert Balfour, 1820), where the entrance-portico is placed on one of the short sides of the house, as at Camperdown.

One of the finest houses of this period is Preston Hall, Midlothian, which was begun by a retired Indian nabob, Alexander Callender, in 1791, and completed by his brother and successor, Sir John Callender, about ten years later. The design was provided by Robert Mitchell, an Aberdonian who appears to have established himself in architectural practice in London by about 1775, and who subsequently gained commissions for the erection of several English country houses, including Moore Place, Hertfordshire. At Preston Hall, as at certain other of Mitchell's houses, the main lines of the composition are conventional, but there is a noticeable refinement of detail, particularly in the sphere of interior decoration. The plan of the main block (following that of Moore Place) revolves about a top-lit staircase, whose first-floor gallery, with its elegant iron balustrade, Corinthian screens and enriched ceiling (the painted decoration was added in about 1830), provides a focal centre of quite unexpected grandeur.

Two other architects whose practices extended across both sides of the Border were Thomas Harrison of Lancaster (1744–1829) and John Paterson of Edinburgh (died 1832). The career of neither has so far been studied in detail but Harrison, in addition to executing a number of public buildings and engineering works in northern England, is known to have designed the modest little mansion of Kennet, Clackmannanshire (for Alexander Bruce of Kennet, c. 1794) (84), and the much larger but equally reticent, Broomhall, Fife (for the seventh Earl of Elgin, 1796–9; alterations by W. Porden, 1809, and J. P. Gandy-Deering, 1827–9). Paterson, too, seems to have had a fairly extensive practice in the north of England, though his most celebrated work was the great sham castle that he built at Eglinton, Ayrshire, for the twelfth Earl of Eglinton in 1798 (now gutted). His principal classical house, Mont-

84 Kennet House, Clackmannanshire

gomerie, Ayrshire, erected for the same patron in 1804, is a long low building in the Adam-Wyatt style with an imposing colonnaded bow-front (74).

More original in conception than any of these, however, was the neo-classical mansion erected in 1791–7 for Charles Gordon of Buthlaw at Cairness, in the remote north-eastern corner of Aberdeenshire, to a design of James Playfair, father of

85   Seton House, East Lothian.
Robert Adam, 1789

86   Taymouth Castle, Perthshire.
Archibald and *James Elliot,*
1806–10, and later

87   Stobo Castle, Peeblesshire.
Archibald and *James Elliot,* 1805–11

88   Balloch Castle, Dunbartonshire.
Robert Lugar, 1809

89 Dunninald, Angus. *Gillespie Graham*, 1819–32

90 Hensol, Kirkcudbrightshire. *Robert Lugar*, before 1828

91 The Pineapple, Dunmore Park, Stirlingshire. 1761

W. H. Playfair of Edinburgh. Like his fellow-Scot Robert Mitchell, Playfair (died 1794) had managed to establish himself in London without sacrificing professional connections north of the Border, and most of his known works were, in fact, executed in Scotland. Cairness is remarkable for its bold stylistic eclecticism, Greek, Roman and Egyptian elements being grouped in striking, if not always harmonious, apposition (75). The house comprises a tall, severe-looking main block of H-plan half encircled at the rear by a low flat-roofed court of offices. The terminal pavilions of the office range are rusticated over all and incorporate arresting Egyptian tomb-portico motifs, while the arched entry to the courtyard is of correspondingly primitive form. Most of the interiors are Greek, but there is one notable Egyptian room decorated with stucco panels containing hieroglyphs.

In the years immediately after the Napoleonic Wars the developed Greek Revival style became extremely popular throughout the country. Sir Robert Smirke (1781–1867), one of the school's most prolific exponents, erected a number of dignified, if uninspired, classical houses in Scotland, including Whittinghame, East Lothian (for James Balfour, 1817) and Kinmount, Dumfriesshire (for the Marquess of Queensberry, before 1819). Ten years after its completion Whittinghame was enlarged by one of Smirke's pupils, William Burn (1789–1870), then at the beginning of a long and successful architectural career in Edinburgh and London. One of the earliest and most distinguished of Burn's own houses is Camperdown Park, Dundee (p. 120; for Viscount Duncan, afterwards first Earl of Camperdown, 1824–8), a subtly refined variant of William Wilkins's Grange Park, Hampshire (1809), and a more remote reflection of a design published by Robert Mitchell in 1801.

Refinement of detail is also a characteristic of the work of the Aberdeen architect, Archibald Simpson (1796–1847), who enjoyed an extensive country-house practice in the north-east during the second quarter of the nineteenth century. Although a pupil of Robert Lugar of London, an architect who played an important part in the popularisation of the Picturesque movement (p. 127), the majority of Simpson's buildings were classical in style, and he was particularly successful in adapting the Grecian vocabulary to the requirements of Aberdeen granite, hitherto regarded as a distinctly inferior building material. The best of Simpson's work achieves a restrained elegance exemplified by Park House, Aberdeenshire (for William Moir, 1822) and Boath House, Nairnshire (for Sir James Dunbar, c. 1830), while at Strathcathro, Angus (for Alexander Cruikshank, 1827–30) (78), external severity is effectively offset by sumptuous interior decoration in paint, scagliola and marble.

As might be expected, the smaller country houses and villas of this period display less regard for stylistic fashions than do the mansions described above, and many are of markedly conservative design. The plain symmetrically planned oblong or T-shaped block with a pedimented frontispiece, first introduced at the end of the seventeenth century, remained popular almost up to the end of the Georgian era, and particularly attractive examples of this class survive at Glendoick, Perthshire (*c.* 1750–60) (*79*), Greenbank, Renfrewshire (*c.* 1763), and Barbreck, Argyll (1790); Invererne, Nairnshire (1818), shows more individuality, but the unorthodox treatment of the centrepiece produces a somewhat disquieting effect. Towards the end of the eighteenth century more sophisticated plans were introduced, with shaped rooms whose geometric forms were often echoed externally by bowed and semi-octagonal fronts. Capelrig, Renfrewshire (1769), which incorporates both traditional and classical elements, is a fairly early instance of this type, while more advanced designs occur at Leuchie, East Lothian (1779–85), and Yair, Selkirkshire (1788). Leuchie, which may have been

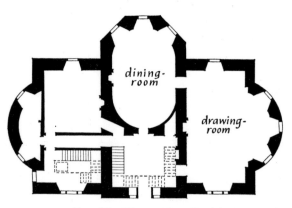

92 Leuchie House, East Lothian

designed by James Peacock of London (?1738–1814), has a noticeably studied plan (*92*), with curved bay-windows on the two side elevations and an oval dining-room which projects in a central semi-octagon at the rear; all the interior decoration is of the highest quality. Yair is representative of a fairly numerous group of late Georgian and Regency villas erected in Tweeddale, and of which other well-preserved examples occur at Haining, Selkirkshire (1794 and *c.* 1819), Crailing, Roxburghshire (1803), and Rosetta, Peeblesshire (*c.* 1810). Finally, mention may be made of the elegant little villa of Downiepark, Angus, erected for a retired Indian army-officer in about 1805, and remarkable for its distinctive external detail and elaborate galleried staircase.

Georgian Gothic Houses

Georgian Gothic houses reflect a bolder and more imaginative attitude to the past than the neo-classical buildings described above. Greek and Roman architecture, like Greek and Roman literature, had for long been accepted as a subject demanding careful and scholarly translation, and much ingenuity had been displayed in adapting the designs of Classical temples and villas to the requirements of upper-class domestic life. For the achievements of western European medieval society, on the other hand, there was, as yet, neither respect nor understanding, and Gothic architecture was esteemed, not for its intrinsic merits or its potentiality for domestic adaption, but for its romantic associations and its ornamental qualities. Most Georgian castles and abbeys were content to wear the very thinnest of Gothic disguises, their plans invariably being of conventional

Palladian or neo-classical type, and their interior decoration often incorporating few if any medieval references. Moreover, Gothic elements were customarily handled with the greatest freedom, Early English, Perpendicular and even Romanesque motifs being mingled together with happy disregard for the stylistic canons of medieval art. Indeed, it was precisely this self-confident and arbitrary approach to their material that enabled Georgian Gothic architects to achieve powers of expression that were denied to the more scholarly, but almost exclusively imitative designers of the Early Victorian Gothic school.

In Scotland, even more than in England, it is hard to say where 'Gothic Survival' ends and 'Gothic Revival' begins. Scottish post-Reformation churches continued to display medieval characteristics right up to the end of the seventeenth century (p. 162), while both Sir William Bruce (at Thirlestane Castle and Holyroodhouse) and James Smith (at Traquair House) were prepared to design in the Baronial manner when occasion demanded. But, if it is accepted that William Adam's quasi-feudal essays at Floors Castle and Duff House were medieval in spirit rather than in substance, the credit for the erection of the first major neo-Gothic house in Scotland belongs to Roger Morris, whose designs for the third Duke of Argyll's new house at Inveraray, Argyll, were prepared in 1745–6. Inveraray Castle is a great square block with circular angle-towers and a clear-storeyed central hall which rises above the main roof-line as a battlemented keep (*80*). Apart from the crenellated parapets, the only external Gothic features are the pointed windows and hood-moulds (the conical roofs of the towers are later additions), while the sophisticated interior decoration, executed by Robert Mylne in 1772–85, is almost entirely classical in character. Morris also prepared designs (in 1744) for remodelling and Gothicising another of the Duke's houses, Roseneath, Dunbarton-shire, upon similar lines to Inveraray, but to what extent the project was carried out is uncertain, for the building itself was destroyed by fire in 1802.

The Adam family made their own distinctive contribution to the development of the romantic style. In about 1757 John and James Adam produced an ambitious design for a courtyard-plan castle at Douglas, Lanarkshire (never completed) with external ornamental detail very similar in character to that at Inveraray, where John Adam had earlier succeeded his father as Master of Works. Then, in the 1770s, Robert Adam built two castellated houses in Berwickshire, Mellerstain and Wedderburn, Adam's design for the latter building being considerably modified by the executant architect, James Nisbet of Kelso. Both houses make only very sparing use of military features and both have classical interiors incorporating imposing double staircases (those at Mellerstain being particularly notable). In each case the principal façade comprises a central keep with flanking curtains and angle-towers. Mellerstain (for George Baillie of Jerviswood, *c.* 1770–8) is an austere composition relying for effect entirely upon the excellence of its proportions, but Wedderburn (? for Patrick Home of Wedderburn, 1770–5), with its turreted upperworks and bold octagonal towers, attempts to strike a more dramatic posture—although its militancy is much subdued by the neat pattern of rustication on the ground floor.

Robert Adam's castellated style achieves maturity in a small, but closely related, group of Scottish houses erected during the last 20 years of his life. These buildings employ a common vocabulary of decoration and all have symmetrical plans and classical interiors; in some cases main block, service quarters and offices are integrated in elaborate courtyard lay-outs. There is a very limited repertoire of ornamental detail, most of it apparently derived from the walled towns and castles of medieval Italy, with which Adam had become familiar during his travels in that country. Open battlemented towers and turrets of rectangular or circular form, corbelled and machicolated parapets, and crosslet loops are the most characteristic decorative features; windows are usually round- or square-headed, the pointed arch being conspicuously absent.

The earliest house in the group, Caldwell, Ayrshire (1771–3), is a flat and rather unimaginative composition, but Culzean, in the same county (1771–92), begins to exploit the full romantic possibilities of the style, its boldness of massing (*81*) deriving additional effect from the superb cliff-top situation. Pitfour, Perthshire (1784), and Seton, East Lothian (1789) (*85*), are compact and well-integrated designs in which castellated features are reduced to a minimum, while at a third Ayrshire house, Dalquharran (1786–90), further simplification induces a distinct note of severity. Finally, at Stobs, Roxburghshire (1792), Adam built a charming miniature version of Pitfour, employing square instead of circular angle-towers, and surmounting Scottish crow-stepped gablets with Latin-Cross finials.

Most of the castellated houses designed by other architects of the period are indebted in some degree to the work of the Adam family. John Paterson (p. 120) was responsible for a number of successful designs, of which Monzie, Perthshire (*c*. 1795), is probably the best surviving example. Caprington, Ayrshire (1797), and Fasque, Kincardineshire (1809), whose designers are so far unidentified, are cast in no less austere a mould than Robert Adam's Dalquharran, while the miniature castle is picturesquely represented by the Hermitage of Braid, Edinburgh (Robert Burn, 1785). James Playfair's Melville Castle, Midlothian (1786), is also of some interest in that it re-introduces the pointed Gothic arch, hitherto employed only at Inveraray and Douglas. More original in conception, however, is Raehills, Dumfriesshire, erected for James, third Earl of Hopetoun, to a design of Alexander Stevens in the same year as Melville. The building was altered and enlarged by William Burn in 1834, but a model of the original design indicates that Stevens's house was not altogether symmetrical in plan, being an L-shaped block with a conventional entrance-front to the north, an imposing east façade overlooking landscaped gardens, and a curiously double-bowed re-entrant angle. The garden elevation is bow-fronted and incorporates a basement terrace above which a quasi-Egyptian colonnade embraces the whole of the principal floor, while an additional upper tier encircles the centre bow. The only castellated features are the battlemented upperworks.

Among the most notable Scottish exponents of castellated Gothic at the beginning of the nineteenth century were the Elliot brothers, Archibald (1761–1823) and James (died 1810), whose important contribution to the development of Georgian Edinburgh did not prevent them from building up an extensive country-house practice. The finest of their surviving works is the main block of Taymouth Castle, Perthshire (86), which they completed for the fourth Earl of Breadalbane in 1806–10, following the Earl's dismissal of the Edinburgh architect, John Paterson. Paterson seems to have been commissioned merely to remodel and enlarge the existing sixteenth-century castle, already much altered by William Adam, but by the time the Elliots took over Lord Breadalbane had made up his mind to have a completely new building. The design is based upon that of Inveraray Castle, but the raised (instead of sunken) basement, and the slender proportions of the angle-towers give the building a much more lofty appearance than its model. Taymouth, moreover, is Gothic inside as well as outside, the most notable features of the interior being the elegant fan-vaulted staircase hall, decorated by the Italian plasterer, Francis Bernasconi, in about 1810, and the extravaganza of painted plasterwork devised by Frederick Crace and Gillespie Graham some 30 years later, when the latter was superintending a final series of alterations of the castle (east and west wings had been added by William Atkinson in 1818–28).

Whilst engaged upon Taymouth the Elliots were also directing the construction of Stobo Castle, Peeblesshire (for Sir James Montgomery of Stobo) (87), where the Inveraray theme is employed once more, but this time with almost exclusively classical interiors. At Newbyth, East Lothian (for General Sir David Baird, 1817–19), however, Archibald Elliot produced a more original composition incorporating high octagonal angle-towers and a rib-vaulted and arcaded portico; the interiors are Gothic.

The symmetry of plan and elevation characteristic of early Georgian Gothic buildings imposed certain obvious limitations upon design, but with the development of the Picturesque movement in landscape and architecture at the end of the eighteenth century architects began to explore the possibilities of the deliberately irregular composition. At the same time stylistic horizons were gradually widening, the neo-Gothic vocabulary being enlarged by the introduction of Tudor, Jacobean and Scottish vernacular motifs, and interspersed by more exotic themes derived from Asia and the Continent.

The first asymmetrical Gothic house in Scotland appears to have been Tullichewan, Dunbartonshire, erected to a design of Robert Lugar (c. 1773–1855) in 1792. Tullichewan was demolished about ten years ago, but a comparable work by the same architect is preserved near by, at Balloch, its most remarkable feature being the concave ground-plan of the entrance façade (88). William Atkinson (c. 1773–1839), a pupil of James Wyatt, is represented by two important houses of this class, Scone Palace, Perthshire (1803–6), and Tulliallan, Fife (1817–20), and Sir Robert Smirke by a single major example, Kinfauns, Perthshire (1822), although, in contrast to Balloch, irregularity of composition is, in all these cases, conceived primarily in terms of the picturesque grouping of individually symmetrical components.

The most accomplished exponent of the irregular Gothic house in Scotland, however, was undoubtedly Gillespie Graham, who produced many fluent compositions both in the castellated and in the monastic idiom. Born in humble circumstances in Dunblane, James Gillespie (*c.* 1777–1855) had risen from the joiner's bench to assume a leading position in the Scottish architectural profession while still comparatively young, setting the seal on his success by marriage to the heiress of an old Perthshire family, whose name he thereafter coupled with his own. Duns, Berwickshire (*c.* 1812), and Dunninald, Angus (1819–32) (*88*, *93*), rank among the best examples of Gillespie Graham's castellated style and demonstrate both his talent for imaginative composition, and his ability to devise rich Gothic interiors in carved stone, timber, paint and plaster. It is noticeable, moreover, that his ornamental detail has a more authentic medieval character than that of most of his contemporaries, for Graham took his Gothic almost as seriously as Pugin, with whom he was to enjoy an intermittent professional association during the later years of his life. Graham's ecclesiastical Gothic is most eloquently represented at Cambusnethan, Lanarkshire (1819), where crocketed finials and traceried windows are skilfully blended with more familiar castellated elements to produce a distinctly secular brand of monasticism. Similar combinations of ecclesiastical and secular motifs appear in most other Gothic abbeys of the period, including Inchrye, Fife (1827, now partially demolished), and the 'Perpendicular-Tudor' Millearne, Perthshire (1825), both probably designed by the Edinburgh architects R. and R. Dickson, whose most outstanding essay in this idiom, Abercairny, Perthshire (with R. Crichton, 1803–42), was demolished as recently as 1960.

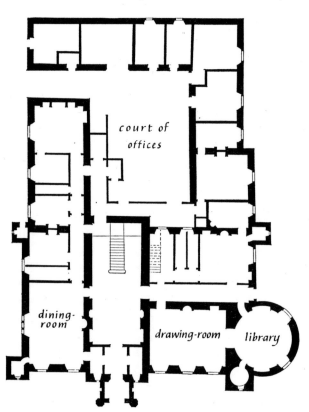

93 Dunninald Castle, Angus

By this time 'Tudor Gothic' was much in favour as a style in its own right, having been introduced into Scotland by William Wilkins (1778-1839) at Dalmeny, West Lothian (1818–19), and Dunmore Park, Stirlingshire (1820–2), and further popularised by William Burn at Carstairs, Lanarkshire (1820), and Blairquhan, Ayrshire (1824). It is hard to evaluate the architectural merits of these vast, painstakingly detailed buildings, and even contemporaries appear to have regarded them primarily as objects of academic interest, 'erected after a very correct design' (Dunmore), or 'displaying a most curious example of the taste of former times' (Dalmeny). Some of the most effective compositions in this style are to be found amongst houses of quite modest size, such as Smirke's uncompromisingly austere Cultoquhey, Perthshire (1819), and, at the opposite extreme, Robert Lugar's spirited Hensol, Kirkcudbrightshire (before 1828) (90), with its sparkling granite masonry, ogee-roofed turrets, and spacious vistaed interiors.

Lugar was also responsible for an interesting Italianate house, Glenlee, Kirkcudbrightshire (1822), while a similar broad-eaved 'Campagna' style was employed to considerable effect by Archibald Simpson at Thainston, Aberdeenshire (c. 1820–30), and by the Angus architect, David Whyte, at Keithick, near Coupar Angus (1818–23). Among the more interesting examples of contemporary work in other styles mention may be made of David Hamilton's 'Norman Castle' at Lennox, Stirlingshire (1837–41), of William Burn's 'Jacobethan' Falkland, Fife (1839), and, representing the small rustic villa that was such a conspicuous feature of Picturesque architecture in England, the charming little *cottage ornée* at Stuckgowan, Dunbartonshire. Abbotsford, Roxburghshire (Edward Blore and William Atkinson, 1816–23), with its conical roofed angle-turrets and crow-stepped gablets, foreshadows the Early Victorian revival of the Scottish Baronial style, while the strapworked pediments and tall clustered chimneys of Dunlop, Ayrshire (David Hamilton, 1833), proclaim a similar re-awakening of interest in the domestic architecture of the early Scottish Renaissance.

The ornamental garden-architecture that forms such an attractive feature of the English Romantic landscape seems never to have achieved much popularity in Scotland —a state of affairs no doubt accounted for more by differences in the meteorological than in the aesthetic climates of the two countries. Nevertheless, a few hardy Scottish noblemen and lairds did venture from time to time to adorn their policies with follies, grottoes and other such fashionable conceits, some devised for them by professional architects, others of their own invention. One of the earliest surviving structures in the former category is Roger Morris's hilltop Gothic tower at Inveraray (1748), while the handsome dovecot-folly erected by Sir John Clerk at Penicuik House is only a year or so later in date. Some of the picturesque grottoes and obelisks built for the Dukes of Atholl at Dunkeld House and Blair Castle in the third quarter of the eighteenth century still survive, although the 'beautifull Chinese house' at Dunkeld that Bishop Pococke so much admired during his visit in 1760 has unhappily disappeared. Other interesting groups of garden buildings occur at Culzean Castle, where there may be seen some rustic cottages and an aviary, and at Taymouth, where there is a curious Gothic mock-fortification, but for originality of conception and brilliance of execution none of these can quite rival the extraordinary garden-pavilion at Dunmore Park. Designed as the central feature of a range of hot-houses and gardeners' dwellings, this comprises a Palladian portico and a superimposed summer-house in the form of a colossal stone pineapple (*91*), complete with cantilevered bracts and realistically sculptured fruits, the whole composition (1761) ranking as one of the most memorable of British follies.

Buildings Specially Worth Visiting

Since most of the buildings described in this chapter are occupied as private dwelling-houses the following list includes only those which, at the time of writing, are the subjects of long-standing arrangements giving either regular or occasional public access. Buildings marked by an asterisk may usually be visited only by appointment; those currently managed as hotels are indicated by the initial (H).

Aberdeenshire	Cairness House, Fraserburgh (H)
	Haddo House, Methlick
Angus	Dun House, Montrose (H)
Argyll	*Inverary Castle*
	Stonefield Castle, Tarbert (H)
Ayrshire	*Culzean Castle*, Maybole
	Montgomerie, Tarbolton (H)
Banffshire	*Duff House*, Banff (exterior only)
Berwickshire	Gunsgreen, Eyemouth (H)
	Mellerstain, Gordon
	*Thirlestane Castle, Lauder
Dumfriesshire	Moffat House, Moffat (H)
Dunbartonshire	Stuckgowan, Tarbet (H)
East Lothian	*Yester House
Fife	*Melville House, Ladybank
Kinross-shire	*Kinross House
Kirkcudbrightshire	Cally House (H)
Midlothian	*Arniston House, Gorebridge
	Duddingston House, Edinburgh (H)
	Holyroodhouse, Edinburgh
	Melville Castle, Dalkeith (H)
	*Penicuik House
	Prestonfield House, Edinburgh (H)
	*Preston Hall, Pathhead
Peeblesshire	*Traquair House*, Innerleithen
Perthshire	*Blair Castle*, Blair Atholl
	*Pitfour Castle, Perth
Renfrewshire	*Pollok House*, Glasgow
Roxburghshire	*Abbotsford House*, Melrose
West Lothian	*Hopetoun House*, South Queensferry

IV ABBEYS AND CHURCHES

Early Churches

The period of Scottish history between the ending of the partial Roman occupation in the third century and the beginning of the main Anglo-Norman penetration in the late eleventh century is one upon which even the combined researches of historians, linguists and archaeologists have so far shed comparatively little light. Yet it was during these 'Dark Ages' that the four principal constituent peoples of post-Roman Scotland, the Picts of the north and east, the Britons of Strathclyde, the Dalriadic Scots of Argyll (all of whom may broadly be described as Celtic speaking), and the Teutonic-speaking Angles of Bernicia, were gradually united to form a single Scottish kingdom; a kingdom, however, whose boundaries stopped short of the Western and Northern Isles and adjacent portions of the mainland, where Norse settlers were established as early as the beginning of the ninth century. It was during this same period that Christianity was introduced and widely propagated, Continental and Irish traditions in due course mingling to produce a Church which, whilst acknowledging the authority of Rome, and ultimately conforming to her customs and usages, yet for long remained fundamentally monastic in organisation, having no regular system of territorial bishoprics and parishes.

At more than a millennium's remove Celtic society stands most vividly revealed in the art of its sculptured stones, metalwork, and illuminated manuscripts. Architectural remains are scanty and, although among surviving monuments ecclesiastical buildings are rather better represented than are domestic ones, our knowledge of building customs in Dark-Age Scotland is very incomplete. Documentary sources suggest, however, that in most parts of the country building in stone was the exception rather than the rule, and that the materials most commonly used in the construction of churches and houses alike were timber, wattle, clay and turf. In considering the buildings now to be described, therefore, it is worth remembering that even if their Early Christian origin is granted (and all are notoriously difficult to date), none can unreservedly be accepted as typical of its period.

It has already been stressed that the Celtic Church was primarily monastic in character, and while bishops exercised the sacramental functions appropriate to their order, they appear to have had no administrative responsibilities. The larger monasteries were independent self-governing units, each ruled by its own abbot. They were frequently located in lonely and inaccessible places, such as small off-shore islands, the remoteness of their situation reflecting the austere and anchoretic lives of their founders in the 'Age of Saints'. The monastic buildings were usually grouped within an enclosure, bounded either by a wall or by a ditch and bank, and included one or more churches together with a number of small huts or cells for the monks; there would also be a guest-house, a refectory, and in some cases a school.

A community of this sort appears to have been established at a very early date at Whithorn, Wigtownshire, where the origins of Christianity can be traced back to about the middle of the fifth century on the evidence of surviving memorial-stones. Writing in the eighth century Bede records a tradition that long before the time of Columba (d. 597), the missionary of the northern Picts, the southern Picts had been converted by the preaching of Ninian, 'a most reverend bishop . . . of the British nation', and that Ninian's monastery was called 'Candida Casa' (the white house) because he had there built a church of stone 'which is unusual among the Britons'. The identification of the site of Ninian's church and monastery with Candida Casa in Galloway is scarcely in doubt, and in 1949 excavations at the eastern end of the medieval cathedral brought to light the lower portions of the walls of part of a small rectangular building having an internal width of 15 ft.; the masonry was of rubble laid in clay and the external wall-surfaces appeared to have been daubed with coarse cream mortar of poor quality. In view of its position, orientation and structural characteristics this building has a better claim than any other to be regarded as the earliest known church now surviving in Scotland, and some scholars are prepared to accept it as St Ninian's own White Church, whose shining stone walls were to win a more than local renown.

No other structural remains have so far been identified at Whithorn, but at Iona, Argyll, where in 563 Columba founded a community which rapidly became one of the most famous in western Christendom, recent excavations have defined the general position and extent of the original monastic enclosure. As at Whithorn many of the early buildings are thought to lie beneath the medieval ones, being thus inaccessible to the spade. On the summit of the rocky outcrop known as Tor Abb, which lies immediately to the west of the abbey church, however, traces were found of a small square hut, built of turf and wattle, which the excavator has suggested may have been the cell of St Columba himself. The monastic buildings appear to have stood within a roughly rectangular enclosure which measured 1100 ft. by 500 ft. internally and was bounded by an earthen bank and outer ditch.

According to Columba's biographer, Adamnan, many of the miracles and other incidents in the Saint's life took place not on Iona itself, but at the near-by island monastery of Hinba, which some scholars have identified with Eileach an Naoimh, the southernmost islet of the Garvelloch group in the Firth of Lorne. This island, which is frequently rendered inaccessible by heavy seas and strong tidal currents, and is today entirely uninhabited, has additional and appropriate associations with St Brendan of Clonfert, the sailor-monk, whose successful establishment of a monastery there in 542 was as much a witness to his seamanship as to his sanctity. The existing remains include two churches, the earlier of them, built in drystone masonry, standing within a substantial ring-wall of similar construction. Massive enclosure-walls of this type are characteristic of early ecclesiastical sites in Celtic Britain and Ireland, two of the most conspicuous Scottish examples occurring at Loch Chaluim Chille in Skye, and Strathcashel on the eastern shores of Loch Lomond, Stirlingshire. There are also two graveyards on Eileach an Naoimh, as well as a puzzling complex of domestic buildings, a barn, a kiln, and a double 'bee-hive' hut (*188*). This latter structure comprises a pair of small circular cells which abut against each other and communicate by means of a short passage in the mid-wall. Their roofs are of corbelled stone built without mortar, the courses oversailing as they rise to produce a converging bee-hive profile. Buildings of similar construction also occur at certain early church sites in the Western Isles, including that on the island of North Rona, and there are a number of well-preserved examples in Ireland, notably at the remote island monastery of Sceilg Mhichil off the coast of Kerry. More general comparisons can be drawn between the structures on Eileach an Naoimh and those at St Blane's Monastery, Kingarth, Bute, and at Sgor nam Ban-naomha, Canna, in the Small Isles, though in all three cases it is hard to say how many of the buildings visible today belong to the Early Christian period. A primitive aspect does not necessarily imply an early date—a point that is clearly brought out by the fact that bee-hive huts are known to have been in fairly general use as summer-pasture shielings in the Hebrides within comparatively recent times (p. 230).

In the far north, within the area once occupied by the northern Picts, the most spectacular evidence of Early Christian occupation is provided by the silver hoard discovered during excavations at St Ninian's Isle, Shetland, in 1958. This site offers little guidance as to the general appearance and character of a Celtic ecclesiastical establishment of the Northern Isles, however, for few remains of actual buildings of the Pictish period have so far been brought to light. At the Brough of Deerness in Orkney, on the other hand, the position is reversed for, although surface traces of buildings survive, no serious archaeological excavation has yet been attempted. Here a small cliff-bound headland has been sealed off on its landward side by a stout drystone wall. Upon the summit there may be seen the remains of a single-chambered chapel measuring about 25 ft. by 18 ft. externally, and constructed of flagstones set in clay and pointed with lime mortar, a technique which recalls that employed in the early church at Whithorn. Round the chapel there are scattered the foundations of 19 rectangular buildings and of a similar number of circular huts. To judge from the surface remains (*94*) the site is probably a monastic one, and the character and lay-out of the buildings can be paralleled at the Celtic monastery of Tintagel, Cornwall, which was in course of occupation between the fifth and the eighth centuries. At the opposite extremity of the Orkney mainland from Deerness a small offshore island known as the Brough of Birsay appears to have housed another important Pictish settlement. Most of the Celtic

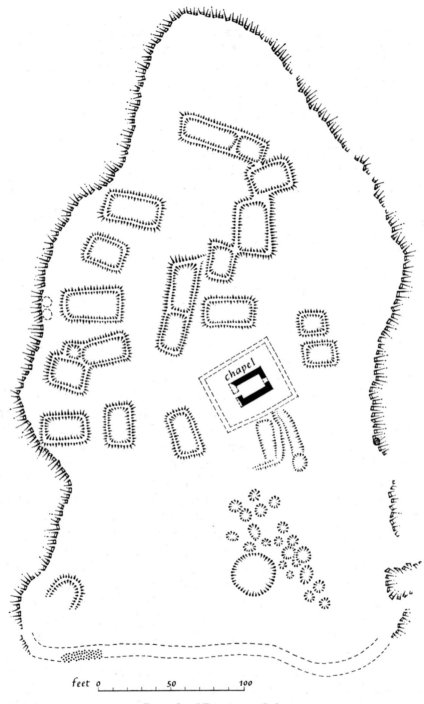

94 Brough of Deerness, Orkney

buildings have been overlaid by later ones, but the ruins of a small church have recently been identified beneath the Norse cathedral, while other excavations have revealed an early cemetery and part of an enclosure-wall, as well as a unique Pictish symbol-stone.

But the most substantial surviving remains of early ecclesiastical architecture are found in southern Pictland, in and about the valley of the Tay, a locality which seems always to have formed the heart of the Pictish kingdom. It was almost certainly from one of his strongholds in this area that in 710 Nechtan MacDerile, King of the Picts, wrote to the abbot of the Anglian monastery of Wearmouth about certain differences that had arisen between the practices of the Celtic Church and those of the Church of Rome, and which Nechtan was seeking to resolve. The King's letter also contained a request that 'architects should be sent to him to make a church of stone . . . after the manner of the Romans' and, although the site of the proposed church is not named, it has been conjectured that it was at Restenneth, Angus, the locality traditionally associated with Nechtan's own baptism by St Boniface. The majority of the buildings now seen at Restenneth were erected in medieval times, when the site was occupied by an Augustinian priory, but the most conspicuous of them, a tall square tower capped by a broach spire, evidently contains work of several different periods and its lower portions exhibit a number of archaic features. There is no consensus of opinion as to the precise age of this tower, but there is little doubt that the structure dates in part from Celtic times, and it has recently been suggested that its lowermost courses may even have formed part of the stone church contemplated by King Nechtan in the early eighth century.

If the Restenneth tower reflects the influence of Northumbrian building traditions in Pictland, the more famous round towers at Brechin, Angus, and Abernethy, Perthshire, as clearly demonstrate how firm were the ties binding the Celtic monasteries of Scotland and Ireland during the period following the union of the Picts in the middle of the ninth century. For the two Scottish towers are closely related, though scattered, members of a single family group of which no less than 80 survivors may still be counted in Ireland. All were built between the tenth and the twelfth centuries to serve, it may be supposed, both as belfries and as places of security for monks and their valuables in time of war. They were strongly constructed of stone and lime-mortar, but their numerous floors—Brechin, for example, had seven—were usually of timber; each tower had a minimum of windows and a single doorway, which was invariably placed some distance above ground level. The Brechin tower (*98*), probably erected about the year 1000, rises to a height of 86 ft., excluding its later spire; the doorway is notable for its sculptured ornament, which includes a representation of the Crucifixion, a subject rarely found in Pictish art. The tower at Abernethy is probably of later date than its companion on the north side of the Tay, and the windows in its upper portion (which has been rebuilt) are Romanesque in character.

Finally mention may be made of the most remarkable of all surviving fragments of Celtic architecture, the segmental-headed lintel stone found many years ago in the

River May, near Forteviot, Perthshire, and now preserved in the National Museum of Antiquities, Edinburgh. This stone, carved with a vigorous representation of human figures and animals grouped on two sides of a nimbed cross, was presumably incorporated within the fabric of some ninth- or tenth-century church. The carved ornament is closely related to that of certain contemporary sculptured stone monuments and, unless the fragment was as unique in its own time as it is today, it is an indication that stone churches were becoming more common by the time of the Pictish-Scottish union, and that the established schools of monumental carvers were prepared to carry their artistic traditions into the potentially much wider field of architectural decoration.

The Middle Ages. Monasteries

Although the early Celtic Church in Scotland had ultimately been brought to acknowledge the authority of Rome, it became increasingly difficult for her to maintain connections either with the Continent or with Anglo-Saxon England after the commencement of the Norse attacks upon Britain at the end of the eighth century. Thrown back upon her own resources the Scottish Church seems to have lost much of her former vitality. Some monasteries appear to have become defunct, while others came to be served by communities of 'Culdees' (Servants of God), whose organisation and practices were more akin to those of later medieval colleges of secular priests than to those of the reformed monastic orders that were then establishing themselves in other parts of western Christendom. This ecclesiastical isolationism was abandoned only when the rulers of the Canmore dynasty, and notably David I (1124–53), made clear their intention to bring the organisation of the Church in Scotland into line with that of the Roman Church as a whole. Thereafter, new monastic foundations, colonised initially from England and the Continent, followed each other in rapid succession, King David himself founding some dozen abbeys and priories, among which the Cistercian and Augustinian Orders were particularly well represented. By the end of the thirteenth century the great majority of Scotland's medieval religious houses were already in being, southern and eastern counties containing a disproportionately large number of foundations, while the north and west were only sparsely endowed. A few more houses continued to be founded in the later Middle Ages, while certain others became defunct, the total number of monastic establishments at the advent of the Reformation being rather more than a hundred.

In contrast to the informal lay-out of the Celtic monastery, the buildings of the new medieval foundations were erected upon a regular plan, whose main features had already become standardised on the Continent in Carolingian times, and which had been further developed and refined in the great reformed houses of Burgundy and Normandy. Such standardisation was appropriate to the more highly organised structures of the principal medieval religious Orders, in which the individual monastery was

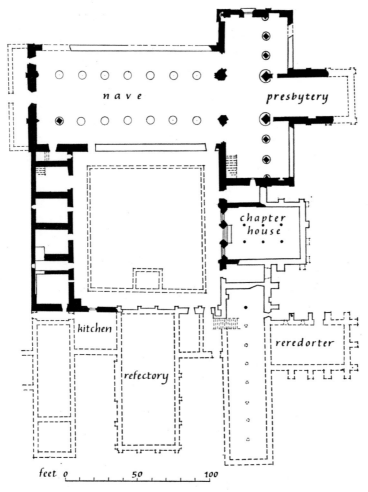

feet 0   50   100

95 Dundrennan Abbey, Kirkcudbrightshire

as closely bound to other houses of the same Order as was the individual monk to the community of which he was a member. The most distinctive characteristic of this plan (*95*) was the cloister, a quadrangular enclosure around which there were grouped the living quarters and administrative buildings of the monks, as well as the church whose choir and altars were the focus of the daily life of the community. Outside this claustral nucleus there were disposed the various offices, together with certain other buildings for which a degree of seclusion was advantageous, such as the infirmary, the abbot's or prior's lodgings and, in some cases, the guest-house.

Architecturally the great Scottish abbeys could stand comparison with their sister houses in England and the Continent and, in a country possessing few notable cathedrals or large parish churches, their construction and adornment provided an all too rare opportunity for the display of a full range of the visual arts. It is doubly unfortunate, therefore, that so little now remains of their carved decoration in wood and stone, of their mural paintings, coloured tiles and rich furnishings, and that the buildings within which such treasures were housed are for the most part mutilated and incomplete. Partly through neglect and mismanagement, partly through the ill chance that placed so many of the wealthier monasteries in the direct path of invading English armies, and partly through deliberate suppression in the days 'when ruine bare rule, and Knox knock'd downe churches', the noblest and most sumptuously furnished buildings in the country were successively destroyed or abandoned, as little regret being shown at their passing as at that of the communities whose dwelling places they had been.

One of the earliest of the Anglo-Norman foundations was Dunfermline, Fife, where a small Benedictine community appears to have been established by Queen Margaret in about 1070. The monastery was raised to abbatial status by David I, who brought Geoffrey, prior of Canterbury, to be first abbot there in 1128. A new church, replacing an earlier one of very modest dimensions, was probably begun about the same time, and work was sufficiently well advanced to allow part at least of the building to be dedicated in 1150. Of this great cruciform structure little now remains but the nave, and even this has been shorn of its eastern bay. Nevertheless, the surviving portion ranks as one of the finest Romanesque interiors in Scotland (96), and the massive cylindrical piers with chevron and twisted-band ornament, the octagonal scalloped capitals, and the triple arch-mouldings all go to suggest that the lower storey at least was the work of master-masons familiar with the bay-design of Durham Cathedral. The nave doorways provide a typically varied display of twelfth-century carved decoration, the east processional door of the south aisle in particular being so well preserved that the individual mouldings and enrichments have lost little of their original crispness. The conventual buildings have mostly disappeared, but something may still be seen of the undercrofts of the monks' dormitory and of the rere-dorter (or latrine), both of which stood at the south end of the east range of the cloister, as well as of the refectory that occupied the greater part of the south range; further west, on the far side of Monastery Street, there stand the monastic kitchens and the guest-house. All these buildings are of fourteenth-century date, the guest-house, however, having been partially reconstructed for use as a royal palace during the reign of James VI. Among the smaller Benedictine houses one of the most interesting is Coldingham Priory, Berwickshire, a twelfth-century foundation which succeeded an earlier Celtic monastery on St Abb's Head. The long aisleless choir of about 1200, almost the only part of the church to survive, is a most unusual composition, the two-storeyed division of the elevations, and the free use of multiple arcading, accentuating the horizontal character of the design.

The reformed Benedictines of Tiron were well represented in Scotland, and two of their larger houses, Kelso and Arbroath, made particularly notable contributions in the

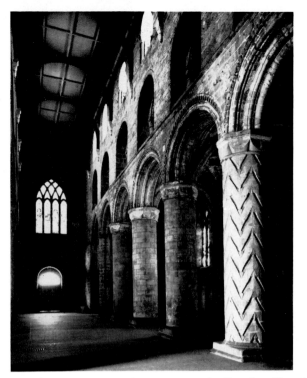

96　Nave arcade, Dunfermline Abbey, Fife. Mid twelfth century

97　Kelso Abbey, Roxburghshire. Late twelfth century

98　Brechin Round Tower and Cathedral, Angus. *c.* 1000, thirteenth century and later

99　St Rule's Church, St Andrews, Fife. Twelfth century

100 Reconstruction drawing of Melrose Abbey, Roxburghshire

101 Melrose Abbey, Roxburghshire. Late fourteenth and fifteenth centuries

sphere of ecclesiastical architecture. Kelso, Roxburghshire, one of the wealthiest and most influential of Scottish abbeys, was colonised directly from the mother house of Tiron, the great monastic church being founded near the royal castle and burgh of Roxburgh in 1128, after another Tweedside site near Selkirk had turned out to be unsuitable. The design of the church is remarkable in that it incorporates transepts at both ends, a plan probably derived in this case from the Carolingian and Romanesque churches of the Rhineland, and otherwise occurring in Scotland only at the sister house of Kilwinning, Ayrshire. Only the west crossing and a fragment of the nave now remain to demonstrate the ambitious nature of the original composition. The nave arcade has squat compound piers and elliptical arches, above which there run the continuous arcades of the triforium and clerestory passages, each storey being further defined by a string-course. All this creates a strong horizontal emphasis which contrasts most effectively with the vertical character of the crossing itself, where the central lantern-tower soars above the tall bays and angle-turrets of the transepts and west Galilee porch (97). Among other notable features of the design mention may be made of the richly decorated gabled portals of the north and west arms, while the galleried and arcaded treatment of the internal wall-surfaces provides a link with contemporary work at Arbroath.

It was from Kelso that a community was sent to Arbroath, Angus, when the abbey of St Thomas Becket was founded by King William the Lion in 1178. The founder was buried in front of the high altar in 1214, some 20 years before the monastic church was completed, and what is thought to have been the royal tomb was rediscovered in 1816, its handsome marble effigy now being preserved in the sacristy. The church is of regular cruciform plan, the most interesting portions to have survived being the south transept and the west front. The former is notable for the boldness and simplicity of its window composition, while the latter incorporates, between heavily buttressed towers of massive proportions, a remarkable centrepiece in which the west doorway is recessed beneath an arcaded gallery open both to the nave and to the exterior of the church. This elevated gallery was intended for liturgical use, as, for example, upon occasions when the great west doors were opened for processional purposes; similar but less elaborate galleries existed at St Andrews Cathedral and at Holyrood Abbey. Above the gablets of the gallery roof there is a band of blind arcading surmounted by a huge circular window of which only the lower portion now survives. Although the conventual buildings have for the most part disappeared, the outlines of the main cloister and of the adjacent kitchen-court can be traced, while to the west of the church there is a fairly well-preserved gatehouse range of late thirteenth-century date.

The third main branch of the Benedictine family, the Order of Cluny, had only two Scottish houses, Paisley, Renfrewshire, and Crossraguel, Ayrshire. The abbey church of Paisley is for the most part of late medieval date, but the general design and proportions of the nave evidently follow those of a thirteenth-century building of which certain fragments remain, notably an elaborate west doorway. The bay-design of the nave incorporates a curious clerestory-gallery which, instead of being wholly contained, as is customary, within the wall thickness, is carried round the main piers upon projecting corbels—a rather clumsy variation of a structural expedient that may be seen employed to better effect at Rouen Cathedral. The general character of the fifteenth-century work is superior to that seen in certain other major Scottish buildings of the period, however, and goes some way to justify Bishop Lesley's comment that for 'bewtie of biging' the Abbey 'may esilie contend with mony kirkes quhilkes this day ar halden maist ornat in uthir cuntreys'.

At Crossraguel the long narrow aisleless church of early fifteenth-century date terminates in a three-sided apse, a type of ending more usually associated with the collegiate churches that were then becoming such a prominent feature of the Scottish architectural scene. Considerable portions of the claustral buildings survive, the east range retaining its vaulted sacristy and chapter-house, above which there may be seen traces of the monastic scriptorium and library. The abbot's lodgings were evidently grouped round a triangular courtyard situated beyond the east range of the cloister. Their most conspicuous feature is a sixteenth-century tower-house of uncompromisingly secular aspect, presumably the residence either of one of the latter-day abbots or of a lay commendator holding a grant of monastic revenues.

The close and friendly intercourse that existed between the court of David I and the leaders of the Cistercian movement in England ensured the rapid establishment of the White Monks in the northern kingdom. In 1136, only seven years after the foundation of the first English community of the Order, a colony was sent north from Rievaulx to establish a monastery at Melrose, Roxburghshire, in its turn to become the parent of no less than five of the eleven Cistercian houses that were in existence at the end of the thirteenth century. Little now remains at Melrose of the small plain church that served the early needs of the community—a generation whose ears were still ringing with St Bernard's eloquent denunciations of all forms of architectural elaboration and embellishment. By the time the abbey came to be rebuilt at the end of the fourteenth century, after suffering fire and pillage at the hands of Richard II's armies, this negative attitude towards art had been abandoned and the new church was conceived upon much more ambitious lines (*100*). The plan itself was to be an enlargement of the original one, the east end retaining its echelon form, and the south nave-aisle being provided with an additional series of chapels. A complete scheme of rib vaulting was envisaged (a rare occurrence in Scotland), and the sculptured decoration was to be of the highest quality. The project was still unfinished when work stopped about the beginning of the sixteenth century, but even so the completed portion ranks as the most accomplished example of late medieval ecclesiastical architecture in the country (*101*). On stylistic grounds the design can be attributed to master-masons of the northern English school, the east arm in particular bearing the stamp of the York masons' yard. The curvilinear tracery of the great south transept-window, however, suggests influences from northern France rather than from Yorkshire, and may probably be ascribed to John Morow, a master-mason of French extraction ('born in parysse certanly'), whose professional career is set out in some detail in a contemporary mural inscription. The claustral buildings at Melrose were erected not, as was customary, upon the south side of the church, but upon the north side, where the waters of the River Tweed could more conveniently be harnessed for drainage purposes. The buildings themselves are now for the most part reduced to their foundations; portions of the great drain are exposed and bear impressive witness to what in its entirety, was a thoroughly comprehensive system of water engineering.

Two other houses of the Order are of special interest, Dundrennan, because it illustrates the early Cistercian Gothic style that was being developed in Britain in the second half of the twelfth century, and New Abbey because its church is more complete than that of any other Scottish Cistercian monastery. The plans of these two Kirkcudbrightshire houses were very much alike (95), each church having had a western porch, aisled nave, transepts with eastern chapels, and square-ended unaisled presbytery. The Dundrennan transepts, the best-preserved features of the remains, are simple but dignified compositions which make use of the pointed as well as of the round arch; the transeptal chapels and the presbytery were rib vaulted. The rectangular aisled chapter-house has a strong family resemblance to those at certain sister-houses in the north of England such as Fountains and Jervaulx. New Abbey was not founded until 1273; its alternative and more familiar designation of 'Sweetheart' was a tribute to the devotion of its foundress, Dervorguilla of Galloway, towards her husband John Balliol, whose embalmed heart lies buried with her before the high altar. Although comparatively well preserved, the fourteenth-century church is architecturally undistinguished, much of its detail, such as the geometric window-tracery of the presbytery, being heavy and uninspired. The conventual buildings have almost entirely disappeared, but considerable traces may still be seen of the massive stone wall, some 12 ft. in height, that bounded three sides of the monastic precinct.

Closely allied to the Cistercian Order was that of Vallis Caulium, which had three Scottish houses, all founded within a year or two of one another; each priory was directly dependent upon the mother house of Val de Choux in France. The most important architecturally is Pluscardine, Morayshire, founded as a Valliscaulian house by Alexander II in 1230, but transferred to the Benedictine order in the middle of the fifteenth century. The plan of the church evidently dates from the original foundation, though much restoration work was undertaken during the Benedictine period. The aisleless choir is square-ended and each transept has two eastern chapels; the nave seems never to have been completed. The east range of the claustral buildings is well preserved, the rectangular chapter-house having apparently been re-vaulted in the fifteenth century. Pluscardine was re-occupied by a Benedictine community in 1948 and the buildings are now once again being restored for religious use.

Beauly, Inverness-shire, has a simple cruciform plan, and the long unaisled nave and short transepts recall the form of the first English Cistercian churches, erected 100 years earlier. The third member of the trio, Ardchattan, Argyll, is closer to Pluscardine in plan, though the transeptal chapels are unusually shallow, and the nave includes a narrow north aisle; the original choir was enlarged during the fifteenth century. The remains are now for the most part incorporated within a later mansion, whose nucleus is the monastic refectory of the fifteenth century. Recent discoveries in this part of the house have revealed the existence of the refectory pulpit (from which readings were customarily made during meals), and of much of the original open timber roof, one of the very few medieval timber roofs now surviving in Scotland.

The Augustinians were among the most popular of the religious Orders in medieval Scotland, having two nunneries and 18 houses of canons, of which one was the monastic cathedral of St Andrews. The smaller foundations have left few traces, though two West Highland houses, Oronsay Priory and Iona Nunnery, have remains of some curiosity and interest. The larger and more generously endowed Augustinian monasteries, however, form a notable architectural group, Holyrood, Jedburgh and Cambuskenneth all retaining substantial fragments of their medieval buildings; of Scone, on the other hand, one of the wealthiest houses of the Order, hardly a stone survives.

Holyrood, Edinburgh, was one of David I's own foundations and, like its sister house of Inchcolm, owed its existence to an apparently miraculous local deliverance of its royal patron from accidental death. The choir and transepts of the abbey church were dismantled after the dissolution of the community at the Reformation; the nave, however, became absorbed within the buildings of the adjacent royal palace and was adapted at first for parochial use and latterly as a Chapel Royal. The high vault remained intact until the third quarter of the eighteenth century when its collapse brought down the clerestory and much of the north pier-arcade. The quality of the original design must now be judged primarily from the early thirteenth-century west front, which stands out as one of the most harmonious and well-balanced compositions of its kind. Above the elaborate west doorway and its tribune gallery the two great west windows originally rose to the nave vault, while tiers of sculptured arcading bound this central unit to square flanking towers capped with pointed spires.

At Jedburgh, Roxburghshire (*102*), another of David I's foundations, a good deal of mid-twelfth-century work remains in the choir and crossing of the church, though the nave was begun not long before that of Holyrood. As at Melrose the choir was echelon ended, while the short north and south transepts appear originally to have had eastern apsidioles. The most striking feature of the choir is the manner in which the triforia are included within the main pier-arcades, a device intended to give an appearance of height to what would otherwise have been a relatively low interior. There are no Scottish parallels to such an unorthodox variation in design, but it occurs here and there in England, notably at Romsey Abbey, Hampshire, a house with which King

David had close family connections. Although comparatively small in scale the late twelfth-century west façade has much in common with the contemporary west front of Kelso. The west portal itself is exceptionally lofty, and its round-arched head of six orders displays a rich variety of Transitional decoration.

Neither at Holyrood nor at Jedburgh does very much remain of the conventual buildings, while at Cambuskenneth, Stirlingshire, there survives almost nothing but a detached belfry-tower of late thirteenth-century date—a unique feature among Scottish medieval churches. Fortunately, however, one Augustinian house retains its claustral buildings in a fairly complete state of preservation. This is the island monastery of Inchcolm, Fife, founded by Alexander I in about 1123, but progressively rebuilt in later medieval times. The cloister belongs largely to the fourteenth century, but its east range incorporates an earlier chapter-house whose polygonal plan, although much favoured in medieval England, was seldom employed in Scotland, where it is now elsewhere found only at Elgin Cathedral. Above the chapter-house there is a warming-house communicating with the monks' dormitory in the main east range, while at the far end of the same range is the rere-dorter, whose latrine shafts are designed to be flushed directly by the sea. The frater, or refectory, occupies its usual position in the south range and the west range contains the guest-house. The most singular feature of the design is the cloister walk, which, instead of having a separate arcade and lean-to roof as is customary, is wholly contained within the ground-floor area of the three main claustral ranges.

The Premonstratensians had only six Scottish communities, and one of these served the monastic cathedral of the Bishops of Whithorn. Apart from Whithorn Cathedral itself, the only surviving remains of any importance are those of Dryburgh Abbey, Berwickshire, which was founded by Hugh de Moreville in 1150, and ranked as the first house of the Order in Scotland. The late twelfth- and early thirteenth-century church comprised an aisled nave, short transepts with eastern chapels, and a square-ended presbytery having side chapels in echelon. The best preserved portions are the crossing and transepts, and only here is it possible to appreciate the unorthodox nature of the elevational design. This offers another solution to the problem of incorporating a conventional three-storeyed system of pier-arcade, triforium, and clerestory within a building of comparatively modest height, but whereas the triforium of the Jedburgh choir is encompassed within the main arcade, the Dryburgh triforium retains separate identity by its compression into a series of small quatrefoil openings set one in each bay. The scanty remains of the nave provide evidence of a fifteenth-century reconstruction, and the west doorway is of some interest as an example of the quasi-Romanesque style that occurs sporadically in later medieval Scottish work. Due to the fall of the ground on the south side of the church the conventual buildings are stepped down to form two distinct levels. The east range is fairly entire, and incorporates a fully representative series of the apartments that customarily occupy this position. The oblong chapter-house is barrel-vaulted and, like the combined library and vestry, contains traces of painted mural decoration of a type that must originally have been commonplace in Scottish medieval churches. For the most part the design comprises simple geometric patterns, such as the chevron, executed in black and red upon a white plaster ground; it may be compared with other styles of painted decoration now represented by fragments at Glasgow Cathedral and Inchcolm Abbey, the former exhibiting a late twelfth-century abstract design and the latter a thirteenth-century figure composition.

Finally some mention must be made of houses of friars. These were quite numerous, but as nearly all were situated in burghs their buildings have shared in the general destruction that has overtaken most other categories of medieval urban architecture in Scotland. Apart from some fragments of the guest-house of the Franciscan convent at Inverkeithing, Fife, there are now no significant remains of any conventual buildings of this class, but the friary churches themselves have fared slightly better, and one or two of them even remain in religious use. The Carmelite friary of Queensferry, West Lothian, was founded by a local laird, James Dundas of Dundas, in 1441, and the existing church was evidently commenced at that time or shortly afterwards. The plan comprised a short nave (now destroyed), a south transept and an aisleless choir, the conventual buildings being on the north side of the church. The choir is ceiled with a pointed barrel-vault, carrying a roof of heavy stone slabs, a type of construction much favoured in Scotland both for secular and for ecclesiastical buildings during the later Middle Ages. As in a number of other churches of monastic or collegiate status, the upper portion of the crossing tower contains apartments designed for domestic use. Greyfriars, Elgin, follows an even simpler plan, the church being a long narrow rectangular building without any structural division between nave and choir. This is a form that was widely adopted for small churches of all categories, and became especially characteristic of the later medieval parish kirk.

Cathedrals

David I's reorganisation of bishops' sees left the kingdom with ten dioceses, and an eleventh was created towards the end of the twelfth century when Lismore was separated from Dunkeld. Three other sees remained outside the Scottish province until the second half of the fifteenth century, at which time Whithorn was formally transferred from the province of York, and Orkney and the Isles from the province of Trondheim in Norway. The administrative changes of the first half of the twelfth century resulted in considerable building activity as new cathedrals were erected and existing ones restored and enlarged. As in the case of the monastic churches, however, these early medieval structures were often remodelled, or replaced by more elaborate edifices, in later times, many of them during a notable period of cathedral building in the thirteenth century.

Apart from the tall primitive-looking tower of Dunblane Cathedral, substantial remains of these early buildings survive only in the dioceses of Orkney and St Andrews, where the later cathedrals were erected upon new sites. The cathedral at Birsay occupies the site of the Celtic monastery to which reference has already been made. Although small in scale it is a structure of considerable interest, the plan comprising a western tower, aisleless nave, and apsidal-ended choir. The most remarkable surviving features are the two circular altar-recesses at the eastern end of the nave, for which parallels must be sought among the twelfth-century churches of Norway and Greenland. Whether the existing building should be ascribed to the early twelfth century or to the middle of the preceding century is not altogether certain, as the site as a whole is still undergoing intensive archaeological exploration. It has been suggested, however, that the remains are those of the 'splendid minster' known from the Norse sagas to have been erected by Earl Thorfinn the Mighty after his return from a pilgrimage to Rome in about 1050, and that the structure was remodelled early in the twelfth century when it became the cathedral of Orkney. A group of buildings lying immediately to the north of the church has been identified as an episcopal palace.

Like Birsay, St Rule's Church, St Andrews (99), is of markedly individualistic character, and neither building is likely to have been typical of Scottish cathedrals of the Norman period. Of narrow proportions and massive construction, its towering walls pierced by small double-splayed windows set high above the ground, the choir of St Rule's at once recalls Northumbrian building practice of pre-Conquest times. The tall square tower with round-headed two-light windows at belfry level belongs to the same tradition, but can be paralleled elsewhere in Scotland, notably at Dunblane and at the parish churches of Dunning and Muthill, Perthshire. It is generally accepted that St Rule's was built as a monastic cathedral of the Augustinian Order by Bishop Robert of St Andrews shortly before the middle of the twelfth century. The distinctive architectural detail so closely resembles that of the slightly earlier church of Wharram-le-Street, Yorkshire, as to make it virtually certain that the two buildings were the work of the same group of masons and this can probably be explained by the fact that both churches had links with the Augustinian priory of Nostell, where Bishop Robert had formerly served as a canon. The building is evidently incomplete in its present form however, the tower formerly having opened westwards into a nave, and the choir eastwards into a sanctuary. Whether this arrangement reflects the incorporation of an earlier building, represented by the tower and choir, within the mid-twelfth-century church is debatable, but in either case the plan is a most unusual one and appears quite unsuitable for the purpose that Bishop Robert had in mind.

The little church on the Brough of Birsay retained its cathedral status for no more than a generation, for in 1137 Earl Rognvald founded a new cathedral at Kirkwall, dedicating it to his murdered kinsman St Magnus. Orkney's political and cultural affiliations were with the Norse world, but the Earl, like his compatriots in Norway itself, maintained artistic contacts with the Anglo-Norman and Scottish kingdoms. It must have been due to his initiative, or to that of his formidable ally, Bishop William the Old, that the influence of the Durham school, already apparent in the design of the nave of Dunfermline Abbey (p. 138), now penetrated to Orkney. As first laid out the plan of St Magnus, Kirkwall, appears to have comprised an aisled nave of eight bays with western towers, transepts with eastern apsidioles, and an aisled choir of three bays terminating in a central apse; the choir aisles may have been apsidal-ended internally but square-ended externally, as at Durham. The work of construction was not completed for more than three centuries, but although many modifications to the original scheme were made during this period, the building still retains a strong underlying unity, while the excellence of the proportions effectively disguises its relative smallness in size (*103*). As it stands today the oldest portions of the cathedral are the transepts and the adjacent bays of the nave and choir, which seem to have been completed by about the middle of the twelfth century. The bay design is tripartite, the cylindrical piers of the main arcades being much more massive than those of Dunfermline, though the general scheme is much the same in both churches. In the late twelfth and thirteenth centuries the nave was carried westwards, though not finished, the crossing and the transeptal chapels were reconstructed, and the choir was extended to a length of six bays; all apsidal terminations were now abandoned, the choir and the transeptal chapels being completed with square eastern ends. The most notable features of this building period are the high vaults of the nave and choir, the latter being skilfully contrived so as to extend over the three Romanesque bays, which had formerly been unvaulted.

St Rule's Church can hardly have been considered a satisfactory building to serve as a monastic cathedral and some doubt arises as to the extent to which it did in fact fulfil this role. But the great cathedral church whose walls began to rise on an adjacent site about the year 1160 was conceived as a building of the first rank, its nave of 14 bays making it one of the longest churches in Britain. Unhappily this 'new kyrk cathedralle' of St Andrew, so proudly consecrated by Bishop Lamberton in 1318, was allowed to fall into total ruin after the Reformation. Enough remains, however, to show that the east gable incorporated three tiers of three round-headed windows—a treatment which seems to foreshadow that at Arbroath—and that the west end was reconstructed in the late thirteenth century, when the two western bays of the nave were replaced by a Galilee porch. Surrounding the cathedral there is a well-preserved precinct wall (p. 173), fortified with round and rectangular towers, and having a stately entrance-gateway on its west side.

Among the cathedrals that took shape during the intensive building activity of the thirteenth century, the most important are Glasgow, Dunblane and Elgin. Apart from certain broad similarities of detail, however, the three buildings have little in common, for in each case the thirteenth-century lay-out was partially determined by the form of an earlier cathedral occupying the same position. Indeed, the site upon which Bishop Bondington of Glasgow began to raise his new cathedral (*104*) some time after 1233 had

102　Jedburgh Abbey, Roxburghshire. Twelfth and thirteenth centuries

103　Kirkwall Cathedral, Orkney. Mid twelfth century and later
104　Glasgow Cathedral. Thirteenth century and later

105　Elgin Cathedral, Morayshire. Thirteenth century and later
106　Holy Rude Church, Stirling. Fifteenth and sixteenth centuries

107　Leuchars Church, Fife. Twelfth century and later
108　Chapel Royal, Stirling Castle. 1594

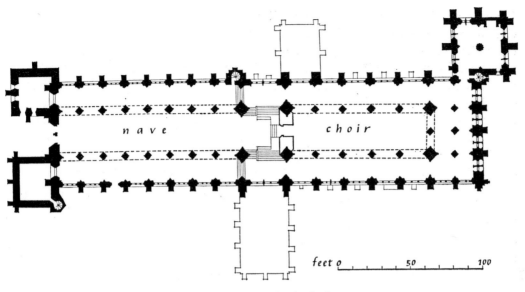

nave   *choir*

feet 0   50   100

109 Glasgow Cathedral

been held sacred since Early Christian times, and must already have borne a succession of churches, each in turn enshrining the relics of St Mungo. Bondington's cathedral incorporated no more than a few fragments of its immediate forerunner of the late twelfth century. More important, however, was the fact that it retained its predecessor's distinctive two-level arrangement of the eastern arm, for this gave the designer an opportunity to create a lower church of unusual dignity and splendour in which St Mungo's shrine could be made more accessible to increasing numbers of pilgrims. The plan adopted (*109*), although apparently novel in Scotland, was already well established in England, where it continued to be employed to good effect throughout the thirteenth century, as at Salisbury and Wells. At Glasgow the choir is of five bays, the side aisles returning to form an eastern ambulatory beyond which there are four chapels; this scheme is repeated in the lower church where the ambulatory plan, coupled with the use of double stairways, enabled pilgrims to make a complete circuit of the central shrine. The western portion of the cathedral comprises an aisled nave and rudimentary transepts of the same width as the main vessel; the original design provided for a crossing tower and for two western towers, but the latter were demolished during the course of the nineteenth century. Alone among Scottish cathedrals Glasgow retains its stone screen, or pulpitum, dividing the ritual choir from the nave; this was erected by Bishop Blackadder (1483–1508), first archbishop of the see, whose building achievements are further commemorated in the richly decorated undercroft that bears his name.

About the time that Bishop Bondington was beginning his work of reconstruction at

Glasgow another ambitious building scheme was commenced at Dunblane. A new church was laid out to comprise an aisled nave of eight bays and a spacious unaisled choir some 80 ft. in length, against the north wall of which there was placed a self-contained two-storeyed structure whose precise function it is now hard to determine; no provision was made for transepts. At some stage during the building operations an older church was swept away, but its freestanding Romanesque belfry-tower was carefully, if somewhat incongruously, preserved by absorbing it within the fabric of the new cathedral, an expedient that was also adopted at Restenneth Priory. The most successful feature of the composition is the nave, where the elegant proportions of the main arcade and of the galleried and arcaded clerestory more than compensate for the omission of a triforium storey. The west end incorporates a deeply recessed central doorway flanked by acutely pointed blind arches containing trefoiled inner heads. Above, there rise lofty triple lancets whose generous dimensions recall those of the south-transept windows of Arbroath, while the design is completed by the provision of a central vesica in the upper gable-wall.

In the diocese of Moray a start was made upon the reconstruction of an existing church at Elgin when the transference of the episcopal seat thither from Spynie was contemplated in the opening years of the thirteenth century. The first cathedral was a comparatively modest structure comprising an aisled nave, transepts, and a square-ended aisleless choir; there were two western towers and a third above the crossing. The partial destruction of the building by fire in 1270 opened the way for a far-reaching scheme of enlargement in which the nave was provided with double aisles on each side —a rare occurrence in Britain—and the choir was extended eastwards to a length of seven bays and flanked by slightly shorter aisles; at the same time an octagonal chapter-house was erected on the north side of the choir. This great cathedral church (*105*), 'the ornament of the realm, the glory of the kingdom, the delight of foreigners and stranger guests', was once more slighted and burnt by Alexander Stewart, 'Wolf of Badenoch', in 1390. Again the damage was laboriously made good, however, and, although abandoned at the Reformation, the fabric remained fairly intact until the morning of Easter Day, 1711, when the fall of the central tower led to the destruction of the greater part of the nave and crossing. The most notable features of the existing remains are the massive western towers flanking the recessed entrance-portal, and the slender arcaded lancets of the choir.

Although none of the buildings just described achieves the purity and refinement of the developed Gothic style of the Ile de France, all exhibit certain general characteristics of that style such as are common to contemporary structures in other western European countries. After the end of the thirteenth century, however, Scottish architecture rapidly lost touch with developments in England and on the Continent, and apart from one or two obviously derivative compositions such as the east end of Melrose Abbey, ecclesiastical buildings of all ranks were absorbed within the vernacular tradition. Scottish church architecture of this period is characterised by a reversion to earlier forms such as the round arch and cylindrical pier, by the development of an increasingly whimsical repertoire of carved detail, and by the adoption of certain structural features of secular origin of which the most conspicuous is the barrel-vault. The native ecclesiastical style of the later Middle Ages cannot be said to possess great aesthetic merit, nor does it always conform to accepted principles of architectural design, but its directness of form and frankness of expression give it an attraction of its own.

Many of these vernacular mannerisms appear in the cathedrals that were rebuilt in the fifteenth and early sixteenth centuries. St Machar's, Aberdeen, for example, retains an aisled nave and western towers of the second quarter of the fifteenth century. The main arcades incorporate plain cylindrical piers having simply moulded bases and capitals; the clerestory windows, on the other hand, and the remarkable seven-light window in the west wall, are round arched, the latter being enriched with cusped inner heads. The severity of the west front reflects the nature of the material of which it is built, every part, with the exception of the spires, being constructed of Aberdeen granite; there is a complete absence of carved decoration, and the mouldings of the processional doorway are rudimentary in character. The barrel-vaulted towers are defensive in aspect if not in function, the heavily buttressed walls rising to a corbelled and machicolated parapet such as might have crowned a contemporary tower-house.

The lay-out at Dunkeld has a good deal in common with that of the neighbouring cathedral of Dunblane, and may reflect the plan of a thirteenth-century building, of which only a few fragments now remain. The extensive unaisled choir was almost entirely reconstructed in the early nineteenth century, but the aisled nave of seven bays and the north-west tower are of fifteenth-century date, the cylindrical columns and pointed arches of the main arcades being similar in character to those at St Machar's. The triforium openings are semicircular and have pointed inner arches with trefoiled heads, while the clerestory comprises a series of small pointed windows of the plainest description. An attempt to improve the design of the west front by the insertion of a new entrance-portal and of a great west window, has produced a curiously unbalanced composition in which the ogee canopy of the inserted window tries to jostle an earlier gable-light out of its central position.

In the more remote parts of the country local stylistic pecularities became pronounced at this period as they had never done in the thirteenth century. This is particularly noticeable at Iona, where an extensive programme of building operations was carried out at about the time that the revived Benedictine monastery became the cathedral church of the Scottish diocese of the Isles in 1499. No attempt was made here to introduce conventional Late Gothic forms, the new work being for the most part closely modelled upon the old. Transitional and Early Gothic mouldings reappear, and the elaborate carved decoration of the late medieval West Highland school characteristically includes a number of revived motifs, among them the 'dog-tooth'. At the same time errors of construction were made with results more far-reaching even than those noticed at Dunkeld for, by placing the clerestory windows of the choir directly above the arcade piers, the builders so weakened the wall as to make necessary the construction of crude flying buttresses that cut across the interior of the south choir-aisle.

Churches

There is no evidence of the existence of an organised parochial system in Scotland before the twelfth century, but with the introduction of Anglo-Norman feudalism the parish church soon became as familiar a feature of the landscape as the baronial castle. Indeed the boundaries of parish and barony were often co-terminous, while the parish church built, endowed and patronised by the lord, frequently stood in close proximity to the baronial residence. Thus, the great earthen mound that today marks the site of Robert de Quincey's motte-and-bailey castle of Leuchars, Fife, stands only a few hundred yards from the parish church that he erected, while at Skipness, Argyll, the early thirteenth-century chapel lay so close to the lord's residence (p. 35) that when the time came to enlarge the castle the chapel had to be replaced by an entirely new church upon another site. Although of Anglo-Norman origin, however, the Scottish parish church rarely achieved the architectural splendours of its medieval counterparts in England and France, being in most cases small in size and undistinguished in appearance. This was no doubt due partly to the fact that in many parishes, and particularly in highland areas, the pattern of settlement was so scattered that spiritual needs could most effectively be met by the erection of a number of small dependent chapels, and partly to the fact that a very high proportion of Scottish parish churches soon became appropriated to religious houses, a considerable portion of the parochial revenues being thus diverted to serve the purposes of a distant monastic community little interested in such local matters as the upkeep of a church fabric.

The typical Romanesque parish church of the eastern lowland counties comprised an oblong nave and a small square-ended chancel; the timber roof was covered with thatch or shingles, and the narrow deeply splayed windows admitted a bare minimum of light to the interior. There was little carved stone detail and the liturgical furnishings were of the plainest, while the broad expanses of the internal wall-surfaces were lime-washed or plainly rendered, perhaps sometimes bearing a simple pattern of painted decoration. Although a considerable number of such churches were built, the majority are now represented only by fragmentary remains incorporated within the fabrics of much later buildings, as for example at Legerwood, Berwickshire, and Borthwick, Midlothian. The parish churches of Duddingston, Edinburgh, and Aberdour, Fife, retain the substance of their Romanesque forms, however, while the little hilltop kirk of St Brandon, at Birnie, Morayshire (110), survives almost intact, its narrow chancel-arch of two plain orders springing from heavy scalloped capitals of conventional

Norman pattern which provide almost the only example of decoration in the entire building. In a few cases churches of a rather more elaborate type were erected for parochial use, though only at St Nicholas, Aberdeen, is there any evidence of the existence of a fully developed aisled and cruciform building of Romanesque

110 Birnie Church, Morayshire

date. The well-preserved mid-twelfth-century parish church of Dalmeny, West Lothian, has a western tower, an oblong nave and a square choir with an apsidal termination; both choir and apse are vaulted. The whole fabric is executed in ashlar masonry of good quality and there is a fine display of carved detail, notably in the south portal of the nave and upon the arches that separate the three main internal divisions of the church. Other closely related examples of the same type survive in rather more fragmentary condition at Tynninghame, East Lothian, and at Leuchars (*107*), where the external wall-surfaces of the choir and apse are enriched with two tiers of ornamental arcading.

A number of churches stand apart from the main categories considered above. The most famous of these is the tiny oblong chapel that crowns the rock summit of Edinburgh Castle. Though traditionally associated with Queen Margaret, the building is probably of late twelfth-century date, the plain exterior concealing a fairly developed plan comprising a nave and an apsidal chancel separated by a narrow chancel-arch. There is another small Romanesque chapel on the island of Iona, while further north the fragmentary remains of a church of most unusual form—the only surviving example of its class in Scotland—stand close to the site of the Norse Earls' palace at Orphir in Orkney. The nave was circular on plan, having an internal diameter of 20 ft.; it was covered with a vault pierced by a central orifice to admit light, while on the east side there was a small barrel-vaulted chancel, this being the only portion of the building that today remains intact. Round churches of this type were erected in a number of European countries during the period of the Crusades, their ultimate source of origin being the Church of the Holy Sepulchre at Jerusalem; the one at Orphir probably dates from the first half of the twelfth century. Not all Orkney churches were as cosmopolitan in form as Orphir, however, for St Magnus, Egilsay, presents a number of features otherwise peculiar to Irish ecclesiastical architecture of the period, though in this instance readily explicable in view of the close contacts that obtained between Ireland and the Northern Isles in Norse times. In size and in basic form the church resembles the cathedral at Birsay, but the round tower at the west end of the nave and the chamber over the barrel-vaulted chancel are both of Irish derivation.

By the end of the twelfth century a large number of parishes in the more developed parts of the country must have been provided with serviceable churches of fairly recent construction. Thereafter church building became more sporadic until the later Middle

Ages when a rise in economic prosperity led to the erection of new burgh kirks and to the foundation of collegiate churches. The plan of the typical post-Romanesque parish church was an aisleless and somewhat elongated rectangle; there were neither tower nor transepts and the only structural differentiation between nave and chancel was provided by a simple timber screen. Good examples of thirteenth-century churches of this type occur at Abdie, Fife, and Auchindoir, Aberdeenshire, while the well-preserved remains of the old parish kirk of Cawdor at Barevan, Nairnshire, are of particular interest by virtue of the fact that the character of the architectural detail associates the building with the near-by hall-house at Rait (p. 34). Barevan Church measures about 70 ft. by 20 ft. internally; the nave and chancel were more or less equal in size and each was provided with its own entrance-doorway in the south wall. The chancel was lit by a series of simple lancet-windows having monolithic arch-heads and heavily chamfered rear-arches. Structures of this type went on being built right up to the Reformation and beyond, and the plan and dimensions of Barevan can be closely paralleled in later medieval parish churches such as Kinkell, Aberdeenshire, whose sixteenth-century character becomes apparent only when account is taken of the surviving fragments of carved detail.

In the more remote parts of the west and north the parochial system was slow to develop, and the typical Anglo-Norman parish church does not appear to have penetrated to these areas. There was a good deal of church building in Argyll during the late twelfth and thirteenth centuries, however, and the Kintyre peninsula alone contains several buildings of standard form, the most notable of these being Skipness, which was evidently constructed by the masons responsible for the conversion of the adjacent manor-house into a great castle of enclosure at the end of the thirteenth century (p. 35). At Dunstaffnage, near Oban, there is an unusually elaborate, but somewhat earlier, church of the same type. The angles are defined by heavy roll-mouldings and the tall lancet windows are enriched with banded nook-shafts and with well-carved dog-tooth ornament of late Transitional character—features which occur at the near-by monastery of Ardchattan (p. 144) and also in the chancel of the parish church of Killean, in Kintyre. The long aisleless rectangle was not the only, nor the most common variety of medieval church in the West Highlands or in the Western and Northern Isles, however, for these areas were more effectively served by the small dependent chapels of which some mention has already been made. Most were single-chambered buildings measuring between 20 ft. and 30 ft. in length and having a single doorway placed towards one end of the south wall or in the centre of the west gable. The extreme simplicity of these chapels defies chronology, but they evidently reflect the influence of Celtic prototypes, and some may antedate the introduction of parochial organisation, as do the closely related 'keeils' of the Isle of Man.

Nearly all the larger Scottish burghs must have been provided with their own parish churches from the earliest times, but with the exception of some fragments of the late

Romanesque church of St Nicholas, Aberdeen, no major burgh kirks of twelfth- or thirteenth-century date now survive. Sometimes, as in the cases of Linlithgow and Stirling, these earlier churches were destroyed by accident or assault; more frequently, perhaps, they were pulled down on account of structural decay, or because their accommodation facilities were felt to be inadequate. During the fifteenth and early sixteenth centuries an improvement in the economic position of a number of the more important towns provided an opportunity for fresh building projects to be undertaken, and burgh vied with burgh in the erection of costly new edifices, whose numerous chapels and altars bore witness to the prosperity, no less than to the piety, of the merchants and craftsmen who endowed them.

Some of these churches bear a strong family resemblance to each other and most are comparable in size to the smaller Scottish cathedrals, being designed as aisled cruciform buildings with one or more towers (*III*). The reconstruction of the parish church of Edinburgh began in the late fourteenth century, the new building comprising a vaulted nave of five bays flanked with double aisles, a crossing tower, short transepts and an aisled choir of four bays. Further additions continued to be made right up to the second decade of the sixteenth century, one of the most notable being the erection of the Preston Aisle in commemoration of a benefactor who had secured a relic of the burgh's patron saint, and bequeathed it 'to oure mother Kirk of Sant Gele of Edinburgh withoutyn ony condicion'. Much interesting carved detail of the period has survived an insensitive restoration of the fabric in 1829. Second only to St Giles', Edinburgh, among the burgh kirks of the Lothians was St Mary's, Haddington, which was completed about the middle of the fifteenth century, and today stands with its choir in ruins but with its restored nave still

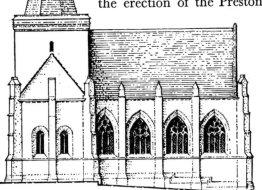

III St Monance Church, Fife

in parochial use. Some of the detail, including the fine round-arched west doorway, recalls work at St Giles', while the crossing tower is known originally to have been crowned with an open-work spire similar to those at St Giles' and at King's College, Aberdeen. These distinctive 'crown spires' are one of the more pleasing features of late medieval Scottish architecture, and examples formerly occurred also on the western towers of the parish churches of Linlithgow and Dundee.

In central and eastern Scotland there may be seen some fragments of the old burgh kirks of Dundee and Aberdeen, the interesting but over-restored remains of St John's,

Perth, and two well-preserved major churches of some importance, Holy Rude, Stirling, and St Michael's, Linlithgow. Both these churches replaced earlier churches destroyed or damaged by fire in the early fifteenth century, and both took a century or more to complete, the Church of the Holy Rude being in fact still unfinished when work upon the fabric stopped about 1540. A similar design was adopted in each case, the plan (*112*) comprising a west tower, an aisled nave and choir of five and three bays respectively, transepts, and an apsidal presbytery of polygonal form; at Stirling it was intended to erect a second tower above the crossing, but the project was abandoned before any of the massive supporting piers had been carried to their full height. Both churches make full use of the natural advantages of their sites, St Michael's commanding the adjacent royal palace of Linlithgow no less than the burgh, and the stepped east end of the Church of the Holy Rude (*106*) forming an equally impressive terminal feature to the upper nucleus of the burgh of Stirling.

During the later Middle Ages the munificent piety of the Scottish baronial class found its chief expression not, as previously, in the foundation of monasteries, but in the endowment of non-monastic communities of secular clergy known as collegiate churches. Many of these colleges of canons or chaplains were new foundations having no parochial

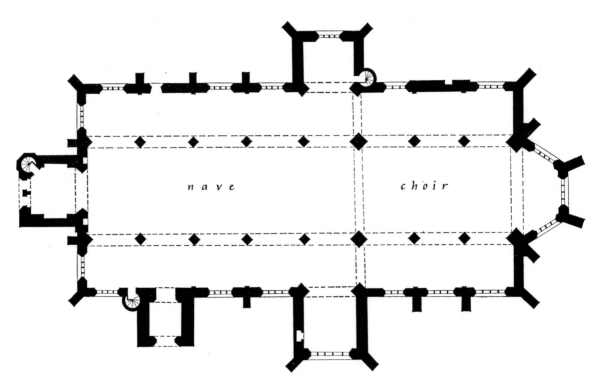

112 Linlithgow Church, West Lothian

114 Greyfriars Church, Edinburgh. 1616–20 and later

116 Penicuik Church, Midlothian. *Sir James Clerk, 1770–1*

113 Dairsie Church, Fife. 1621

115 Canongate Church, Edinburgh. *James Smith, 1688*

117 St John's Episcopal Church, Edinburgh. *William Burn*, 1816

118 St George's Church, Charlotte Square, Edinburgh. *Robert Reid*, 1811–14

119 Dunfermline Abbey Kirk, Fife. *William Burn*, 1821

commitments, while others were established within existing parish churches. Indeed, so popular did such establishments become that a number of the larger burghs found it desirable to secure collegiate status for their own mother churches and, of the seven burgh kirks mentioned above, all but three had become collegiate by the time of the Reformation. Whether a church was newly founded or simply raised in status some form of building activity was likely to be necessary, and it is noticeable that priority was invariably given to the erection of a choir and chancel, thus allowing the full round of the divine office to be commenced. In many cases, however, the endowments appear to have been insufficient to permit the construction of a nave, and churches were left in an unfinished condition.

One or two of the smaller collegiate churches, such as Innerpeffray, Perthshire, and Fowlis Easter, Angus, followed the standard oblong form of the simpler parish kirks. Fowlis Easter itself, founded by a local laird about the year 1453, is a particularly well-preserved example; it retains part of its original timber rood-screen, an elaborate sacrament-house and some notable painted decoration. More typically, however, collegiate churches were of cruciform plan, having well-defined choirs with square or polygonal eastern ends; choir and transepts were unaisled, being ceiled with heavily buttressed barrel-vaults whose comparatively low springing level restricted the height of the window openings. Many of the surviving churches of this group are in the Lothians, where polygonal-ended choirs can be seen at Dalkeith and Seton, and square-ended ones at Corstorphine, Crichton and Dunglass; only at the latter church does a pre-Reformation nave remain intact. Quite the most ambitious of all Scottish collegiate churches was Roslin, Midlothian, which was founded by William St Clair, Earl of Orkney, in 1446. This was intended to be a fully-developed cruciform structure, but the choir only was completed, together with an adjacent sacristy or chapel, which extends eastwards at a lower level. Both in its plan and in the quality of its ornamental detail the church is of quite exceptional interest. The aisled choir is of five bays, the aisles returning across the eastern end to form an ambulatory beyond which there are four eastern chapels. This plan may have been modelled upon that of Glasgow Cathedral, but there are also indications of borrowings from other and perhaps more distant sources in the curious transverse barrel-vaults of the side aisles and in the rich Plateresque decoration, and these go some way to confirm the account of a late seventeenth-century family historian who records that the Earl 'caused artificers to be brought from other regions and foraigne kingdomes'.

Post-Reformation Churches

The general introduction of the Reformed pattern of worship in the third quarter of the sixteenth century brought about a number of important changes of architectural usage. The compartmentation of medieval churches was condemned by the Reformers, to whom the customary divisions of nave and chancel, transept and chapel, were so many obstacles to the observance of fully congregational worship. Their principal requirement was a single-chambered building in which people could freely hear the preaching of the Word and take part in the celebration of the Lord's Supper, the congregation being accommodated for this purpose at long communion-tables placed within the body of the church. Baptism, too, was a congregational service and it was found convenient to attach the baptismal basin to the pulpit, which usually occupied a prominent position against the south wall of the church. The only major subdivision of the building was of social rather than of liturgical significance, the laird and his family, and the burgh magistrates, invariably preferring to be seated within their own private pews or galleries. These 'lairds' lofts' were frequently placed above a family burial-vault, the whole structure thus forming a separate appendage that commonly projected from the centre of the north wall of the church. Sometimes, as in the sumptuously appointed Hopetoun Aisle at Abercorn, West Lothian, and at St Bridget's Church, Dalgety, Fife, the loft incorporated a comfortable retiring-room in which meals could be taken in the intervals between services.

The smaller medieval churches were quite easily adapted to meet these new requirements, but some difficulty was experienced in the case of cathedrals, abbeys, and the larger burgh kirks, all of which were inherently unsuitable for congregational worship. Thus it often came about that part only of a church was preserved, as for example at Melrose and Dunblane, or, conversely, that two separate places of worship were formed within the same building, a state of affairs that persisted at Holy Rude, Stirling, until the restoration of 1936–40. Whether it was a question of adapting existing churches, or of building new ones, there were always liable to be financial problems. Much of the not inconsiderable wealth of the medieval church had passed into secular hands at the Reformation and the responsibility for fabric maintenance and for the provision of stipends usually fell upon the local landholders, or heritors, who were often unable or unwilling to meet their commitments. This is probably the main explanation of the comparatively modest size and demeanour of the average post-Reformation kirk, as also for the neglect and disrepair so frequently commented upon by seventeenth- and eighteenth-century travellers, one of whom went so far to remark that 'in many parts of Scotland our Lord seems still to be worshipped in a stable'.

Of the new churches erected in the first century and a half after the Reformation a large number were of the simple oblong type that had become customary during the later Middle Ages. Stylistically, too, many followed medieval precedents, Gothic forms persisting even more noticeably in the ecclesiastical than in the domestic architecture of the period. The attractive little Tweedside church of Lyne, Peeblesshire, is a fairly representative example of its class (*120*). Built by Lord Hay of Yester between 1640 and 1645 it measures about 54 ft. by 21 ft. over all and is lit by a series of heavy traceried Gothic windows; the single entrance-doorway is placed towards the west end of the south wall. Lord Yester's original canopied pew survives, together with a contemporary oak pulpit which formerly stood against the south wall, directly opposite the pew. Less typical of the period, but of greater architectural interest, are two other rectangular kirks, the Chapel Royal at Stirling Castle, and the parish church of Dairsie, Fife. The former, which was hastily erected for the baptismal ceremonies of Prince Henry in 1594, has a

120 Lyne Church,
Peeblesshire

remarkable south elevation (*108*) in which two-light semicircular-headed windows are symmetrically disposed about a central doorway framed within a rather clumsy classical frontispiece. The internal arrangements have been altered, but some interesting and well-documented fragments of early seventeenth-century painted decoration survive. Dairsie was built by Archbishop Spottiswoode in 1621, and it has been suggested that its original internal lay-out (which included a choir screen) reflected current attempts to introduce Anglican liturgical practices into Scotland. The external elevations (*113*) are a strange mixture of Renaissance, Scottish Baronial and debased Gothic; buttresses divide the long walls into four bays, each of which contains a broad three-light window incorporating plate tracery, while at the south-west angle a corbelled belfry of octagonal form rises to a balustraded parapet surmounted by a spire.

A natural development of the simple rectangle produced the equally characteristic T-plan, in which the projecting wing or 'aisle' frequently housed the laird's burial vault and loft. Two seventeenth-century Fife churches, Anstruther Easter (1634) and Tulliallan (1675), may serve to illustrate this type. In the former the aisle is quite small, but at Tulliallan it is of the same width as the main body of the church, access to a gallery having been obtained by means of a forestair rising against the east wall. Both churches have western towers, that at Anstruther being little more than a belfry, while the one at Tulliallan, like its near neighbour at Airth, on the Stirlingshire side of the Forth, is a full-scale structure of some architectural refinement. One of the most ambitious T-plan churches of the period was the Tron Kirk, Edinburgh, begun in 1637 to a design of the King's Master-Mason, John Mylne, younger. The plan is now incomplete for, when the building was altered and truncated in the late eighteenth century, the original south aisle was entirely removed; the surviving architectural detail is of considerable interest, however, some of it evidently reflecting the current Anglo-Flemish style, and some apparently being of direct Low Country origin.

Among those churches that fall outside the two main categories considered above, a small group of centrally planned buildings deserves special consideration. The earliest of them, and one of the few churches erected by the first generation of Reformers, is the parish kirk of Burntisland, Fife, which was built at the expense of the local inhabitants in 1592 at a time when the burgh was enjoying a period of some commercial prosperity. The building is almost square in plan and is surmounted by a central tower carried on semicircular arches springing from four rectangular piers; additional support for the tower is provided by heavily buttressed diagonal arches. Although unique in Scotland this design is not necessarily of foreign inspiration for it has recently been demonstrated that the supposed 'Dutch models' of popular tradition in fact post-date Burntisland itself. Edinburgh's first post-Reformation church, on the other hand, was of much less enterprising design, Old Greyfriars (1612–20) (*114*) being no more than a reproduction of a typical medieval aisled nave with the pulpit placed near the centre.

All the centrally planned churches erected in the seventeenth century appear to have been cruciform and most were of Greek-Cross plan. One of the best preserved is Lauder, Berwickshire, which was designed in 1673 by Sir William Bruce, who was then remodelling the near-by castle of Thirlestane for the Earl of Lauderdale (p. 94). In the original arrangement of the interior three of the limbs seem to have contained galleries, while the fourth accommodated the communion-tables; the pulpit stood in the crossing. Apart from its distinctive plan Bruce's design is firmly set within the vernacular tradition, but the aisled Latin-Cross church of Canongate, Edinburgh (*115*), attributable to his versatile fellow-architect and contemporary James Smith, is much more ambitious in character. Its basilican plan is more reminiscent of Continental Catholicism than of Scottish Presbyterianism and may reflect the mutal religious sympathies of James VII and II, by whose command the building was commissioned in 1688, and of the architect (p. 101). The architectural detail includes both classical and Gothic elements, a combination of styles which also appears in the slightly later parish church of Durisdeer, Dumfriesshire. This building, too, is associated with Smith, though his precise share in its design is uncertain; the plan is cruciform, with a western appendage in the form of a two-storeyed school building. The north limb comprises the Queensberry Mausoleum, whose plain external walls conceal a Baroque interior no less dramatic than the show-front of Drumlanrig itself; this, certainly, is Smith's creation and it forms a fitting repository for John Van Nost's magnificent marble tomb of the second Duke and his wife.

Although varying in style in accordance with current architectural fashions, post-Reformation churches of the eighteenth and early nineteenth centuries showed little novelty of plan. Outside the towns narrow rectangular kirks of the plainest description remained popular almost throughout the Georgian period. The type is particularly well represented in the north-east, as for example at Auldearn, Nairnshire (1757) (*121*), and Alves, Morayshire (1769), while at Tynet, in the same county, there survives one of the earliest of Scottish Roman Catholic chapels, a low plain building of 1755 which was subsequently extended to a length of no less than 120 ft. During this

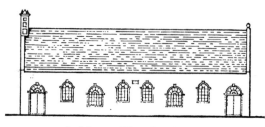

121 Auldearn Church, Nairnshire

period imported timber scantlings of large dimensions became more generally available, thus facilitating the erection of buildings of somewhat greater width. Roxburghshire contains a series of simple eighteenth-century churches of this class, including Roxburgh itself (1752), Morebattle (1757) and Sprouston (1781), each of which has a gable belfry at the west end and a range of tall round-headed windows in the long walls.

Town churches, too, were frequently of oblong plan, many of the larger ones being dignified by a tower or steeple placed either at the west end or at the centre of one of the side walls. One of the most attractive is St Andrew's, Dundee, erected by Samuel Bell, a local architect, in 1772 to plans prepared by James Craig of Edinburgh. The steeple, like many others of its period, follows the pattern first introduced in the London city churches a generation or more previously, while the classical details of the main block are equally old-fashioned in character. Later in his career, however, Bell showed his willingness to conform to Gothic tastes, choosing this style for a second rectangular kirk, St Clement's, which he designed for his native city in 1787. Some of the best steepled churches of this class are found in the smaller towns and burghs, those at Catrine, Ayrshire (1792), and Fochabers, Morayshire (1798), having been planned to conform with regular 'new town' layouts. Lanark Old Kirk, with its round-headed keystoned windows and many-storeyed tower, is a near contemporary of St Andrew's, Dundee, as is also the correct little classical church of Penicuik, Midlothian (*116*), erected by the local laird and gentleman architect Sir James Clerk (p. 118). By retaining the near-by tower of the old church the heritors of Penicuik saved themselves the expense of building a new one—a measure of economy similar to that which had earlier ensured the preservation of the fine domed steeple of St Ninian's, Stirlingshire (1734), after the adjacent church had been blown up by the Jacobite army in 1746.

T-plan churches continued to be built throughout this period, some of the most attractive examples dating from the opening decades of the eighteenth century. Polwarth, Berwickshire, a trim harled structure of 1703, has a west tower capped with a broach spire, while at Yester, East Lothian (1710), and at the two Midlothian kirks of Carrington (1710) and Newbattle (1727), the tower is placed laterally, balancing the central limb of the T. More modest buildings such as Gargunnock, Stirlingshire (1774), and the little Gothic church of Newlands, Peeblesshire (1838), made do with simple gable belfries of standard pattern. Internally most churches of this type, like those of plain rectangular form, were galleried on three sides, the pulpit occupying its customary position against the centre of the south wall.

More particularly characteristic of the later eighteenth and nineteenth centuries is the 'hall church', a term applied to buildings of oblong plan having galleries running along both side walls and one end wall; the main entrance-doorway, vestibule, and gallery staircases are grouped at one end of the church, while the pulpit usually stands towards the centre of the opposite wall. This plan was first introduced into England by Wren, and appeared in Scotland half a century later in the developed form popularised by James Gibbs. At St Nicholas West, Aberdeen (1755), Gibbs himself provided the design, making no charge for this notable service to his native city despite the considerable difficulties involved in replacing the nave of a medieval church while leaving the old choir and transepts standing. Gibbs's influence is equally apparent in Allan Dreghorn's almost contemporary church of St Andrew, Glasgow, whose impressive pedimented portico and elegant steeple, no less than the boldly rusticated window-architraves, clearly recalls St Martin-in-the-Fields. Among buildings of the second rank special attaches to the double church designed by Robert Mylne for the new town of Inveraray in about 1794. This is a plain oblong building, pedimented at each end, with a central partition-wall which divides the interior into two separate but identical compartments intended for the celebration of Gaelic and English services respectively. During the first half of the nineteenth century many towns were dignified by the erection of fine hall kirks in either the Gothic Revival or the neo-classical style, but the more modest buildings provided by the heritors of innumerable country parishes were all too often of pedestrian design. Thus at one end of the scale this period produced buildings of the calibre of Gillespie Graham's and A. W. Pugin's Tolbooth St John's, Edinburgh (1844), and Archibald Simpson's St Giles's, Elgin (1828), while at the other it contributed largely to the aesthetic poverty of numerous Scottish villages.

Other plans were employed more sparingly, their effectiveness being enhanced by their comparative rarity. Architects working in the Gothic style occasionally adopted medieval precedents wholeheartedly enough to design aisled and arcaded churches (*117*)—the earliest example appears to be Craig, Angus (1799)—while William Burn's Dunfermline Abbey Kirk (1821) is a fully developed cruciform structure with a crossing tower (*119*). There are also several notable centrally planned buildings (*118*), including William Adam's parish kirk of Hamilton, Lanarkshire (1732), and Captain Andrew Frazer's elegant New Town church of St Andrew, Edinburgh (1785). The plan of the former is that of a circle within a Greek Cross, of which one arm is reserved for the private use of the Hamilton family, while another houses the entrance-portico and vestry. Frazer's design is no less original in its conception, comprising as it does an elliptical body set behind a pedimented portico and steeple. The only round church of the period seems to be the remote island kirk of Bowmore, on Islay, but the octagonal form is less uncommon. Kelso, Roxburghshire, has an interesting classical church of this type (1773), while St Paul's, Perth (1807), designed by the Edinburgh architect John Paterson, is a more developed example of the same class executed in the Gothic manner. Neither of these buildings, however, has the charm of the two Gothic Revival village kirks of Dalmally (1811) (*122*)

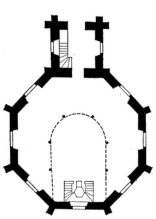

122 Glenorchy Church, Dalmally, Argyll

and Cairndow (1816), Argyll, whose white harled walls and pinnacled towers stand out with unexpected precision against the rugged West Highland landscape.

Sites or Buildings Specially Worth Visiting

The use of italics signifies that a structure is, at the time of writing, the subject of a long-standing arrangement giving either regular or occasional public access.

Early Churches

Angus	*Round Tower, Brechin Cathedral*
Argyll	*Eileach an Naoimh,* Garvelloch Isles
	Iona Cathedral
Orkney	*Brough of Birsay*
	Brough of Deerness
Perthshire	*Round Tower,* Abernethy
Wigtownshire	*Whithorn Cathedral*

MONASTERIES

Angus	*Arbroath Abbey*
Argyll	*Iona Nunnery*
	Oronsay Priory
Ayrshire	*Crossraguel Abbey*
	Kilwinning Abbey
Berwickshire	*Coldingham Priory*
	Dryburgh Abbey
Fife	*Dunfermline Abbey*
	Inchcolm Abbey
Kirkcudbrightshire	*Dundrennan Abbey*
	New Abbey (Sweetheart Abbey)
Midlothian	*Holyrood Abbey,* Edinburgh
Morayshire	*Pluscardine Priory*
Renfrewshire	*Paisley Abbey*
Roxburghshire	*Kelso Abbey*
	Jedburgh Abbey
	Melrose Abbey
Wigtownshire	*Glenluce Abbey*

CATHEDRALS

Aberdeenshire	*(Old) Aberdeen*
Fife	*St Andrews*
Lanarkshire	*Glasgow*
Morayshire	*Elgin*
Orkney	*Kirkwall*
Perthshire	*Dunblane*
	Dunkeld
Ross and Cromarty	*Fortrose*
Sutherland	*Dornoch*

Medieval Churches

Aberdeenshire	King's College, Aberdeen
	Auchindoir
Angus	Fowlis Easter
Argyll	*Dunstaffnage*, Oban
	Killean, Kintyre
	Kilmory, Knapdale
	Skipness, Kintyre
Banffshire	*Deskford*
Berwickshire	*Ladykirk*
East Lothian	*Dunglass Collegiate Church*, Cockburnspath
	St Mary's, Haddington
	Seton Collegiate Church, Cockenzie
	Tynninghame
Fife	Abdie
	Aberdour
	Leuchars
	St Monance
Inverness-shire	*Rodil*, Harris
Kirkcudbrightshire	*Lincluden College*, Dumfries
Midlothian	*Corstorphine*, Edinburgh
	Crichton
	Duddingston, Edinburgh
	St Giles', Edinburgh
	St Margaret's Chapel, Edinburgh Castle
	Midcalder
	Roslin Chapel
Morayshire	Birnie
Nairnshire	Barevan, Cawdor
Orkney	*St Magnus's*, Egilsay
	Orphir
Perthshire	Dunning
	Grandtully
	Innerpeffray
	Muthill
	St John's, Perth
Stirlingshire	*Holy Rude*, Stirling
West Lothian	*Dalmeny*
	Kirkliston
	St Michael's, Linlithgow

Post-Reformation Churches

Aberdeenshire	North Church, Aberdeen
	St Nicholas West, Aberdeen
Angus	Craig
	St Andrew's, Dundee
Argyll	Bowmore
	Dalmally
	Inverary
Ayrshire	Catrine
	Dreghorn

Berwickshire	Lauder
	Polwarth
Caithness	Reay
Dumfriesshire	St Michael's, Dumfries
	Durisdeer
East Lothian	Yester
Fife	Anstruther Easter
	Burntisland
	Ceres
	Dairsie
	Abbey Kirk, Dunfermline
	Fordell
Inverness-shire	Garrison Chapel, Fort George
Lanarkshire	St Andrew's, Glasgow
	Hamilton
	Lanark
Midlothian	Carrington
	Cannongate, Edinburgh
	St Andrew's, Edinburgh
	St John's Episcopal, Edinburgh
	St Stephen's, Edinburgh
	Tolbooth St John's, Edinburgh
	Tron, Edinburgh
	Penicuik
Morayshire	Alves
	St Giles's, Elgin
	Fochabers
	Tynet
Nairnshire	Auldearn
Peeblesshire	Lyne
Perthshire	Kincardine-in-Menteith
	St Paul's, Perth
Roxburghshire	Kelso
Stirlingshire	Chapel Royal, Stirling Castle

V BURGH ARCHITECTURE

Medieval Survivals

Like the castle and the parish church the Scottish burgh owes its origin primarily to the Anglo-Norman kings of the Canmore dynasty. The earliest burghs came into existence not by any process of casual growth, but as a result of deliberate acts of royal policy designed to promote economic expansion by the establishment of fixed centres of trade and industry. In some cases, as for example at Edinburgh and Stirling, burghs were erected in existing centres of population, but many were entirely new foundations to which settlers were encouraged to come by the special privileges granted to the king's burgesses. Since regular trade fairs and markets could be held only in conditions of security, the early burghs were usually situated in close proximity to royal castles, whose strategic and administrative importance further promoted economic intercourse.

By the end of the twelfth century about 15 royal burghs had been established in Scotland, and there were already one or two episcopal and abbatial burghs, such as St Andrews and Canongate, Edinburgh, which had been founded by ecclesiastical corporations with royal consent. Lay lords, too, were permitted to establish burghs of their own and as time went on these 'burghs of barony', as they were called, became increasingly common, notwithstanding the fact that their privileges were limited to exclude overseas as opposed to local trade. Once established, burghs were constitutionally self-perpetuating, but no foundation charter could confer perpetual prosperity. Thus it came about that, whilst most sizeable towns eventually became burghs of one sort or another, many once thriving communities ultimately declined into obscurity. James VI's description of the province of Fife as 'a beggar's mantle with a fringe of gold' (the busy coastal burghs) was already in need of revision in Cromwellian times and the fringe wore much thinner during the early eighteenth century. But whether their burghs were large or small, rich or poor, townsmen always formed a distinct social group, and their way of life differed markedly from that of the great mass of their contemporaries. Nor did the essential quality of burgh life change much before the municipal reforms of the nineteenth century. John Galt's Provost and Council of Gudetown would have felt quite at home among the Edinburgh merchants of William Dunbar's time and their motives and policies would have earned the poet's censure no less.

Contrary to popular belief scarcely a single urban building of medieval date now remains in Scotland. Apart from a few notable late medieval burgh kirks, all structures older than the late sixteenth and seventeenth centuries have either been swept away or been so much altered as to become unrecognisable. Nor do we have any detailed knowledge as to the probable form and appearance of these early burgh dwellings—though timber, wattle-and-daub and thatch rather than stone, slate and pantile should be visualised as the standard building materials. Archaeological excavation could provide a good deal of the required information and, although no advantage has been taken of recent opportunities to investigate key sites in such important burghs as Edinburgh and Stirling, one complete and undisturbed medieval burgh lay-out still awaits the spade. It is that of the former county town of Roxburghshire, whose deserted site occupies a grassy haugh at the confluence of the Rivers Tweed and Teviot about a mile above Kelso. Formerly one of the most important and influential of Scottish medieval burghs, Roxburgh fell into decline during the late fifteenth century and was virtually abandoned before the middle of the following century; its site presents opportunities for systematic excavation such as occur almost nowhere else in Britain.

While the successive replacement of individual buildings can drastically alter the character and appearance of a town, it rarely obliterates basic features of topography and many existing street-plans preserve medieval lay-outs. Most burghs originated as a single main thoroughfare—usually known as the High Street—from which lesser streets led off at right-angles. When the burgh was associated with a castle the main street was invariably axial to the castle, an arrangement which is still clearly perceptible

at Jedburgh, Peebles and Forres (*123*), as also at Inverness, where the burgh seems always to have embraced both banks of the river. The High Streets of Edinburgh and Elgin preserve, in addition, another characteristic medieval feature, namely a widening of a short section of the thoroughfare to form a market place. Two early bishops' burghs retain the outlines of less orthodox plans. At Glasgow there is a

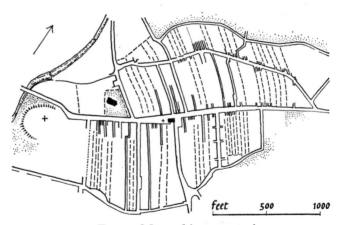

123 Forres, Morayshire: street-plan

double-cross layout in which the High Street, although axial to the bishop's castle and cathedral, is traversed at two points by important subsidiary routes, the lowermost of these intersections forming the site of the market-cross and tolbooth. St Andrews, on the other hand, has two main thoroughfares running westwards from the cathedral linked at intervals by cross streets. Between the two principal streets there is a third, Market Street, whose name sufficiently explains its original function. A rather similar grid-plan of even greater regularity occurs at Perth, whose lay-out resembles those of many English and French new towns, or 'bastides', of the thirteenth century.

Street names, too, frequently reflect long-vanished features of burgh topography or are evocative of past customs and usages. Kirkgate, Castlegate, Seagate, Bridgegate, Cowgate, Gallowgate, Trongate, Wellgate are all directly expressive of former functions or destinations. The term gate, or gait, was reserved for main thoroughfares, where the houses stood side by side, presenting narrow frontages to the street but having long strips of enclosed land extending behind them. As these enclosures, or 'closes', themselves came to be built upon, subsidiary access-streets were formed, some, by a simple transfer of nomenclature, becoming known as closes and others as wynds or vennels. Some of these likewise bore descriptive names—Baxter's Wynd, Fleshmarket Close and so on—but many were known simply by the names of their principal occupants; a walk down the High Street of Edinburgh will still reveal numerous examples of each class. Only the main thoroughfares were likely to be paved, and even there projecting fore-stairs and piled up middens restricted traffic to the crown of the causeway. The lesser streets tended to be narrow, steep and nasty, like the wynds of Southey's day 'into which no English nose would willing venture, for stinks older than the Union are to be found there'.

Although many medieval burghs could look to a near-by castle for protection in times of danger, most were provided with some independent means of defence. In the early medieval period, when the majority of castles were themselves constructions of earth and timber, the burgesses naturally made use of similar materials. A charter of William the Lion (1165–1214) to the burgh of Inverness mentions an agreement whereby the king was to be responsible for building an earthen rampart round the town, after which the burgesses were to crown the rampart with a palisade and thereafter keep the whole in good repair. During the Wars of Independence there are references to the fortification of Dunfermline with a ditch by Edward I, and to the successive refortification of Perth, in one case by a ditch and palisade and in the other by a wall of clay. By this time some burghs are likely to have been enclosed with walls of stone and lime; Edinburgh, for example, is known to have had a substantial stone wall by the middle of the fifteenth century, and excavations carried out in 1833 revealed traces of a still earlier wall of unknown date.

It is at Edinburgh that the oldest surviving remains of such defences can now be seen. The 'Flodden Wall' is traditionally associated with the refortification of the burgh after the disaster of September 1513, but its completion appears to have been delayed until towards the end of the sixteenth century. The line taken by this wall shows that it enclosed a much greater area than its predecessors. Fragments of two towers survive, one round and the other square, and there are a number of short sections of the wall itself, which appears to have had an average thickness of about 3 ft. 6 in. After work had begun upon the erection of Heriot's Hospital in 1628 the wall was again extended to take in this new ground, the remaining sections of this portion—the 'Telfer Wall'—being distinguished by their greater width and by the more massive character of the masonry.

Stirling, like Edinburgh, occupies a naturally strong site, but artificial defences were probably always considered necessary, except perhaps on the north side, where the River Forth formed an effective barrier. The existing wall was begun following a resolution passed by the Burgh Council in October 1547 for 'the strengthing and bigging of the wallis of the toun, at this present peralus tyme of neid, for resisting of oure auld innimeis of Ingland'. Considerable portions survive on the south side of the old town where the wall skirted the edge of a natural rock out-crop. Some sections stand to a height of more than 20 ft. and are equipped with crudely formed wide-mouthed gun-ports; there are also two circular bastion-towers, one of which now wears the less martial aspect of a dovecot. There is no evidence of a specially constructed defence on the north side of the burgh where the rear enclosure-walls of the various burgess tenements were presumably felt to offer sufficient protection. Peebles Town Wall, too, is of sixteenth-century date, having been erected between 1570 and 1574 under the direction of Thomas Lauder, a local mason. The building contract specified that the wall was to be 'four elnis half ground and all, thre futtis half ane fut of breif' and the surviving sections indicate that these dimensions were followed fairly closely. There were also to be 'blok houssis' at intervals, and one of these is still well preserved; it is circular on plan and its two wide-mouthed gun-ports are so placed as to provide covering fire along both adjacent sections of the wall.

With one or two exceptions, such as Haddington, East Lothian, other burghs now retain no trace of their former defences, the numerous 'ports', or gateways, having fallen victim to successive schemes of street improvement no less universally than their walls have surrendered to the demands of urban expansion. The only town gateway to survive in anything like its original condition is the West Port at St Andrews (124), which was built in 1589. The structure was supposedly modelled upon the newly recon-structed Nether Bow Port at Edinburgh, but in fact bears a much closer resemblance to the somewhat earlier entrance-gateway at Linlithgow Palace. It comprises a central archway between two semi-octagonal gun-looped towers, but the present appearance of the structure owes a good deal to a restoration carried out just over a century ago.

Perhaps some mention should also be made here of the well-preserved precinct wall of St Andrews Cathedral, for this takes precisely the same form as a burgh fortification. The wall was originally nearly a mile in length and enclosed an area of about 30 acres; the greater part survives to an average height of 20 ft., together with 13 of the original 16 towers, of which a few were oblong but the great majority round. An additional feature of interest is provided by a number of associated armorial panels and inscriptions, while the principal gateway, the 'Pends', is an important survival from an earlier precinct-wall of fourteenth-century date.

Burgh Architecture of the Sixteenth and Seventeenth Centuries

When MacGibbon and Ross were preparing their monumental survey of the domestic architecture of Scotland some 80 years ago, they found that many of the older burgh houses had already disappeared and that others were vanishing before their eyes. Since then the pace of demolition has greatly increased and, although this process has been counterbalanced to some extent by the restoration of individual structures of outstanding interest, little effort has been made until recent years to preserve homogeneous groups of historic buildings of the second rank, such as rows of individually unimpressive street-fronts, which are in some respects more representative of their period. Thus, while a certain number of important public buildings and noblemen's town houses of the later sixteenth and seventeenth centuries still remain intact, the general character of post-Reformation burgh architecture has been almost everywhere lost.

Contemporary travellers give very mixed reports of the urban scene, one impressed by the 'lofty and stately buildings' of Edinburgh, another contemptuous of the mean houses of 'dirty Dumblain' (Dunblane); and not infrequently two writers produce conflicting accounts of the same locality. On one point of architectural importance, however, they are all agreed, namely that many burgh houses were constructed wholly or partially of timber. Writing in 1656 Richard Franck noted that the buildings of Aberdeen were 'framed with stone and timber', while a French traveller who visited Glasgow five years later reported that 'the houses are only of wood, ornamented with carving'. Some visitors to Edinburgh were more specific, noting that, although the best houses were basically of stone construction, most were timber fronted. At ground-floor level these wooden forescreens usually contained a continuous covered passage, while on the upper floors a series of open or enclosed galleries, supported on posts, overlooked the street. The passage served partly as a pedestrian thoroughfare and partly as a space for shops and booths, while the galleries were integrated with the main residential accommodation within.

Some houses were self-contained, but flatted buildings several storeys in height became increasingly common in the more prosperous towns, where shortage of space made vertical expansion a necessity. Thus there were evolved the tall tenement-buildings that remain one of the most characteristic features of the Scottish burgh—though vertical living can hardly have come as a novelty to a nation whose upper classes had for so long resided in tower-houses. Standards of accommodation varied widely, but the well-to-do Edinburgh merchant of the early seventeenth century would have reckoned himself comfortably housed if he had a hall and kitchen, three or four chambers, a gallery and one or more cellars; if he lived on one of the upper floors of the building, part of the ascent would be made by means of a stone forestair rising directly from the street.

Quite a number of part-timbered houses still existed in Edinburgh a century or so ago, a particularly fine group at the corner of West Bow and Lawnmarket having been demolished only in 1878. Apart from one or two buildings with wholly reconstructed timberwork, such as Huntly House, the only structure of this class now to be seen in the city is 'John Knox's House', High Street (*128*). This, too, would certainly have been pulled down had not popular tradition (almost certainly ill-founded) associated the building with the Reformer. The structure has a long and complex building-history, but evidently assumed its present appearance in about the third quarter of the sixteenth century when it was occupied by James Mosman and his wife, whose initials and armorial bearings appear upon the west front. Timber galleries project from the south front at first- and second-floor levels, and there are gabled projections, also of timber, on both main elevations. The building seems originally to have contained two separate dwellings, which made common use of a forestair, but had individual internal staircases. Similar buildings must once have existed in other burghs, and some may remain, heavily disguised beneath later accretions. Lord Kinnoul's modest three-storeyed town house in Perth, for example, seems to be a galleried structure, and beneath the cement rendering that now covers it there may be seen traces of heavy supporting timbers; analysis and restoration of a building such as this might prove unexpectedly rewarding.

Timber-framed and timber-fronted houses standing in close proximity to one another presented a considerable fire hazard, and burgh councils increasingly advocated the erection of buildings of stone and lime. Some traditional methods of timber construction readily lent themselves to reproduction in stone. Thus, the upper storeys of a building might be projected on individual or continuous stone corbel-courses, as at Huntly House, Edinburgh, and Sailors' Walk, Kirkcaldy, while galleries might be boldly corbelled out over the street, a particularly fine example of this type of construction being preserved at Moray House in the Edinburgh Canongate. In the same way timber posts carrying the front upper portion of a house over a pedestrian thoroughfare were translated into stone columns, thus producing the arcaded fronts that became one of the chief characteristics of later seventeenth-century burgh architecture. The only surviving example in the High Street of Edinburgh is Gladstone's Land, where the existing stone front is thought to have been formed in about 1630, but some interesting groups of arcaded houses of the last two decades of the seventeenth century are preserved at Elgin. Most of these are three-storeyed buildings with crow-stepped gables and heavy stone-slated roofs punctuated at eaves level by dormer-windows; the segmental-headed arches of the arcades rest upon sturdy columns, which have simply moulded bases and capitals.

The pace of transition from timber to stone construction varied a good deal from place to place, but nowhere were more substantial stone-built houses erected in the later sixteenth and seventeenth centuries than in the thriving seaport burghs of Fife. At this period the development of coastal shipping and the growth of trade with Low Country and Baltic ports brought great prosperity to an area that was naturally endowed with almost unlimited supplies of freestone of the highest quality. Thus, as burgh after burgh obtained its formal charters of privileges—no less than five towns on the south coast were erected into royal burghs between 1541 and 1588—so was each dignified by handsome new houses constructed for wealthy merchants and sea captains.

Culross itself, deservedly the best known of the historic coastal burghs, owed much to the ingenuity and enterprise of a member of a distinguished local family, Sir George Bruce of Carnock, whose impressive marble funeral-monument now stands within the near-by Cistercian abbey. For almost half a century before his death in 1625 Bruce showed great resource in the development of the long established industries of salt-panning and mining, and the underwater coal-pit that he established beneath the River Forth became one of the wonders of the day. The earliest surviving dated house in Culross was built in 1577, 11 years before the town became a royal burgh, but the majority of the existing buildings of architectural interest can be ascribed to the seventeenth century. Thanks to an imaginative policy of restoration by the National Trust for Scotland over the past 30 years, the centre of the burgh now looks much as it must have done in the days of its greatest prosperity, wanting only the reek and dirt of industrial activity to complete the authentic atmosphere of the period. Most of the houses rise to a height of two or three storeys and are constructed of harled rubble masonry with dressings of yellow sandstone (138); they have crow-stepped gables and roofs of red pantile, which was a standard roofing material in eastern counties during the seventeenth and eighteenth centuries. (Pantiles are commonly supposed to have been first introduced into Scotland as ballast for incoming boats from the Low Countries, but tiled roofs of one sort or another were not unknown in medieval times, and the 'tyill for building and sclaitting of houssis at lowe raittis', for whose manufacture a royal licence was sought in 1611, no doubt included pantiles.) Some of the houses are flatted, the upper floors being approached by means of open forestairs. Many display the carved stone embellishments that were so popular at this period—ornate dormer-window pediments, trade symbols, family initials and pious inscriptions; one, for example, incorporates a panel showing a butcher's cleaver accompanied by a spring-balance, while the door-lintel of another bears a Greek inscription 'God provides and will provide'. In one or two buildings the type of window treatment that was customary before the introduction of sash-windows in the later seventeenth century has been carefully restored. At this time it was usual to glaze only the upper half of a window opening, the small lozenge-shaped panes of glass being set within fixed lead frames; the lower portion of the window was provided with shutters. Among the most attractive features of the burgh are the irregular cobbled causeways that run between the houses, and the finest of these, Tanhouse Brae, must have caused many an honest burgess some shortness of breath during Sabbath ascents to the parish church.

The closely packed burghs of the East Neuk of Fife also contain a number of individual houses of architectural merit as well as many good groups of less

124 West Port, St Andrews, Fife.
Thomas Robertson, 1589

125 Pittenweem Harbour, Fife.
Seventeenth century and later

126 Rope-works, Cromarty, Ross
and Cromarty. Late eighteenth
century and later

127 Main Street, Inveraray,
Argyll. *Robert Mylne*, 1775

128 (*Left*) John Knox's House, Edinburgh. Sixteenth century
129 (*Top right*) George Square, Edinburgh. *James Brown, c.* 1763–85
130 (*Bottom right*) St Bernard's Crescent, Edinburgh. *James Milne,* 1824

distinguished buildings. The materials and methods of construction are generally similar to those described above, but each burgh possesses a charm and character of its own. Thus, the two Anstruthers, although separated only at high tide, developed quite independently of each other, the one with its main street crammed in axially to the tiny harbour, the other with its principal buildings spaciously disposed along the harbour front. At St Monance, too, the huddle of buildings round the harbour constitutes the nucleus of the burgh, but at Crail and Pittenweem an additional focal point is provided by an orthodox High Street lay-out on the higher ground above the harbour. The land-ward end of the main street of Crail broadens out to form a market-place, but most of the existing houses here are of eighteenth- and early nineteenth-century date. The older houses stand at the south end of High Street and at the foot of the steep cobbled wynds that lead down to the harbour. Fewer boats now tie up at the sandstone-block jetties than in former days, and one fishing smack has long since found safe anchorage ashore, where it adorns the pend lintel of the 'Custom House' in Shoregate. Pittenweem, too, has some particularly fine harbour groups (*125*), including one or two sea captains' houses of the seventeenth century.

The historic towns of the middle reaches of the Forth valley are of more varied origin than the coastal burghs of the East Neuk. Clackmannan, for example, developed under the protection of the Bruce family as a small market-town and received burghal status and the right to erect a market-cross in 1551. Despite modern industrial expansion the old street-plan remains almost intact, the single main thoroughfare, defined by its cross and tolbooth, descending like a formal avenue from the gates of the baronial castle to which the burgh owed its origin. A number of seventeenth- and eighteenth-century houses are preserved, one of them displaying a curvilinear 'Dutch' gable such as may also be seen at Parleyhill House, Culross. Linlithgow, on the other hand, was established beneath the walls of a major Crown stronghold as a royal burgh and the seat of a sheriffdom by the third quarter of the twelfth century. The T-shaped street-plan probably goes back to the earliest days of the burgh's history, the base of the T, Market-gate, being axial to the palace, and the horizontal bar, High Street, following the historic line of communication from east to west. Writing in 1636 Sir William Brereton described Linlithgow as a 'a fair, ancient town, and well built, some part of it of stone', but many fine houses have been destroyed during the past century (some within recent years), and apart from the palace environs the burgh now contains little historic architecture. One or two rubble-built houses of the seventeenth century with crow-stepped gables fronting the thoroughfare survive here and there in High Street.

Stirling, too, has lost many of its older buildings, but efforts are now being made to bring out the best features of those that remain through a policy of partial restoration and conversion, and by the recreation of a sympathetic environment. The lay-out of the old town in relation to the castle recalls that of Edinburgh, and is the result of similar topographical and historical factors. The main street and its principal subsidiaries follow the alignment of the rock outcrop south-eastwards from the castle summit. This alignment is broken, however, by two offshoots, St Mary's Wynd and Friars' Street which point the way respectively to the Forth crossing and the harbour, both of which were in existence in the twelfth century. Two of the oldest houses in the burgh, Glengarry Lodge, Spittal Street, and Bruce of Auchenbowie's House, St John Street, have circular stair-towers projecting into the street, and the second displays a relatively uncommon form of crow-stepped gable in which each step is surmounted by a weathered coping. These plain four-storeyed buildings are probably representative of the more substantial undetached houses of the late sixteenth and early seventeenth centuries, but both show extensive signs of later alterations. 'Darnley House', Bow Street, evidently dates from the same period, but the principal elevation is more sophisticated in treatment. The masonry of this portion is of ashlar and there is an ovolo-moulded eaves-cornice interrupted by a row of pedimented dormers. The building is L-shaped on plan, the wing at the rear being entered by means of an arched pend. The principal street of the old town was Broad Street, known at one time as High Gait, and subsequently as Market Place. Here, no doubt, in close proximity to the tolbooth and cross dwelt the chief municipal dignitaries. One of them, Town-Clerk Norrie, erected a particularly fine house for himself and his wife Agnes Robertson in 1671. The rather narrow street-frontage of four storeys and an attic is of ashlar; the ground floor has angle pilasters decorated with lozenge-shaped facets, while above there are three tightly packed rows of pedimented windows whose tympana contain texts and initials. More typical, perhaps, of its period is an adjacent twin-gabled flatted house of harled rubble with simply dressed window-margins.

The principal cities of the east coast, Dundee, Aberdeen and Inverness, contain few houses of the class now under review, but examples survive in some of the smaller burghs such as Stonehaven and Thurso. The former developed as a fishing port under the watchful eyes of the Earls Marischal of Dunnottar Castle. Already a burgh of barony, 'Stenhyve' replaced Kincardine as the county town in 1607, and some time afterwards received a grant of two yearly fairs and a weekly market. The old town and harbour stand on the south bank of the River Carron and within the parish of Dunnottar. The older houses date from the seventeenth century, but most are in poor condition and it seems unlikely that more than one or two will be preserved. They exhibit the roll-moulded surrounds, crow-stepped gables and angle-turrets characteristic of their period, and one has a chimney boldly corbelled out of one of its long walls a few feet above street level. Thurso became a burgh of barony in 1633 and one or two picturesque two- and three-storeyed houses of this period may still be seen here and there in the old town.

But by far the most comprehensive series of burgh houses of the later sixteenth and seventeenth centuries in the north of Scotland occurs at Kirkwall in Orkney. The origins of the burgh must go back to the stormy days of the Norse earls, but little is known of its history before the formal annexation of Orkney to the Scottish Crown in 1471. The growth of the fishing industry and a general increase of trade during the following two centuries led to the rebuilding of the greater part of the burgh with substantial stone houses. The plan comprises a long straggling main street, which broadens out into a market-place between the cathedral and the site of the old castle. The harbour area to the north may have developed independently, for the alignment of its principal thoroughfare, Bridge Street, bears little relation to the main street-plan. The subsidiary thoroughfares run at right angles to the main street and many of the houses have narrow gabled frontages with paved wynds and closes running between them. In their general appearance the houses resemble those seen in other parts of the country and there is a fine array of inscribed skew-puts, lintels and pediments. Regional characteristics are also well marked, however, many of the buildings being constructed of local flag-stone laid in clay mortar, and roofed with heavy stone slates.

In conclusion, attention may be drawn to an interesting scheme of early suburban development carried out at Inveresk, Midlothian, during the later seventeenth and early eighteenth centuries. The houses themselves are similar in size to those erected in other parts of the country by lairds of the middle rank, but the absence of extensive policies and the relatively close grouping of the buildings and their enclosure walls creates a distinctively urban atmosphere. Two houses of contrasted type deserve more detailed description. The first, Inveresk Lodge, may be considered as typical of its class and period. It is a tall narrow L-shaped structure having a semi-octagonal stair-tower projecting from the re-entrant angle of the main block and the wing; the tower contains the original entrance-doorway. This portion of the house dates from the year 1683, but a few years later the wing was extended in length and a range of offices added. The second house, Halkerston, is quite different in conception, being almost square on plan with an internal turnpike stair which gives access to all four storeys. There is a part basement containing a vaulted kitchen and well-house, while on the two principal floors there are four main apartments, one in each corner. The massive pyramidal roof rises to a central chimney flanked by two others rising from the level of the eaves. The plan shows a determination to break away from the traditional elongated lay-out found in the majority of comparable Scottish houses of the sixteenth and seventeenth centuries, and anticipates certain features that were to become general during the next generation or two. Curiously enough the only existing parallel, Preston Lodge, Cupar, is of considerably earlier date, having probably been erected in the year 1623. Some of the detail bears a strong resemblance to that at Abbey House, Culross.

The Great Town Houses of the Sixteenth and Seventeenth Centuries

The houses described in the preceding section of this chapter were for the most part the residences either of moderately wealthy merchants or of prosperous craftsmen—skinners, goldsmiths, surgeons, hammermen and the like—between which two classes (and to the considerable advantage of the former) the responsibilities and privileges of burgh life were chiefly divided. But in most burghs, certainly in the larger ones, there were also a number of more substantial dwellings erected by men of higher rank. The possession of a private residence at either Edinburgh or Stirling, where the Court was most frequently to be found at this period, came to be regarded almost as a necessity by members of the church and nobility who aspired to the highest offices of state. In other towns the local gentry, unwilling to endure the hardships involved in regular travel to and from their estates, erected lodgings of more modest character where private business could happily be combined with family pleasures. And, not to be outdone, the richest merchants—and some were rich enough to be personal creditors of the Crown—housed themselves in a manner clearly indicative of their pre-eminence in burgh affairs.

If due allowance is made for the restricted nature of urban sites, it will be found that buildings of this class are comparable in size and appearance to those erected by the upper classes upon their country estates. For the largest houses the courtyard lay-out was favoured, for most others a variety of the tower-house form, and for a few the traditional urban plan comprising a narrow street-frontage with a long and somewhat irregular range of buildings extending to the rear.

Among the larger Edinburgh town houses the most noticeable example of this latter group is 'Huntly House', Canongate, of which some mention has already been made elsewhere in this chapter. The building has been extensively reconstructed on several occasions, but the fine ashlar street-front probably dates from about the year 1570, when the property was owned by the Aitchison family. Close by, but standing well back from the main thoroughfare, is Acheson House, an attractive four-storeyed building of irregular plan entered from a paved fore-court giving on to Bakehouse Close. Many of the best Edinburgh houses seem to have occupied similarly withdrawn situations, for when he visited the city in 1618 John Taylor, the Water-Poet, observed that 'the gentle-mens mansions and goodliest houses are obscurely founded in the . . . by-lanes and closes'. More ambitious in conception than either of these two houses was the 'great ludging' erected by the Dowager Countess of Home on another Canongate site about the third decade of the seventeenth century. Moray House, as it has been called since 1643, was originally quadrangular on plan, the extensive grounds to the south of the building being laid out as gardens and orchards. Only the north and west sides of the early house now remain, but these are of considerable interest in view of the fact that the design may probably be attributed to William Wallace, the King's Master-Mason. The Anglo-Flemish detail and the tall diagonally set chimneys recall Wallace's work at Linlithgow Palace and Heriot's Hospital (p. 54), while the rich Jacobean plasterwork that is such a notable feature of the interiors is a no less typical ingredient of the current Scottish Renaissance style. One of the last great town houses to be erected before the Act of Union abruptly deprived the city of the financial and social benefits that it had enjoyed as the meeting place of the Scottish Parliament was Lord Hatton's lodging in the lower Canongate. Soon after its erection in 1681–2 Hatton sold the property to the Duke of Queensberry, whose name has since been associated with the house. The plan comprises an oblong main block from which two wings project at right angles towards the street to form an entrance-forecourt. The elevations are plain but dignified, although the general external appearance of the building has been marred by the addition of a fourth main storey and by the removal of the original ogee roofs from the angle pavilions of the main block.

Although Edinburgh had succeeded in establishing her claim to be the Scottish capital by the reign of James IV, Stirling remained a favourite seat of the Court for another century, before declining into what John Ray described, somewhat patronisingly, as 'an indifferently handsome town' having 'a good market-place and two palaces'. Of the two buildings thus referred to in 1662 only the first, Mar's Work, dates from a period when the burgh was an important centre of political and social activity. It is a structure of exceptional interest, built during the most violent years of Mary Queen of Scots' reign as the private residence of a great nobleman who was shortly to become Regent of Scotland. The plan adopted makes little concession to the urban environment, being in all respects similar to that of a contemporary courtyard-castle such as Tolquhon. Begun in 1570, the building was still unfinished at the time of the Earl of Mar's death two years later. Today only the east range of the courtyard survives, its octagonal-towered gatehouse and gun-looped basement fronting the main approach to Stirling Castle. The principal façade is of regular design, but the main lines of composition are somewhat overlaid by an abundance of ornament, much of which seems to derive from James V's palace within the castle. The gatehouse presents a good display of heraldic carving together with a prominent inscription well calculated to disarm all criticism:

> *I pray al lvikaris on this lvging*
> *Vith gentil e to gif thair ivging,*

though a second couplet, less prominently displayed, is perhaps more likely to represent the Earl's true attitude to his critics:

> *Esspy speik fvrth and spair notht*
> *Considdir veil I cair notht.*

The second house that caught Ray's eye as he made his way up to the castle, Argyll Lodging, ranks as the finest surviving of its class in the country. Its principal creator, William Alexander, Viscount Stirling, was one of the most colourful figures at Charles I's court; poet, scholar, statesman and adventurer, he succeeded in making himself one of the best known, if least loved, men of his day only to have his career shattered in mid course by financial ruin. Alexander remodelled and enlarged an existing building on the site to form two ranges of a quadrangular house and part of a third range (*131*); the

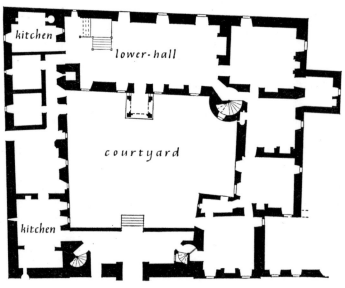

131 Argyll Lodging, Stirling

plan was completed by the Earl of Argyll in 1674, the courtyard being closed on the remaining side by a handsome screen-wall containing an entrance-gateway. There is a very generous provision of accommodation, and it is noticeable that a number of the principal apartments, instead of occupying their customary position above a vaulted cellarage, are disposed at ground-floor level, an arrangement which marked a decisive step forward in architectural design. Good vertical circulation is provided by a series of conveniently placed turnpike-staircases, while the main rooms in the south range are additionally served by a dignified scale-and-platt stair of timber. The external elevations are typical of the Scottish Renaissance style, some of the richly carved ornamental detail being so like that seen at Heriot's Hospital, Edinburgh, as to suggest that the same craftsmen were employed in both buildings.

In Aberdeen the tower-house form and the traditional urban plan seem to have been favoured more than the courtyard lay-out, and the three surviving examples of greater town houses all correspond with one or other of these types. 'Wallace's Tower', recently removed from its original site in Nether Kirkgate and re-erected for preservation in another part of the city, makes no attempt to disguise its affinities with contemporary Aberdeenshire castles. Its Z-plan, comprising a tall rectangular main block having round towers at diagonally opposite corners, may be compared with such tower-houses as Terpersie and Pitcaple, although specifically defensive features, such as gun-ports, are absent. The house is more correctly known as Benholm's Tower, after its builder Sir Robert Keith of Benholm, who died in 1616; the celebrated sculptured figure that adorns the building, though traditionally reputed to represent William Wallace, may in fact be a contemporary portrait of the founder.

Provost Skene's house in Guest Row (*133*), on the other hand, originated in the middle of the sixteenth century as a plain three-storeyed block having its gable fronting the street in the manner characteristic of most small urban dwellings; access to the two upper floors was gained by means of a forestair. During the course of the next 100 years the building was twice extended in length, but its present aspect is due largely to an extensive scheme of alterations carried out by George Skene after he acquired the property in 1669. Skene, a rich Aberdonian merchant trading in Danzig, gave the building something of the appearance of a contemporary laird's house, regularising the fenestration, and emphasising the horizontal character of the elevations by the substitution of a flat roof for a pitched one. Internally the most noteworthy feature is the painted gallery of about 1626, which displays the full range of late medieval imagery with a boldness that would be inconceivable in any other part of the country at that time.

Much the same range of house types is found in the smaller burghs. At Culross the loose courtyard-plan of Sir George Bruce's 'palace' was the result of successive additions to an original freestanding house of quite modest dimensions. Most of the work was completed between 1597 and 1611, these dates, together with the initials of the builder, being visible on different portions of the house. As at Provost Skene's house at Aberdeen, there are some notable painted interiors, while Bruce also took care to provide himself with a fireproof safe-room in which his papers and valuables could be securely housed. It was from the hospitable doors of the Palace that John Taylor, the Water-Poet, was escorted upon his memorable tour of Bruce's underwater mine (p. 176) in 1618, whence he returned dreaming of bigger and better Gunpowder Plots, and of the unlimited facilities available for the storage of 'Beere and Bottle-ale'.

Across the Forth, at Leith, 'Andrew Lamb's House' bears a marked resemblance to Skene's House, although its architectural evolution is much less complex. The building dates from the late sixteenth or early seventeenth century and comprises a tall, narrow, rectangular block with a square staircase-tower projecting from the centre of one of the long sides. The upper portion of the stair is handsomely corbelled, and its gabled cap-house and flanking chimney-stacks rise high above the wall-head, giving considerable individuality to the roof line. Successive alterations have obscured the original internal arrangements, but it seems likely that the ground floor was devoted to storage space, and that the principal apartments were grouped on the two main upper floors. The building has recently been restored as a social centre, but the visual qualities of the external elevations have been preserved by sympathetic restoration (*134*).

The influence of the tower-house is most clearly seen in the design of some of the smaller town residences. Kellie Lodging, Pittenweem, for example, although erected in a busy burgh high street as the town house of a local laird, could as well be the seat of some modest country estate. The same might be said of 'Queen Mary's House', Jedburgh, a building whose castellated aspect has led to its supposed identification as a bastel-house (p. 45). Both structures date from the last decade or so of the sixteenth century, and each comprises a tall oblong main block with a rectangular staircase-wing having a subsidiary stair-turret corbelled out in the re-entrant angle. Kellie Lodging was a residence of the Erskines of Kellie, while heraldic evidence associates 'Queen Mary's House', not with that much travelled monarch, but with the families of Wigmer and Scott.

As the tower-house was gradually domesticated, so did its derivative urban forms slowly change character. Plewlands House, South Queensferry, and Fordell's Lodging, Inverkeithing, both bear a strong family resemblance to the typical laird's house of the seventeenth century. The former, built in 1641 for Samuel Wilson and his wife Anna Ponton, and successfully restored within recent years, is a three-storeyed building designed on an L-plan. The principal entrance-doorway is placed at the foot of a polygonal staircase-tower, which rises in the re-entrant angle of the main block and the wing; the initials of the builder and the date of erection are inscribed upon the door lintel. Sir John Henderson of Fordell's town house at Inverkeithing is of slightly later date and, although the L-plan is repeated, the staircase is wholly enclosed within the wing. Not all features of the design are so advanced, however, for a basement cellarage is provided and there is a corbelled angle-turret of traditional character at one end of the principal frontage.

The picture is much the same in the more remote areas of the country. A number of interesting town houses survive in the south-west, notably at Kirkcudbright and at Maybole, where there were formerly 'many pretty buildings belonging to the severall gentry of the countrey, who were wont to resort thither in winter, and divert themselves in converse together at their owne houses'. The finest of these to be seen today, the former residence of the Earls of Cassillis, is a typical L-shaped tower-house of the early seventeenth century. Typical, that is to say, in its plan, for the rich Anglo-Flemish detail seen in the chimney copings and pierced dormer-window pediments, and the lofty three-sided oriel window that adorns the staircase-tower, gives the building a character of its own. Sir Thomas Maclellan of Bombie, a onetime provost of Kirkcudbright,

132 Maclellan's House, Kirkcudbright

133   Provost Skene's House, Aberdeen. Seventeenth century and earlier

134   Andrew Lamb's House, Leith, Edinburgh. Late sixteenth or early seventeenth century

135   Charlotte Square, Edinburgh. *Robert Adam*, 1791–3

136   Moray Place, Edinburgh. *Gillespie Graham*, 1822

provided himself with a town residence of unusual size and splendour, taking as his model one of the more substantial lairds' houses of the day, such as Elcho Castle (p. 72) in which castellated and domestic features are found in combination. The plan (*132*) is basically L-shaped, but there is a double projection within the re-entrant angle as well as a projecting tower at one corner of the main block. Apart from the provision of a few splayed gun-ports little care has been taken to make the building defensible. The principal apartments, set over a vaulted basement, are reached by means of a straight stair rising directly from the entrance-doorway, while the upper floors are served by a series of conveniently placed turnpike-stairs.

Returning, in conclusion, to the courtyard plan, mention may be made of two notable town houses of this class whose comparative remoteness has prevented them from attracting the attention they deserve. The first stands in a quiet back-street of the Ayrshire burgh of Irvine. It appears to have been erected by the third Earl of Eglinton sometime between 1562 and 1585, and was occupied until about the middle of the eighteenth century. Like Mar's Work, Stirling, the existing remains seem to represent an unfinished building of courtyard plan entered from the street through a vaulted pend placed centrally in the principal frontage. The accommodation arrangements are unremarkable, but the nature of the ornamental detail deserves further comment. This is an inspired blend of Scottish Baronial elements, including chequer and cable ornament, with the revived Gothic forms more frequently seen in the ecclesiastical architecture of the period, of which the curious round-arched pend gateway with dog-tooth decoration provides the most conspicuous example.

The second building referred to, Tankerness House, Kirkwall, has ecclesiastical connections of a much more convincing character. Standing almost within the shadow of St Magnus's Cathedral, it appears to have originated in 1574 as the residence of the principal dignitaries of the cathedral, of whom there were several at this period. During the seventeenth century the building came into the hands of the Baikie family, who subsequently remodelled it as a town house. As it stands today Tankerness House comprises four main ranges of buildings grouped round a rectangular courtyard, which is entered from Broad Street by means of a round-arched gateway. Above the entrance there is a corbelled balcony incorporating an inscribed panel together with the initials of Archdeacon Gilbert Fulzie and his wife. The courtyard buildings show work of several different periods, only the north range being as old as the sixteenth century.

Burgh Architecture of the Eighteenth and early Nineteenth Centuries

For the greater part of the eighteenth century Scottish burgh architecture retained much of its vernacular character. Despite the gradual acceptance of more uniform standards of domestic taste, the widespread use of local building materials ensured the preservation of regional mannerisms. Stone was by now employed almost universally, and efforts were being made to prohibit the use of thatch for roofing. An act of 1681 had laid down that all houses thereafter to be built in Edinburgh, Glasgow, Aberdeen, Dundee and Stirling were to be roofed with 'lead, slate, scailzie, or tile, and no otherwise', and the magistrates of other royal burghs were encouraged to make similar provision in their own towns. Window openings were becoming larger, and the practice of half-glazing was dying out as casement and sash-windows came into fashion. Most urban houses made little concession to the principles of classical design, only the somewhat greater regularity of their plans and elevations, and their more correct vocabulary of ornament, distinguishing them from their predecessors. Except in the more crowded burghs, where shortage of space encouraged the development of the multi-tenement form, the height of houses tended to diminish, buildings of more than two main storeys becoming less common than hitherto. At the same time an increased understanding of the use of classical mouldings made for greater restraint in the employment of applied surface-decoration. Carved panels containing heraldic or trade insignia remained popular, but the heavy roll-mouldings and wide chamfers of the late sixteenth and early seventeenth centuries were replaced by plainer forms, occasionally relieved by the more elegant bolection-moulding.

The small coastal burghs of Fife and the Forth Valley continued to produce many good examples of minor domestic architecture. Airth and Kincardine, which face each other across the river some eight miles below Stirling, both flourished as seaports during the eighteenth century. The former had become a royal burgh as early as the reign of William the Lion, but the foundation was a failure and, when at last the town began to prosper, the old hilltop site was abandoned in favour of a riverside position giving ready access to the docks and harbour. Here, in 1723, a traveller noticed that ships of quite large size were being built 'very ingeniously and frequently as in any dock in the firth'. Most of the older houses in the burgh date from this period; they are plain two-storeyed buildings with steeply pitched pantiled roofs, crow-stepped gables and moulded eaves-courses (*137*). They show little variety of plan, most of them having the main rooms equally disposed on each side of a central entrance-lobby and staircase; some are flatted and incorporate stone forestairs.

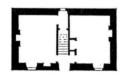

137 House near the Market-cross, Airth, Stirlingshire

A recent re-development scheme has deprived Airth of a number of attractive buildings that could well have been preserved, while at the time of writing Kincardine affords a scarcely less gloomy prospect, neglect and slow decay going far to achieve a similar and equally regrettable result. Two hundred years ago the town was at the summit of its fortunes, the old-established industries of salt-panning and coalmining having given way to boat-building for the West Indian traffic and Greenland fisheries, and to the development of coastal and overseas trade. The houses are similar to those at Airth; a large number of them bear their date of erection and some incorporate such characteristically nautical motifs as the cable and anchor.

Further down the coast there are some good groups of buildings at Kinghorn, and others at Crail, Pittenweem and West Wemyss. Inland, Falkland, with its interesting Y-shaped street-plan, provides a representative series of eighteenth-century houses, as well as one or two notable examples of rather earlier date; there are also a number of single-storeyed weavers' cottages. Thatched roofs still occur here and there, as they do also in the neighbouring burgh of Auchtermuchty.

But the most important architectural centre in East Fife at this period was unquestionably St Andrews which, while never quite regaining the position that it had held in medieval times, nevertheless enjoyed a modest degree of prosperity as a university seat and a small trading-port. Much rebuilding had already been done during the later sixteenth and seventeenth centuries and quite a few houses of this period survive, some of them openly parading their antiquity and others disguising it behind later street-fronts. It is the domestic architecture of the Georgian era that predominates, however, the vernacular style of the earlier eighteenth century blending happily with the more formal manner in vogue at the time of the first *Statistical Account* (1794), whose author observed that 'new houses on an improved plan of size, accommodation, and elegance, are yearly rising, and there is every reason to believe, that St Andrew's will continue to flourish'.

On the south side of the River Forth a similar mingling of the vernacular and academic styles can be seen in the county towns of East Lothian and Roxburghshire. Haddington has an interesting series of Georgian houses, some of them rising to a height of as much as four storeys; many have arched pends at ground-floor level leading to yards or closes at the rear. Here, pantiled and slated roofs stand side by side, but in Kelso, where a number of the street-fronts are attractively painted or stuccoed, slate is the standard roofing material. Both burghs have distinctive and well-preserved street-plans, Haddington having its two main streets running parallel to one another, and Kelso exhibiting a curiously un-Scottish lay-out in which all the principal thoroughfares converge upon a spacious cobbled market-square. Less well known is the picturesque little Wigtownshire burgh of Whithorn, where the single broad main street is lined with groups of plain two-storeyed houses built of local flagstone rubble. Most are harled or colour-washed, and some are roofed with heavy stone slates that are said to have been shipped across the Solway Firth from Cumberland.

In Perthshire interest is concentrated upon the two small cathedral towns of Dunkeld and Dunblane, where steps are now being taken to preserve the best of the older houses. The mid-eighteenth-century traveller who drew attention to houses in Dunkeld that were 'composed of blocks of peat, stones, and broom' says nothing of the trim two-storeyed buildings of harled rubble that had recently been erected in Cathedral Street. Nor does Bishop Pococke, who made equally unflattering remarks about Dunblane some 20 years later, give credit to the builders of the solid stone houses that stand round the Cathedral Square. Such buildings were then commonplace, but familiarity is less likely to leave the modern visitor blind to their true qualities of scale and proportion, which are accentuated by good grouping and sympathetic environment. The same attributes can be recognised at Little Causeway, Forfar, where a number of late eighteenth- and early nineteenth-century houses are ranged informally round a roughly cobbled square. Most are two-storeyed structures having either stuccoed or rubble-faced street-fronts, and roofs of heavy Angus stone slate.

In the north and east it is again the coastal burghs that provide the main focus of interest. Arbroath and Banff both prospered in the second half of the eighteenth century, the former as a manufacturing centre producing thread, sail-cloth and other linens, and the latter gradually concentrating upon stocking manufacture. Ship-building, together with a fairly extensive coastal and overseas trade, was developed in both towns, a new harbour being built in Arbroath about the year 1725, and one in Banff some 50 years later. Arbroath High Street contains some substantial late-Georgian houses in the classical style, while nearer the harbour, in Oldshorehead, there are one or two attractive colour-washed buildings of more vernacular character having fore-stairs and stone-slated roofs. There is rather more variety at Banff, where the continuous street-fronts of the principal thoroughfares are occasionally broken by large detached houses standing well back within their own gardens. The older houses, some of them dating from the seventeenth century, are grouped round the harbour; one of them is of courtyard plan, access to the interior being gained by means of segmental-arched pend leading from Water Path.

At Cromarty (*126*) the destruction of the old town by sea-erosion, followed by a sudden spurt of prosperity during the second half of the eighteenth century, led to the creation of a new and homogeneous urban centre. To supplement the traditional native activity of herring fishing the manufacture of imported flax and hemp was developed, as well as nail-making and brewing, capital for these new ventures being provided almost entirely through local initiative. The houses of the merchants and manufacturers—charmingly unsophisticated interpretations of mid-Georgian classicism—were for the most part erected in Church Street, and few seem to have undergone any substantial alteration since their construction. They are dignified two- and three-storeyed buildings composed of red sandstone rubble with darker pinnings, the general plainness of their elevations being relieved here and there by rusticated quoins, or by the provision of a handsome radial fan-light above the principal entrance-doorway. Some have their gable ends fronting the street, while others stand back within leafy walled gardens. In complete contrast are the early nineteenth-century fishermen's cottages in Shore Street, whose closely spaced rows and narrow cobbled alleys, running at right angles to the

138   Tanhouse Brae and The Study, Culross, Fife. Late sixteenth and seventeenth centuries

139   Market Cross, Prestonpans, East Lothian. Early seventeenth century

140   Culross Tolbooth, Fife. Seventeenth century and later

141   Sanquhar Tolbooth, Dumfriesshire. Eighteenth century

142 Town House and High Street, Old Aberdeen. *George Jaffray*, 1788, and later

143 Crail Tolbooth, Fife. Sixteenth century and later

144 Jedburgh Jail, Roxburghshire. *Archibald Elliot*, 1823

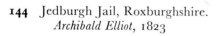

main street and water-front, reflect the separate identity of this very different social group.

Further north still the cathedral town of Fortrose can boast a few solid late Georgian houses grouped round the main square, while its twin burgh of Rosemarkie retains some traces of former maritime enterprise. Lerwick's position depended largely upon its status as a market town and a seat of a sheriffdom, together with the seasonal occupation provided by the ling fishery. The old street-plan is well preserved and makes little concession to vehicular traffic. A number of two- and three-storeyed houses of traditional aspect survive in the principal thoroughfare, some of them being gable fronted.

Most of the buildings so far described in this section were designed and executed by local master-masons or contractors who were more familiar with practical details of building construction than with the theoretical principles of classical architecture. The latter could be acquired only by the study of London or Edinburgh pattern-books, of which a considerable number seem ultimately to have found their way to Scottish provincial towns, or, if opportunity offered, through first-hand acquaintance with the works of leading architects. Tobias Bauchop, the Alloa master-mason, for example, who erected a small but well-proportioned and carefully detailed house for himself in his native town in 1695, evidently gained his knowledge during the course of his long professional association with Sir William Bruce (p. 97). In these circumstances it was inevitable that burgh architecture should remain predominantly vernacular in character almost up to the end of the Georgian period—'the 18th.', as Lord Cockburn succinctly remarked, 'was the final Scottish century'.

But the important developments in urban design that took place in England during the early Georgian era did not altogether escape notice in North Britain. The well-ordered lay-outs and homogeneous street-fronts that had already transformed the appearance of London and Bath could be achieved only when building operations were conducted on a very large scale, and few Scottish towns provided opportunities for this degree of expansion before the end of the eighteenth century. When such a chance did come, through the necessity of relieving the acute congestion that prevailed in the capital by opening up new streets beyond the waters of the North Loch, the city fathers at first procrastinated. But, urged on by the success of the more modest schemes being carried out by private builders on the south side of the burgh (*129*), they finally invited competitive plans for the lay-out of a proposed new town in 1766. The result was James Craig's design for what proved to be the first of a series of urban lay-outs that carried the city boundaries northwards almost to the Water of Leith and eastwards beyond the Calton Hill by the second quarter of the nineteenth century. In the initial stages of Craig's project, as it is seen in St Andrew's Square and Queen Street (*145*), no strict uniformity of frontage was imposed, but after Robert Adam's successful design for Charlotte Square (*135*) in 1791 it became usual to treat whole blocks of houses as individual architectural units. Among the later schemes (*130, 136*) the most ambitious

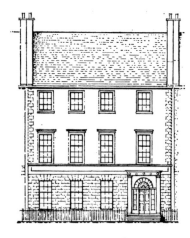

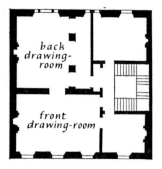

145 No. 64 Queen Street, Edinburgh

were Reid and Sibbald's lay-out of the Great King Street area, which included in Abercromby Place the first curved street-façade in Edinburgh, W. H. Playfair's Calton Hill terraces, and Gillespie Graham's Moray Place project—one of the few classical compositions of an architect who is more familiar as an exponent of the Gothic Revival (p. 128).

No other Scottish burgh of the Georgian era could produce a classical lay-out to rival those of Edinburgh, but a number of the larger towns fostered more modest schemes of improvement, which were not lacking in architectural merit. One of the first in the field was Perth, where well-detailed terraced houses were being erected in Charlotte Street shortly after 1783, to be followed at the turn of the century by the correct but rather severe crescent-front of Atholl Place. Rose Street, where John Ruskin once lived, dates from the same period and has Robert Reid's Old Academy as a centre-piece, while a combination of terraced houses and detached Regency villas makes for rather greater diversity of appearance in near-by Barossa Place. At Stirling a good series of detached and semi-detached villas, two storeys and a basement in height, began to rise in the Allan Park area in about 1820 as a first step in the expansion of the town westwards along the line of the Dumbarton road. Glasgow now exhibits more evidence of compulsive Victorian expansion than of its not inconsiderable Georgian prosperity, but still retains a number of dignified pedimented street-fronts along the south bank of the Clyde, and some well-preserved terraced houses in Blythswood Square, while Dundee can show some interesting neo-classical street architecture in David Neave's Union Street. In Aberdeen Archibald Simpson made effective use of the somewhat intractable local building-materials, producing dignified classical street-fronts with a minimal use of mouldings. The two most successful of his surviving compositions are Bon Accord Crescent and Marine Terrace, whose granitic severity is admirably offset by the adjacent tree-studded gardens—a combination of elements for which Lord Cockburn was forcibly pleading in Edinburgh.

Other coastal burghs were expanding at the same period, some because of the development of trade, and others as health resorts. In the latter class the most interesting example is Ardrossan, which was laid out for the twelfth Earl of Eglinton in 1806 by Peter Nicholson, who at that time had an extensive practice in Glasgow. 'It is built on a regular plan,' wrote the author of the *New Statistical Account*, 'the streets are wide, straight, and cross at right angles. The houses are all of two storeys, well finished, neat and comfortable.' Fairly well-preserved terraced buildings of this type survive today in Princes Street and Montgomerie Street. Ayr, too, was dignified by a new and spacious lay-out on the south side of the old town. Wellington Square, the focal centre of the scheme, retains much of its late eighteenth-century character, while the solid two-storeyed terraced houses of yellow sandstone in Alloway Place incorporate Grecian details typical of the Regency era. On the east coast Montrose has a number of pleasant tree-lined streets of late Georgian origin, together with some early Victorian terraces. Of these the most notable is Panmure Terrace, erected by Messrs. Japp in about 1850, in which the end bays are raised a storey above the remainder and are emphasised by Ionic doorways at first-floor level. At Fraserburgh the reconstruction of the harbour under the direction of Robert Stevenson during the second and third decades of the nineteenth century brought prosperity to the herring-fishing industry. New streets were laid out on a grid-plan in about the year 1815, but building seems to have proceeded rather slowly; most of the surviving houses of this period are of one or two storeys, some being constructed of neatly pinned blocks of local granite and others being rubble-built.

The majority of the schemes so far mentioned involved the extension of existing urban centres, but from time to time the opportunity arose for the creation of a comprehensive new lay-out on a hitherto undeveloped site. The most notable instance of this occurred at Inveraray, where the fifth Duke of Argyll pulled down the old town because of its proximity to the castle and laid out a new burgh on Loch Fyneside at his own expense. In origin the plan—the first project of its kind in Scotland—goes back to the time of the third Duke (1743–61), but although one or two of the more important buildings, such as the Town House and the inn (now the Argyll Arms), were erected during the 1750s, most of the houses date from the closing decades of the century. The focal point of the lay-out is the parish church, which occupies an island site midway along the principal street, but care was also taken to present a well-ordered front to the main, or northern, approach, where arcaded screen-walls are employed to unite the various individual elements of the composition. Most of the dwelling-houses are plain two- or three-storeyed tenements of harled rubble having pitched slate roofs (thatch was then an almost universal roofing material in Argyll) and prominent chimney-stacks (*127*). The architects most closely concerned with the Inveraray lay-out were John Adam and Robert Mylne, who were outstandingly successful in establishing a basic discipline of scale and proportion within the framework of the vernacular tradition.

Another comprehensive burgh lay-out of relatively early date was carried through at Penicuik, Midlothian, by Sir James Clerk in about 1770. By enclosing the immediate environs of the town as gardens the founder tried to ensure that the rapidly developing local industries did not destroy the rural atmosphere of the place, but such ideals held little appeal for subsequent generations and, apart from the parish church, almost nothing of the original scheme now survives. Fochabers, Morayshire, on the other hand, remains almost unspoiled. Transplanted, like Inveraray, by ducal command, the new town was laid out on a grid-pattern immediately beyond the gates of Gordon Castle during the last decade of the eighteenth century. The central square, planted with two rows of sycamore trees, is dominated by John Baxter's handsome parish church and its contemporary flanking-blocks. The remaining streets were not completed for some years—a house in the principal thoroughfare bears the date 1823—but all the buildings are of uniform appearance; most are plain harled structures of either one or two storeys roofed with local slate. Grantown-on-Spey, in the same county, was established by the Grant family in 1765 as a small agricultural and industrial centre, and the street-plan, which is similar to that of Fochabers, no doubt goes back to this period. The majority of the simple granite-built houses in the market-square and in Castle Road, however, are of somewhat later date, while the Charity School, with its charming ogee-roofed clock-tower, was not completed until 1824. Finally, mention may be made of the model fishing-town laid out by the British Fisheries Society at Pultneytown, on the south side of the burgh of Wick, in 1808. Standard plans were prepared by Thomas Telford for one- and two-storeyed houses, the smaller variety being provided with particularly spacious attics designed to accommodate fishing gear, but construction did not begin until 1830. Buildings of this type, some roofed with Caithness slates, can be seen in Argyll Square and Dunbar Street.

Something has already been said about early suburban development at Inveresk in a previous section of this chapter (p. 181). It was not until the late eighteenth and early nineteenth centuries, however, that the advantages of taking up residence on the out-skirts of the larger towns and cities came to be widely appreciated by increasing numbers of professional men, prosperous merchants and industrialists, and retired colonial officials. At first the more substantial suburban villas were architecturally indistinguishable from small country mansions of contemporary date. Gayfield House, for example, erected in the village of Broughton in the northern environs of Edinburgh shortly before 1765, is a plain oblong block comprising a sunk basement, two main storeys and an attic; the elevations conform to a standard pattern, the advanced central portion of the principal front rising to a triangular pediment surmounted by urn finials. Kelso can show several late Georgian villas of the same type, the most accomplished of them, Ednam House (1761), standing within a stone's throw of the abbey, and the remainder scattered through the northern and eastern outskirts of the town. Old Aberdeen (*142*), on the other hand, falls within a different category, being in origin a self-contained university and cathedral town enjoying the status of a burgh of regality, rather than a suburb of Aberdeen. Nevertheless, the architectural character that it assumed during the Georgian era can be described only as suburban. In High Street and College Bounds solid granite-built villas are flanked on the one hand by the small country mansion of the Leslies of Powis, and on the other by a row of pantiled cottages of wholly rural aspect, while beyond the Town House, in Chanonry, the dignified late Georgian houses of the university and cathedral dignitaries stand within secluded walled gardens.

During the first two or three decades of the nineteenth century a more distinctive type of suburban residence emerged, more compact than its predecessors, but carefully planned, and often elaborately ornamented in one or other of the current architectural styles. Many were probably indirectly derived from architectural pattern-books, whose authors, rejoicing as much in confusion of terminology as in variety of invention, contrived innumerable designs for model cottages, villas, villa cottages, mansion villas, suburban villas, marine villas and casinos in every style from Hindoo to Old Scotch. Thus the Gothic and castellated villas of the prosperous Dundee suburb of Newport, and the little classical marine residence, Springfield House, Campbeltown, find many parallels in the pages of J. C. Loudon's *Encyclopaedia of Cottage, Farm and Villa Architecture* (1833), an exhaustive compilation which rapidly became one of the most influential of its kind. Certain other suburban villas show greater originality of design. Walton Hall, Kelso, a neo-classical bungalow erected for John Ballantyne in 1820, is attractively sited on the east bank of the River Tweed; the plan revolves around a central hall, lit by a cupola, and includes a spacious octagonal dining-room overlooking the terraced riverside garden. Castle House, Dunoon, designed by David Hamilton two years later, also takes full advantage of an exceptionally fine situation. According to the author of the *New Statistical Account*, its builder, James Ewing of Glasgow, deserves much of the credit for the burgh's subsequent popularity as a Firth of Clyde watering-place, for 'the taste displayed in the erection of his villa ... pointed out to others the advantages of the locality ... of which several individuals of respectability soon availed themselves'. Most remarkable of all, perhaps, is the 'art-gallery villa' (a variant not anticipated even by Loudon) known as The Vyne, which was built for George Duncan in the Magdalen Green district of Dundee in 1836. Like Walton Hall it is a carefully detailed neo-Grecian bungalow having a central hall with a cupola; the principal front shows a Doric portico, inclined window-jambs and antae beneath a continuous broad frieze.

Public Buildings

After the parish church the two most important buildings in any early Scottish burgh were the market-cross and the tolbooth. The cross, as the essential symbol of burghal status, always occupied a prominent position in the main street or the market-place. Here formal proclamations of local and national import were made, criminals were punished and, on occasions of public rejoicing, there was festivity and banqueting. The earliest market-crosses were probably of timber, but all the surviving examples are of stone except that at Kilwinning, which retains a wooden cross-head. Cruciform examples of any description are, in fact, rare, although Banff Cross, which may be as old as the fifteenth century, incorporates a Calvary scene, while at Campbeltown and Inveraray late medieval ecclesiastical cross-shafts ornamented with typical West Highland relief carving can be seen in secondary use. More usually the shaft rises to a decorative capital bearing a coat of arms or a sundial, and often surmounted by a unicorn or other finial. Sometimes these features are found in combination; the late medieval crosses of Peebles and Inverkeithing, for example, display the armorial bearings of important local families, and both also incorporate seventeenth-century sundials. The shaft itself is usually plain, and of square or octagonal section, though one or two late examples, such as the one at Musselburgh, are of columnar form. In most cases the cross is set upon a roughly-hewn stepped base, but a number stand upon stone platforms of some architectural elaboration. Of this latter group the finest is undoubtedly that of Prestonpans (*139*), which dates from the early seventeenth century. This has a circular base divided by pilasters into eight compartments, two of which contain doorways, and the remainder shell-headed alcoves. One door gives access to a small internal chamber, while the other leads by way of a narrow stair to a parapeted platform.

At the tolbooth, or Town House (as it latterly came to be called), the public affairs of the burgh were transacted. It was the regular meeting-place of the burgh court and of the council, and served also as the municipal prison. For reasons both of prestige and of security the earlier stone tolbooths followed the familiar tower-house pattern, the town bell being conveniently housed in the upper portion of the building. One of the very few surviving buildings of this class is Tain Tolbooth, a substantial three-storeyed structure of about the end of the sixteenth century, surmounted by angle-turrets and a belfry. Canongate Tolbooth, Edinburgh, is of the same period and its tower is of similar design except that its lowest storey incorporates a pend leading to a wynd at the rear. Until about 1880 the tower was roofed with wooden shingles, a type of covering that may have been in fairly common use before the general introduction of slate and pantile. By themselves towers such as these could provide only a limited amount of accommodation and, when more spacious rooms came to be required, the obvious solution (and the one followed also in contemporary tower-houses) was to extend the building horizontally. Whether or not the existing three-storeyed extension containing the Canongate council-chamber is contemporary with the tower is debatable, but certainly when a new tolbooth was erected in Musselburgh in about 1590 it took the form of a long narrow block incorporating a tower at one end. The provision of a stone vault at each level, and of an open parapet carried on stone corbels, maintains the defensive aspect of the building, but the tower itself is little more than a steeple, its ogee-roofed timber spire being wholly domestic in character.

Such developments soon became general. The primitive tower-like tolbooths were gradually replaced by more up-to-date buildings or, if, as in the case of Crail (*143*), they remained in use, they were remodelled and enlarged (*140*). Most of the larger seventeenth-century tolbooths seem to have been provided with prominent steeples, and a particularly handsome example in the Scottish Renaissance style may still be seen at Glasgow, although the tolbooth itself has long since disappeared. In the smaller burghs more modest schemes might be adopted; Dunbar has a well-preserved tolbooth of about the same date as the Glasgow steeple. It is a three-storeyed building of T-plan, the octagonal stair-tower that projects from the centre of the main front terminating in a charming timber spire, partly slated and partly sheathed in lead. This type of plan remained popular for a considerable period, and there are good examples of simple eighteenth-century tolbooths with rectangular bell-towers at Kilmaurs (*146*) and West Wemyss. Both have forestairs leading up to a principal entrance-doorway in the tower, and at West Wemyss the lower storey of the main block is traversed by a vaulted pend from which access is obtained to the prison cells. A panel built into the front wall of the tower bears an explanatory couplet, penned by some eighteenth-century McGonagall:

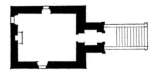

146 Kilmaurs Tolbooth, Ayrshire

> *This fabric was built by Earl David Wemyss and town*
> *For the cribbing of vice and service to crown.*

During the second half of the seventeenth century buildings of more formal design began to appear. One of the earliest is Linlithgow Tolbooth, for which John Mylne, younger, the King's Master-Mason, is known to have provided a number of alternative schemes shortly before his death in 1667. The thorough-going restoration carried out in 1848 makes it hard to determine the precise appearance of Mylne's building, but it seems to have been an elongated rectangular block of three main storeys; a tall square tower projected from the centre of the rear elevation, its lower portion containing a staircase and its upper serving as a belfry. The principal elevation had a central entrance-doorway at first-floor level, approached by a double forestair, while in the two upper storeys all four elevations incorporated ranges of lug-moulded windows having flat triangular pediments with enriched tympana. Dalkeith Tolbooth, too, displays a much altered symmetrical front of simple classical form having a pedimented doorway, regularly disposed windows and rusticated quoins.

When the opportunity came to erect a new Town House in Stirling in 1702 the council commissioned a design from the leading architect of the day, Sir William Bruce. The resulting composition is a compact three-storeyed building having a carefully detailed ashlar front (subsequently lengthened by three bays), and a fine six-storeyed spire which takes full advantage of its corner site. The panelled council-chamber on the first floor is reached by a flight of steps which rises within the tower, passing above the prison, or 'holl beneath the steeple'. Bruce's design was closely followed by Tobias Bauchop of Alloa in his plan for Dumfries Town House (The Midsteeple) a year or two later. Less academic in character are the attractive Georgian tolbooths at Sanquhar (*141*) and Kintore. In both cases plain two-storeyed rectangular blocks of conventional design have been dignified by distinctive ridge-belfries, while Kintore can also boast an elegant double forestair rising to a principal entrance-doorway at first-floor level.

147 Town House, Peebles

At Peebles Town House (*147*), on the other hand, there is neither steeple nor belfry, and the building relies for effect upon its sturdy proportions and robust detail; the wall-head pediment contains a carved shield bearing the burgh arms and the date of erection, 1753, while the burgh motto is boldly painted beneath the eaves cornice.

By the latter part of the Georgian era vernacular styles had been almost completely submerged and the Town Houses of this period were in most cases of conventional neo-classical design, many of the larger ones having imposing steeples of the type so often found in contemporary churches. Ayr Town Hall, erected to a design of Thomas Hamilton of Edinburgh in 1828, has a particularly fine steeple, and there are other notable examples at Falkirk (David Hamilton, 1813) and Haddington (Gillespie Graham, 1830). More individualistic in conception is Montrose Town House, designed by John Hutcheon, a local land-surveyor, in 1763, but remodelled and enlarged by William Smith, of Montrose, half a century later; its most distinctive feature, and one that formed part of the original scheme, is an arcaded 'piazza' opening on to the High Street and market-place.

Other types of public building were few and far between before the end of the eighteenth century, and some of the most notable ones, such as Old College, Glasgow, and the Old Royal Infirmary, Edinburgh, have since been replaced. Most were erected for educational or other charitable purposes, the earliest example of this class being King's College, Aberdeen, founded by Bishop Elphinstone in 1495. The most important of the original buildings that stand today is the chapel, which contains the finest surviving collection of medieval carved woodwork in Scotland; the handsome crown spire is a mid-seventeenth-century reconstruction of the original one. Aberdeen can also boast one of the two earliest school buildings in the country that still fulfil their original function. Like George Heriot's Hospital, Edinburgh (p. 54), Robert Gordon's College was endowed by a wealthy burgess as an orphan school for local children. Within a decade of the institution's foundation in 1730 a plain but dignified three-storeyed granite block (*148*) had been completed to a design of William Adam, the pedimented end-bays of the principal front rising a storey higher than the central portion, where a statue of the founder (by John Cheere), framed within a Venetian window-recess, surmounts the main entrance.

Closely allied in purpose were the municipal hospitals intended primarily to meet the needs of the poor and elderly. The best example of this class is Cowane's Hospital, Stirling (1637-49), a charming courtyard-plan building (*154*) of vernacular character

148 Robert Gordon's College, Aberdeen. *William Adam, c.* 1730–40

149 Edinburgh University. *Robert Adam* and *W. H. Playfair,* 1789–1828;
dome by *R. Rowand Anderson,* 1887

150 Royal High School, Edinburgh. *Thomas Hamilton,* 1829

151 National Gallery, Edinburgh. *W. H. Playfair*, 1845

152 Dollar Academy, Clackmannanshire. *W. H. Playfair*, 1818

153 Montrose Academy, Angus. *David Logan*, 1815

with a prominent lead-roofed steeple; the designer was John Mylne, younger, who himself carved the portrait statue of the pious founder. Dunbar's Hospital, Inverness, dates from the third quarter of the seventeenth century, while King James VI's Hospital, Perth, is a mid-Georgian replacement of an earlier structure of the same name. It is a substantial four-storeyed building of conventional classical design laid out on an H-plan; the leaded cupola formerly

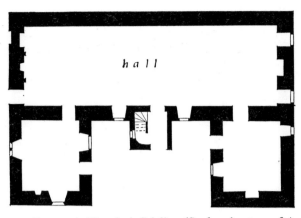

154 Cowane's Hospital, Stirling (Scale 1 in. to 24 ft.)

surmounted the House of Nairne, in Strathtay, summarily demolished by its purchaser, the Duke of Atholl, in 1764. Two much less well-known public buildings of about the same period, both of some architectural interest, are Innerpeffray Library, near Crieff, designed by Charles Freebairn of Alloa, and the Estate Office, Hamilton, which incorporates a spacious Assembly Room of late eighteenth-century date.

The first Edinburgh new town scheme inaugurated more than half a century of intensive public building activity in the capital. Apart from two relatively quiescent decades occasioned by the Napoleonic Wars hardly a year passed without some new church, municipal building or monument thrusting its way into the city's skyline. The two most important of the pre-Napoleonic buildings, General Register House and the University, were primarily the creation of Robert Adam. The former, a repository for the public records of Scotland, was commenced in 1774 on a key site at the intersection of the recently completed North Bridge and the east end of Princes Street, while the latter was begun 15 years later in the less accommodating surroundings afforded by the southern outskirts of the old town. Adam's design for the Register House, echoing his earlier scheme for Syon House, Middlesex, was for a rotunda within a square courtyard, while that for the University comprised a main quadrangle with a forecourt and monumental portico fronting South Bridge (149, 155). In each case, however, the original conception was still unfulfilled at the time of the architect's death and was subsequently modified by other and less sensitive hands.

The years after Waterloo brought great opportunities to a new generation of architects, many of them Edinburgh men who had returned home after a spell in one of the leading London offices. The city had at least awakened to the aesthetic potentialities of its topography and, with what one contemporary described as that 'foolish phrase, "The Modern Athens"' as its watchword, was preparing to adorn its numerous monumental sites with buildings of the purest Grecian style. The Calton Hill, a reluctant

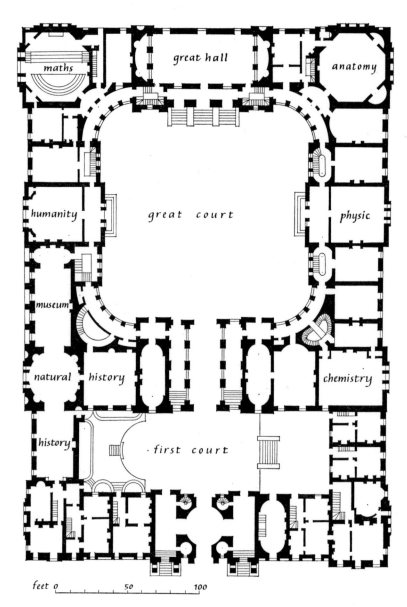

155 Edinburgh University

latter-day Acropolis, bore the main weight of this municipal endeavour. Archibald Elliot's Old Calton Jail (of which the Governor's House alone now remains), a spirited essay in the castellated manner, was soon overshadowed by the many-porticoed New Observatory (1818) and the ill-fated National Monument, or Parthenon (1822–), both designed by W. H. Playfair. Lower down the hill Thomas Hamilton's Royal High School (*150*), by general consent the finest monument of the Scottish Greek Revival, was completed in 1829, its massive stepped profile culminating most effectively in the Doric temple portico of the main hall, while for good measure rival variants of the Choragic Monument of Lysicrates at Athens appeared on each flank, Thomas Hamilton's (1830) commemorating Burns and Playfair's (1832) Dugald Stewart. Another outstanding site, the intersection of the Mound and Princes Street, was also entrusted to Playfair, who burdened it with two of Edinburgh's most familiar Grecian buildings, the Royal Institution (1823–36, now the Royal Scottish Academy) and the National Gallery (1845) (*151*). Nor were the expanding suburbs of the new town ignored, the Doric mantle here being assumed by the young William Burn, who was responsible for the closely related designs of John Watson's school (1825) and the Edinburgh Academy (1823–36).

Late Georgian public buildings in the provinces reflect the same influences as those of the capital, although here the early decades of the nineteenth century were less completely dominated by the Greek Revival. The three major east-coast burghs can all show at least one or two buildings of the first rank, Archibald Simpson's Music Hall at Aberdeen (1820) and Leslie and Taylor's Dundee Custom House (1842–3), in particular, presenting instructive contrasts with the more purist compositions of the Edinburgh Grecian school. Glasgow's most notable public buildings of this period are David Hamilton's Royal Exchange (1829–30), influenced in part by the work of Sir John Soane at the Bank of England, and the no less monumental County Buildings, erected to a design of Messrs. Clarke and Bell in 1844. Among the smaller burghs Elgin can boast good examples of the work of Gillespie Graham (Dr Gray's Hospital, 1815–19) and Archibald Simpson (General Anderson's Institution, 1831), Leith and Greenock have imposing though rather gloomy Custom Houses (Robert Reid, 1811; William Burn, 1818), while Greenlaw's impressively domed Court House (John Cunningham, 1829) commemorates the burgh's former status of a county town. The early nineteenth century also saw the construction of many new prisons, whose architects invariably strove to combine strict functionalism of plan with appropriateness of stylistic expression; the rudimentary classicism of the unobtrusive little jail at Inveraray (*c.* 1820) and the fortress-like aspect of the complex radial lay-out at Jedburgh (1823) (*144*) are illustrative of a wide range of style and plan-types. During the same period a notable series of burgh schools was erected. Of these the most imposing are W. H. Playfair's Dollar Academy (1818) (*152*) and George Angus's Dundee High School (1834), but the trim and compact central block of Montrose Academy (1815) (*153*), designed by a local architect, David Logan, and R. and R. Dickson's Bathgate Academy display a welcome individuality of treatment.

Towns or Buildings Specially Worth Visiting

The use of italics signifies that a building is, at the time of writing, the subject of a long-standing arrangement giving either regular or occasional public access.

Medieval Survivals

Fife	West Port, St Andrews
Stirlingshire	Town Wall, Stirling

Burgh Architecture of the Sixteenth and Seventeenth Centuries

Clackmannanshire	Clackmannan
Fife	Crail
	Culross
	Pittenweem
Kincardineshire	Stonehaven
Midlothian	Edinburgh
Morayshire	Elgin
Orkney	Kirkwall
Stirlingshire	Stirling

The Great Town Houses of the Sixteenth and Seventeenth Centuries

Aberdeenshire	*Provost Ross's House*, Aberdeen
	Provost Skene's House, Aberdeen
Ayrshire	Seagate Castle, Irvine
	Maybole Castle, Maybole
Fife	*The Palace*, Culross
Kirkcudbrightshire	*Maclellan's House*, Kirkcudbright
Midlothian	*Acheson House*, Edinburgh
	Huntly House, Edinburgh
	Moray House, Edinburgh
	Andrew Lamb's House, Leith
Orkney	Tankerness House, Kirkwall
Roxburghshire	*Queen Mary's House*, Jedburgh
Stirlingshire	*Argyll Lodging*, Stirling
	Mar's Work, Stirling

Burgh Architecture of the Eighteenth and early Nineteenth Centuries

Aberdeenshire	Aberdeen
Angus	Montrose
Argyll	Inveraray
Ayrshire	Ardrossan
	Ayr

Banffshire	Banff
East Lothian	Haddington
Fife	Anstruther
	Crail
	Falkland
	Kincardine
	Pittenweem
	St Andrews
Midlothian	Edinburgh
Morayshire	Fochabers
Perthshire	Dunblane
	Dunkeld
	Perth
Ross and Cromarty	Cromarty
Roxburghshire	Kelso
Shetland	Lerwick
Wigtownshire	Whithorn
	Wigtown

Public Buildings

Aberdeenshire	King's College, Aberdeen
	Music Hall, Aberdeen
	Robert Gordon's College, Aberdeen
	Town House, Kintore
	Town House, Old Aberdeen
Angus	Custom House, Dundee
	The Academy, Montrose
Ayrshire	Town Hall, Ayr
	Tolbooth, Kilmaurs
Clackmannanshire	The Academy, Dollar
Dumfriesshire	The Midsteeple, Dumfries
	Town House, Sanquhar
East Lothian	Tolbooth, Dunbar
	Market-cross, Prestonpans
Kincardineshire	Tolbooth, Stonehaven
Midlothian	Calton Hill, Edinburgh
	Canongate Tolbooth, Edinburgh
	General Register House, Edinburgh
	Old College, Edinburgh
	Royal High School, Edinburgh
	Tolbooth, Musselburgh
Morayshire	Dr Gray's Hospital, Elgin
	General Anderson's Institution, Elgin
Perthshire	Library, Innerpeffray
	King James VI's Hospital, Perth
Ross and Cromarty	Tolbooth, Tain
Roxburghshire	Old Jail, Jedburgh
Stirlingshire	*Cowane's Hospital*, Stirling
	Town House, Stirling

VI INDUSTRIAL ARCHITECTURE

The rapid developments in technology and communications during the early years of the Industrial Revolution have left their own architectural legacy in many areas of Great Britain—albeit one that has remained almost totally unappreciated by its heirs until within recent years. Yet it seems likely that the current investigations of 'industrial archaeologists' will show that Scotland has retained a more interesting and representative selection of material remains of the recent industrial past than most other parts of the island. Scotland's possession of extensive mineral resources, and of an abundance of sites suitable for the harnessing of water power, ensured that her industrial contribution was a notable one, while at the same time the challenge presented by her topography brought tremendous opportunities in the field of communication. In the development of the country's two chief industries of textile manufacture and the production of iron and coal much of the initiative came from the south, through the agency of men like Arkwright and Garbett, but for the task of road and bridge building and for the construction of canals, harbours and lighthouses, Scotland produced a race of engineers whose inventive genius restored the balance in full measure.

The pace of technological change varied greatly from one branch of manufacture to another. Thus, the old established linen trade remained primarily a cottage industry until well into the nineteenth century, spinning and weaving usually being done by hand, and often as a part-time occupation. The few specifically industrial buildings that survive from this period, such as the plain, two-storeyed, hip-roofed block (1767) at Spittalfield, Perthshire, and the interesting little mill (1755) at Lornty, Blairgowrie, in the same county, were presumably erected either as warehouses or as 'manufactories' devoted to the partially mechanised preparatory and finishing processes. Later on machine spinning was introduced, the factory organisation of the industry being concentrated in Angus, Fife and Perthshire. Lornty Mill itself, perhaps originally a lint-mill, had become one of a group of five spinning-mills by 1843, and some of the buildings of this period, together with rows of partly ruinous workers' dwellings may be seen on both sides of the Ericht Water. Arbroath, another centre of the linen industry that expanded rapidly during the first half of the nineteenth century, retains a number of its early mills, notably the imposing four-storeyed Baltic Spinning Mill, where the principal frontage is of ashlar with rusticated quoins, the central and end bays being surmounted by triangular pediments.

The cotton industry, on the other hand, developed with exceptional rapidity, new and improved types of spinning machinery becoming available just at the time when Scotland's trade was being re-orientated following the economic disasters brought about by the American War of Independence. Within a decade of the establishment of the first effective cotton-mill at Rothesay in 1779 some 20 mills were in operation, and there were more than twice this number before the end of the century. The most important of these early enterprises were the famous New Lanark Mills, founded by Richard Arkwright and David Dale in 1785, and controlled and managed by the latter's son-in-law, Robert Owen, from 1799 to 1827. The village of New Lanark is one of the outstanding monuments of the Industrial Revolution in Britain, the close inter-relationship of its mills, schools, church, shops and workers' model dwellings reflecting the founders' ideal of a planned community governed by the principles of philanthropic socialism. Although situated within the heart of industrial Lanarkshire the village still retains an air of almost rural detachment, the approach road passing between pedimented entrance-lodges and winding down thickly wooded slopes before it reaches the tall stone buildings that stand so purposefully by the water's edge (*156, 157*). Second only in interest are the Stanley Cotton Mills, Perthshire, established in the same year as New Lanark by a group of local gentry and merchants, together with Arkwright, upon land feued from another supporter of the project, the Duke of Atholl. Here, too, a model village was laid out and, although the mills were forced to close for a period at the end of the Napoleonic Wars, prosperity returned during the second quarter of the nineteenth century. The existing buildings include a six-storeyed mill of stone and brick construction which, like its companions, was formerly powered by giant water-wheels supplied through a tunnel that drew the waters of the Tay from beyond the north side of Shiel Hill. The village has some neat two-storeyed houses, some of stone, but others of brick made on the site from local clays. Similar enterprises were undertaken at about the same time at Deanston, Perthshire, and Catrine, Ayrshire, the former by the Buchanan family, in close association with Arkwright, and the latter by Claud Alexander and David Dale. At Catrine the recent demolition of the original five-storeyed mill of 1787 has robbed the site of its historical centrepiece, but Deanston (*158*), although preserving none of its earliest buildings, retains a late-Georgian mill of some architectural distinction, which employs fireproof brick-arch construction, as well as an interesting vaulted weaving-shed of 1820, and some rows of plain two-storeyed workers' dwellings. Among minor projects of early date the most ambitious was the establishment of a spinning-jenny factory on the shores of the Dornoch Firth by George Dempster, one of the founders of Stanley Mills. This scheme, in which instructors were brought from Glasgow 'to conduct the work, and to teach the natives of the country the arts of spinning and weaving', foundered with the accidental destruction of the factory by fire in 1808, only a burnt-out shell (*159*) and the name 'Spinningdale' now commemorating this first attempt to introduce textile manufacture into the Highlands.

Like the linen trade the woollen industry was organised largely on a domestic basis until the general introduction of improved machinery during the first half of the nineteenth century, and such earlier factories as there were have by now mostly disappeared. At Bannockburn, Stirlingshire, however, where tartans were probably being factory-produced as early as 1770, a small mill of the period survives in part, together with some slightly later workers' tenements and a large handloom-weaving factory—the Royal George Mill (*160*)—of about 1820. One of the first attempts at mechanisation in the Border towns was the introduction of the stocking-frame in the Hawick district in 1771, and two early stocking factories, of very modest size, can be seen in the village of Denholm. Shortly afterwards came the handloom factories like Brodies' late eighteenth-century 'workhouse' at Innerleithen, now incorporated in later buildings, where the two lower floors were originally devoted to spinning, carding and roving by water power, while the three upper were partly occupied by hand-operated machines and partly used for storage. In the later full-scale mechanisation of the woollen industry Galashiels took the lead and both there, and at the neighbouring burgh of Selkirk, a number of the earlier mills are still in production.

Iron smelting by means of primitive 'bloomery' furnaces is known to have been carried out in many parts of Scotland from an early date, but the recent history of the industry may be said to begin with the foundation of the Invergarry furnace, near Fort Augustus, in 1727. Like its successors at Bonawe (1753) and Goatfield (1775), Argyll, the Invergarry enterprise was an offshoot of the Lancashire and Cumberland iron-industry, the ore being transported by sea from these areas to the Highlands, whose abundant woodlands could provide the furnace charcoal that was by this time almost impossible to obtain elsewhere; the smelted pig-iron was carried southwards again by the returning ships. A well-preserved furnace and a number of associated buildings survive at Goatfield (now called Furnace), but the most important group of remains is at Bonawe, where operations did not finally cease until about 1875. Here there may be seen an early industrial lay-out as self-contained as that of New Lanark, the furnace itself (*161*), with its inscribed cast-iron lintels, standing in close proximity to solidly constructed iron-ore and charcoal storage-sheds, while near by there are rows of flatted dwellings, a manager's house, and a pier and storehouse.

The general adoption of coke fuel in place of charcoal during the second half of the eighteenth century led to the large-scale establishment of the industry in the Central Lowlands, where both ironstone and coal were readily available. Carron Ironworks was founded by Samuel Garbett of Birmingham and his two Scottish co-partners in 1759, to be followed after an interval of 20 years by a small coke-furnace at Wilsontown, Lanarkshire, and thereafter by other works in different areas. At Carron itself all the original buildings have been replaced, the most important surviving example of industrial architecture being the early nineteenth-century engineering shop; this displays some interesting peculiarities of cast-iron construction, and its massive open-timber roof incorporates a remarkable suspended upper floor. Cramond, Midlothian, where

156 New Lanark, Lanarkshire. Late eighteenth and early nineteenth centuries

157 Cotton mill, New Lanark. Late eighteenth or early nineteenth century

158 Cotton mill, Deanston, Perthshire. Early nineteenth century

159 Cotton mill, Spinningdale, Sutherland. Late eighteenth century

160 Royal George Mill, Bannockburn, Stirlingshire. Early nineteenth century
161 Bonawe Iron-furnace, Argyll. 1753 and later

the nail trade was established by Carron Company at an early stage in its development, retains two late eighteenth-century iron-mills and some associated industrial housing, while something also remains of the Wilsontown works, which closed down in 1842.

Credit for the construction of what must certainly have been one of the first canals in Scotland is traditionally given to that doughty sea captain Sir Andrew Wood of Largo, who died as long ago as 1515, and the track of the waterway upon which he was supposedly rowed to church each Sunday in an eight-oared galley is still pointed out in the grounds of Largo House, Fife. The history of the main Scottish canal network of the late eighteenth and early nineteenth centuries is a good deal more prosaic. Many of the earliest canals, such as the Monkland Canal (1770–90) and the now almost forgotten Campbeltown–Drumlemble Canal (c. 1790), were intended primarily for the transport of coal. The more ambitious projects, although contributing no less effectively to the expansion of industry, were designed with broader aims in view, the Forth and Clyde Canal and its subsidiaries to facilitate general commerce between the western and eastern lowlands, and the two Highland canals to discourage emigration and to benefit naval and mercantile shipping.

It was the works of this latter class that presented the greatest challenge to the engineer. The Forth and Clyde Canal itself, begun under the direction of John Smeaton in 1768, had to be driven for a distance of 38 miles over unusually difficult terrain, both rock and quicksand being encountered, necessitating massive earthen embankments in certain sections. Its logical successor, the Union Canal, which continued the existing waterway eastwards from Falkirk to Edinburgh, thus providing a direct link between the capital and Glasgow, was completed in 1818–22 by Hugh Baird, of Kelvinhead. In this instance a rock-cut tunnel, 700 yd. in length, had to be constructed, and there were also a number of important river-crossings, notably those over the Almond and the Avon. The Avon Aqueduct (*163*) is a major achievement of civil engineering, its 12 segmental-headed arches, supported on hollow piers, carrying an iron water-trough 13 ft. in width and some 6 ft. in depth for a distance of nearly 300 yd.

Formidable though these problems may have been, they were nothing to the difficulties that confronted Thomas Telford during the construction of the Caledonian Canal (1804–22). Although two-thirds of the total length of the proposed waterway was navigable by means of a chain of freshwater lochs, the construction of the remaining 20 miles made exceptionally heavy demands upon the designer's patience and ingenuity. At the south end of the canal the sharp ascent to Loch Lochy involved the construction of a series of eight massive locks, promptly christened 'Neptune's Staircase' (*164*), which raise the level of the waterway by a total of 72 ft., while at the north end the entrance lock to the Clachnaharry Basin (itself occupying an area of some 32 acres) had to be founded upon piles in mud having a depth of not less than 60 ft. Although opened to shipping in 1822, the project was not fully completed until 1847, the total cost by this time having reached the enormous figure of £1,300,000.

The first systematic attempt to promote the safety of coastal shipping by the erection of lighthouses began only with the creation of the Board of Commissioners of Northern Lighthouses in 1786. A few primitive beacon-towers are known to have existed at an earlier period, however, the oldest surviving one being the little square tower that was constructed on May Island, in the Firth of Forth, in 1636. This was a private light, the owner of the island being empowered to levy tolls on passing shipping; like its companion (c. 1750) on Little Cumbrae Island, Buteshire, the May lighthouse was provided with an open chauffer, or brazier, in which a coal fire was kept burning. The earliest of the Commissioners' lighthouses was no more than a tower (1787) perched on the roof of the sixteenth-century castle on Kinnaird Head, Fraserburgh, but more ambitious projects followed, the most notable being the construction of the Bell Rock Lighthouse, off Arbroath, in 1807–11. Credit for the design must go primarily to John Rennie, who modelled his plan upon that of the Eddystone Lighthouse (1756–9), but the resident engineer, Robert Stevenson, contributed largely to its successful execution. Great difficulties were encountered, the Inchcape reef being exposed for such short periods that no more than a few hours' work was possible each day, and that only during the summer months; the tower rises to a height of 127 ft., including the lantern, the greater part of the masonry being of dovetail-joint construction. Among the most impressive of the other Scottish lighthouses of the period (*168*) are Rhinns of Islay (1825), probably designed by Stevenson, and Skerryvore, Tiree (1840–4) (*167*), one of the principal achievements of the engineer's eldest son, Alan Stevenson. This latter structure, standing 11 miles out into the Atlantic, was carried up to a height of almost 160 ft. (including the lantern) to ensure that its light would be visible throughout the whole area of surrounding reefs.

The extensive harbour improvements carried out at about this time by Telford and other engineers at almost every port in Scotland fall outside the scope of this survey, but some mention should perhaps be made of certain groups of harbour buildings belonging to a rather earlier period. One of the most interesting series can be seen at Portsoy, Banffshire, where the harbour precincts (*170*) seem to have changed little since the eighteenth century, when the burgh was a busy little fishing port, supporting also a linen-thread manufactory. Some of the quays, constructed of large up-ended blocks of variegated sandstone, are said to date from the sixteenth century, but the harbour is known to have been reconstructed more than once during the past 150 years. A number of fine eighteenth-century warehouses (now much in need of restoration) still stand in Shorehead, while houses of similar character line the narrow streets that climb steeply up to the main square. Cromarty Harbour was built by a beneficent local laird, George Ross, in about 1785, to serve his newly established hempen-cloth factory, which contributed largely to the late-Georgian prosperity of the burgh (p. 192). This industry has long since been defunct, but the factory (*126*) still stands behind the harbour, its spacious quadrangular lay-out incorporating a pair of detached buildings in the centre of the courtyard. About 200 people were employed within its walls at the time of the *Statistical Account* (1794), whose author remarks with pride that 'the buildings for this business are large and extensive beyond any for the same purpose in Britain'. At the other end of the town there may be seen another of Ross's enterprises, the brewery, a plain rectangular building of red sandstone with a hipped roof and brick chimneys. Other well-preserved groups of harbour buildings of about the same date survive at Stromness, Orkney, and Ullapool, Ross and Cromarty (*169*), while along the western shores of the Cromarty Firth there are scattered a number of individual warehouses whose precise function is not easy to determine. The most interesting of these is the 'Old Rent House' at Foulis, which is said to have been used to store estate rents, payable in kind, prior to their shipment for sale. It is a long narrow building of two main storeys and an attic, the ground floor being served principally by a series of three

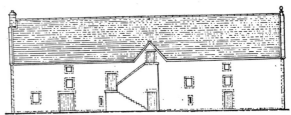

162 Old Rent House, Foulis, Ross and Cromarty

entrance-doorways on the seaward side, and the upper floors by what may originally have been hoisting doors (*162*).

Bridges

Very few early bridges survive in Scotland. The Romans do not appear to have built any stone bridges in Britain (although many so-called 'Roman Bridges' are still pointed out), and throughout the medieval period there were many more bridges of timber than of stone. Nor is it an easy matter to decide the precise age of the older bridges that do exist, for few have any stylistic peculiarities, and methods of construction changed relatively little from one century to another.

It seems likely, however, that the oldest surviving Scottish bridges date from the fifteenth and early sixteenth centuries. They are characterised by narrow roadways, massive piers, and multiple arches of uniform but comparatively restricted span. Dumfries Bridge (*171*), where building operations are known to have been in progress in 1431, clearly belongs to this category, as does Guard Bridge, Fife, and the old bridges of Ayr and Peebles. Stirling Old Bridge (*172*) and Bridge of Earn, Perthshire, where the central spans are rather wider than those at the sides, may also be ascribed to this period, and likewise the single-arch structures at Brig-o-Doon, Ayr, and Brig o'Balgownie, Aberdeen. The ribbed arch was not infrequently employed at this time, good examples of this form of construction being preserved at Bridge of Dee, Aberdeen, and at Haddington, Jedburgh and Tullibody.

Few major bridges seem to have been erected during the century following the

Reformation, although a number of lesser structures of this period are preserved, including Fogo Bridge, Berwickshire, a single-arch construction having a span of 40 ft. and a width of about 10 ft. at the roadway; a carved panel commemorates its erection by Sir James Cockburn of Ryslaw in 1641. With the gradual introduction of coach and carriage traffic towards the end of the seventeenth century, however, bridge building was commenced on a more extensive scale, the number of bridges multiplying rapidly during the following century as the military road-system was driven into the Highlands and the Turnpike Acts were introduced. At the same time carriageways became wider and arch spans were increased, while piers and cutwaters gradually assumed more slender proportions. One of the best of the early improved bridges is Clydseholm Bridge, Lanark, a plain three-arch structure erected in 1694–9 to a design of John Lockhart of Lanark, while Hyndford Bridge (1773) in the same neighbourhood, with its corbelled parapet and rounded, turreted cutwaters, exemplifies the more sophisticated approach of the bridge builders of the turnpike era. The designer was probably Alexander Stevens, one of the best known bridge engineers of the day. The majority of the numerous bridges that belong to the military-road period are severely plain, but the most famous of them, General Wade's Tay Bridge at Aberfeldy (1733) (*173*), is an elaborate structure of some architectural distinction. Regarded by its founder as the summit of his road-building achievements, this bridge was designed by William Adam, and skilfully executed in local freestone by craftsmen drawn from as far afield as northern England. Such refinement of design is unusual in public bridges at this period, but is not uncommonly found in connection with private schemes of estate improvement. Good examples occur at Dumfries House, Ayrshire, and Pollok House, Glasgow, while at Inveraray there is a notable series of estate and highway bridges (*174*) designed by the architects responsible for the lay-out of the town and castle.

The erection of Smeaton's handsome nine-arch bridge at Perth (*175*) in 1766–72 marked the opening of a new era of bridge building dominated by the great engineers of the late Georgian period. Smeaton himself followed up his achievement at Perth with similarly designed bridges at Coldstream (1766) and Banff (1779), while John Rennie, whose first bridge was erected on the outskirts of Edinburgh when he was no more than 23 years of age, went on to produce one of the most influential compositions of his day at Kelso (1803). This was one of the first bridges in the country to have a level roadway; there are semi-elliptical arches of 72 ft. span and the roadway has a width of 23 ft. between the balustraded parapets (*176*). Certain features of the design, including the twin-column treatment of the piers, were subsequently developed by Rennie at Waterloo Bridge, London, while a more direct imitation by another designer spans the Teviot Water just upstream from Kelso itself.

But the greatest individual contribution was undoubtedly that of Thomas Telford, whose report on Highland communications in 1803 led directly to the establishment of the Commission for Highland Roads and Bridges, a body that ultimately succeeded

163 Avon Aqueduct, Union Canal, Stirlingshire. *Hugh Baird*, 1818–22

164 Neptune's Staircase, Caledonian Canal, Inverness-shire. *Thomas Telford*, 1804–22

165 Hutton Suspension Bridge, Berwickshire. *Samuel Brown*, 1820
166 Perth Waterworks. *Adam Anderson*, 1832

167 (*Left*) Skerryvore Lighthouse, Argyll. *Alan Stevenson*, 1840–4
168 (*Top right*) Cromarty Lighthouse, Ross and Cromarty. 1846
169 (*Bottom right*) Ullapool Harbour, Ross and Cromarty. Late eighteenth century and later

170 Portsoy Harbour, Banffshire. Eighteenth century and later

in constructing 730 miles of road and well over 1000 bridges. Telford was personally responsible for the design and execution of many of the more important projects, two of the most notable of these being the fine seven-arch bridge across the Tay at Dunkeld (1809), which opened up the whole of the Central Highlands, and the beautiful cast-iron Spey bridge at Craigellachie, Banffshire (1815). The Spey had a reputation for sudden floods of great violence, and in order to avoid any constriction of the waterway Telford's design comprised a single arch of 150 ft. span; the cast-iron construction is unusually elegant, the light open framework of the arch contrasting most effectively with the rusticated granite of the turreted abutments. Outside the Highlands two of the most interesting of the engineer's Scottish bridges are those at Tongland, Kirkcudbrightshire (1805), and Dean Bridge, Edinburgh (1831), this last coming almost at the end of what was certainly one of the most productive and diversified careers ever achieved in the field of civil engineering. Tongland Bridge, a picturesque structure of pink Arran sandstone in the castellated style, incorporates certain novelties of design, including the piercing of the high approach-walls and the construction of longitudinal load-bearing walls within hollow spandrels. Credit for the construction of the first large British suspension-bridge must go not to Telford, however, but to Captain Samuel Brown, R.N., who having taken out a patent for bridges of this type in 1817, spanned the Tweed at Hutton, Berwickshire, in 1820, the year in which work began upon Telford's Menai Suspension Bridge. This pioneer structure (*165*), which still carries traffic across the Border, has a length of 361 ft., and the total weight of 100 tons is carried on three main double chains of flat-link construction.

The various categories of building so far described in this section by no means exhaust the surviving range of early industrial and engineering works, and comparable structures of architectural or historical interest are liable to be met with in almost every part of the country. Thus, the roads of the turnpike era are studded with a great variety of toll-houses, some of them structures of considerable charm or curiosity, while abandoned mines and quarries may be survived by rows of workers' dwelling or by machine-sheds such as the early pumping-engine houses at Stevenston, Ayrshire, and Prestongrange, East Lothian—this last still containing a well-preserved Cornish beam-engine. In the towns there are water-mills of many different types (p. 253), as well as warehouses, cisterns and wells, although few burghs can boast as ingenious a water-supply system as Perth, where Dr Anderson's waterworks (1832), complete with domed, cast-iron storage tank (*166*) and columnar chimney, stand like some archetypal mosque upon the quiet banks of the River Tay.

Industrial and Engineering Works Specially Worth Visiting

Aberdeenshire	Brig o' Balgownie, Aberdeen
	Bridge of Dee, Aberdeen
	Kinnaird Lighthouse, Fraserburgh
Ayrshire	Old Bridge, Ayr
	Catrine
Argyll	Bonawe, Taynuilt
	Crinan Canal, Lochgilphead
	Furnace, Inveraray
	Bridges at Inveraray
	Mull of Kintyre Lighthouse, Southend
Banffshire	Portsoy
	Spey Bridge, Craigellachie
Berwickshire	Union Bridge, Hutton
Clackmannanshire	Bridgend Bridge, Tullibody
Dumfriesshire	Dervorguilla Bridge, Dumfries
East Lothian	Pumping-Engine House, Prestongrange
Fife	Guard Bridge, St Andrews
Inverness-shire	Neptune's Staircase, Caledonian Canal, Banavie
Kirkcudbrightshire	Tongland Bridge
Lanarkshire	Hyndford Bridge, Lanark
	New Lanark
Midlothian	Cramond
	Dean Bridge, Edinburgh
Perthshire	Deanston, Doune
	Lornty Mills, Blairgowrie
	Perth Bridge
	Perth Waterworks
	Stanley Cotton Mills
	Tay Bridge, Aberfeldy
	Tay Bridge, Dunkeld
Renfrewshire	Mills and Threadworks, Paisley
Ross and Cromarty	Cromarty
Roxburghshire	Tweed Bridge, Kelso
Selkirkshire	Woollen Mills, Galashiels
	Woollen Mills, Selkirk
Stirlingshire	Bannockburn
	Old Bridge, Stirling
Stirlingshire–West Lothian	Avon Aqueduct, Union Canal
Sutherland	Cotton Mills, Spinningdale, Dornoch

VII SMALL RURAL HOUSES, FARMS AND VILLAGES

Few small houses and cottages now in occupation in Scotland are more than 150 years old, and none is likely to have been erected before about 1750. This situation is the result of a revolution in standards of rural housing which swept most parts of the country during the late eighteenth and early nineteenth centuries. Before the commencement of this era of agricultural improvements tenant farmers and rural labourers lived in conditions of deplorable squalor. The witness of contemporary writers and travellers is unanimous. In 1662 John Ray, journeying through East Lothian, observed that 'the ordinary country houses are pitiful cots, built of stone, and covered with turves, having in them but one room, many of them no chimneys, the windows very small holes, and not glazed', while Dr Johnson's celebrated account of his first reception in a Highland cottage, 'constructed with loose stones, ranged for the most part with some tendency to circularity', indicates that a very similar state of affairs still prevailed in Inverness-shire more than a century later. The detailed and well-informed testimony of the authors of the various county volumes of the *General View of Agriculture*, published between about 1790 and 1810, is even more impressive, writer after writer contrasting the lamentable conditions of the very recent past with the improved standards of his own day.

Furthermore, the documentary evidence makes it clear that, because of the rudimentary nature of their construction, these unimproved dwellings had a remarkably short life, total or partial rebuilding being undertaken at frequent intervals. Indeed, in some areas it was customary for tenants and cottars to carry away with them the more important structural components such as roof timbers, when they moved from one farm to another—a common enough occurrence at a period when farms were let either without leases or upon very short tenures. It is clear, therefore, that even the few remaining buildings that do, in fact, antedate the agrarian revolution are unlikely to be of any great antiquity, and that, despite their primitive appearance, most constructions of traditional character, such as the Hebridean 'black houses', that survive to this day in the more remote parts of the country, were built comparatively recently. Fortunately for the historian of vernacular architecture, however, local craftsmen have always been slow to abandon traditional techniques of building construction, and a careful analysis of existing buildings of eighteenth- and nineteenth-century date, together with a consideration of the evidence that is available from documentary sources and from archaeological excavation, can go at least some way towards reconstructing a picture of the medieval Scottish peasant's dwelling.

Buildings of Traditional Character

It is convenient to classify these buildings in accordance with the different kinds of material and the varying techniques employed in their construction. The first type of structure that demands consideration is the timber-framed building which, although now rare, was at one time in general use throughout the greater part of the country. To what extent relatively advanced techniques of timber construction were employed in the houses of the upper and middle classes during medieval and post-medieval times is not easy to determine (pp. 35, 174), but there can be little doubt that before 1800 most Scottish rural labourers and artisans (and not a few lairds) lived in some form or other of primitive timber-framed building.

By far the most common type of construction—and one that is known to have been widespread in western Europe since at least as early as the beginning of the Middle Ages —was that in which the roof rested upon pairs of stout curved, or elbow-shaped, timbers (known generally in Scotland as 'couples', and in England as 'crucks') set at intervals along the side walls, with their feet only a little above ground level. Robert Dinnie's account of the methods employed in erecting houses in southern Aberdeenshire in the third quarter of the eighteenth century provides an excellent description of this form of construction. 'The couples were made with a perpendicular leg on each side of about four and a half feet in length, and were set up when the walls were built to the height of eighteen inches, with the foot of the couple resting on the inner part of the wall. The couples were placed from six to ten feet apart, and the gable tops serving the place of two, only three or four were required for a house of forty feet in length. The couples were sometimes made of whole trees, squared a little with the adze or axe, sometimes with trees cleft down the middle called half tree. In places of nails they used wooden pegs for fixing together the different parts of the couple.'

Considerable numbers of cruck-framed buildings still survive in south-west Scotland, in the Central and Western Highlands and in the northern mainland counties, and it is probable that at one time this method of construction was in general use throughout the country, except, perhaps, in the Outer Isles and in Shetland, where suitable timber was hard to obtain. Techniques varied a good deal from one district to another and, to a lesser degree, from one building to another within the same locality. Thus, in many West Highland areas, and in Skye, the couples are usually jointed at about wall-head level, the lower member (Gaelic, *crùb*) being scarfed and pegged to the upper one (Gaelic, *taobhan*); further east, and in south-west Scotland, most couples appear to be single-membered. Again, in certain of the cruck-framed buildings of the Aberfeldy

171 Dumfries Bridge. Fifteenth century

172 Old Stirling Bridge. Fifteenth century and later

173 Tay Bridge, Aberfeldy, Perthshire. *William Adam, 1733*

174 Aray Bridge, Inveraray, Argyll. *Robert Mylne*, 1775

175 Perth Bridge. *John Smeaton*, 1766–72

176 Kelso Bridge, Roxburghshire. *John Rennie*, 1803

district of Perthshire (*181*) the ridge-pole (Gaelic, *cabar-droma*) is supported by a horizontal yoke (Gaelic, *ad*), which unites the upper extremities of the couples, while in others the couples intersect to form a cradle support for the ridge.

Most, if not all, existing cruck-framed buildings in Scotland have gable walls of stone or clay, but turf- and wattle-walled structures of earlier periods were probably cruck-framed throughout their length. Sometimes, particularly in structures that appear to be of comparatively recent date, the couples do not rise from near ground level, but from a point much closer to the wall-head, thus approaching the form of a normal coupled roof, in which the principal rafters rest upon wall-plates. In treeless areas of Caithness and Sutherland it was customary for crucks to be made up from second-hand materials, such as old ships' timbers, a number of short lengths being joined together to form a continuous rib of almost semicircular section. A similar method of construction, in which materials of even less substantial character are employed, may be observed in the Highland tinker's house of the present day, where a canvas-tarpaulin roof is frequently stretched across hooped branches whose feet have been firmly driven into the ground.

By virtue of the fact that it supported the whole weight of the roof the cruck framework was particularly suitable for use in conjunction with non-loadbearing walls of turf, wattle or clay, and there is every reason to suppose that buildings of this type were formerly common (*182*). Thus, the author of the *Statistical Account* of Dornoch, Sutherland (1793), mentions a part of his parish in which 'every cottage was built of feal (turf), and thatched with divot', while a year earlier Joseph Farington, the artist, made a number of sketches of cruck-framed turf houses in Kincardine Moss, near Stirling, noting that they were constructed not by building up walls of cut turf or peat (as was no doubt customary), but by cutting away the surrounding peat to leave solid upstanding walls—a convenient enough method to employ in areas where new land was being reclaimed for farming. Sod-walled houses (probably not cruck-framed) are known to have been in occupation in the Hebrides within the recent past, while both in the Outer Isles and on the mainland it is still possible to come across buildings in which the upper portion of a gable- or of a partition-wall is constructed of turf; turf dykes were also common at one time.

Another walling material suitable for use in conjunction with a timber framework was wattle, or wicker. An early Scottish reference to a building of this type occurs in the *Register of Paisley Abbey*, where it is recorded that a certain Bede Ferdan was dwelling in a 'great house constructed of wattles' (Latin, *virgae*), close to Kilpatrick Church, about the year 1170, while later writers make it clear that houses of similar construction were to be found in parts of the Highlands until about the end of the eighteenth century. An informative description of these Highland 'creel-houses', as they were called, is given in a report drawn up for the Board of Trustees for Manufactures in 1754. Writing of farmhouses in Wester Ross and adjacent areas of Inverness-shire the author remarks:

'The side walls are made of stakes stuck into the ground, which are wattled with the branches of trees, outside of which is a wall of turf, with divots turfed over it like slates. The roof is supported with coupled trees fixed in the ground. These are wattled with small wood, over which divots are laid, and then it is thatched with straw, stubble or ferns.'

No houses of this type appear to survive today, but internal partition-walls of wattle plastered with clay are still occasionally to be seen, as for instance on the west coast of the island of North Uist, while a barn incorporating wattle side-panels (*183*)—intended to provide ventilation—was observed at Balmacara, near Kyle of Lochalsh, Ross and Cromarty, in 1959.

The two other principal building-materials, namely clay and stone, were commonly utilised in the construction both of loadbearing and non-loadbearing walls. Thus, the 'clay biggins' of the Carse of Gowrie have conventional coupled-rafter roofs, while most of these in Dumfriesshire appear to be cruck-framed. Again, the unmortared, or mud-mortared stone walls, found in most existing cruck-framed Highland buildings, are in many cases capable of supporting the thrust of a coupled-rafter roof, as has frequently been demonstrated when buildings have been successfully re-roofed in modern times— in such cases the crucks are usually sawn off at wall-head level to facilitate the laying of the wall-plates. At first sight it seems puzzling that timber-framed structures should ever have been provided with such substantial walls, for it would appear to have been more economic either to have employed a cruck framework in conjunction with walls of turf or wattle, or to have dispensed with crucks altogether in favour of a stone- or clay-walled building with a coupled-rafter roof. Reluctance to abandon a time-honoured method of construction supplies a partial explanation of this apparently contradictory state of affairs, while it is also worth remembering that an existing cruck framework may be older than its surrounding walls, and that stone or clay may have been substituted for less durable materials during some previous rebuilding operation.

Although building in clay was a relatively laborious process, a soundly constructed clay-walled house afforded its occupants an exceptional degree of insulation and, so long as the external wall-surfaces were kept weatherproof by harling, enjoyed a rather longer life than comparable structures of turf or unmortared stone. When non-viscous earth was used, however, the results were often a good deal less satisfactory. The author of the *Statistical Account* of Kiltearn, Easter Ross, writing of the houses of his parishioners, stated in 1791: 'The greatest number are built of earth, and are usually razed to the ground once in 5 or 7 years, when they are added to the dunghill—they cannot afford to build them of better materials, not even with clay and stone.' As might be expected clay-walled houses are now most commonly to be found in areas where suitable building stone is not readily available. Examples still survive on the shores of the Solway Firth, on Coldingham Moor, Berwickshire, in the Gowrie carselands, and in certain coastal areas of Morayshire and Banffshire, while the eighteenth-century documentary evidence reflects a much more widespread distribution.

Various techniques of construction were employed. A late eighteenth-century account of the method then in use in the parish of Dornock, Dumfriesshire, deserves quotation at length. 'In the first place, they dig out the foundation of the house, and lay a row or two of stones, then they procure from a pit contiguous, as much clay or brick-earth as is sufficient to form the walls: and having provided a quantity of straw, or other litter to mix with the clay, upon a day appointed, the whole neighbourhood, male and female, to the number of 20 or 30, assemble, each with a dung-fork, a spade, or some such instrument. Some fall to the working of the clay or mud, by mixing it with straw; others carry the materials; and four or five of the most experienced hands, build and take care of the walls. In this manner, the walls of the house are finished in a few hours; after which, they retire to a good dinner and plenty of drink which is provided for them, where they have music and a dance, with which, and other marks of festivity, they conclude the evening. This is called a daubing; and in this manner they make a frolic of what would otherwise be a very dirty and disagreeable job.' To judge from existing examples in the locality the clay was usually bedded in horizontal courses a few inches in thickness, separated by thin layers of straw; the walls were about 2 ft. in thickness.

The method of construction described above does not appear to have involved the use of timber framework, or shuttering, but this technique may have been employed in some areas, including Berwickshire and Angus, where the marks of timber shuttering may sometimes be discerned upon the walls of derelict 'clay biggins'. In this process the walls were built up some 2 ft. or 3 ft. at a time and, if a semi-liquid mixture was employed, each course, after being rammed home, was allowed to dry out before the next one was formed. The ingredients and proportions of the clay mixture varied in accordance with the availability of materials. In the village of Kingstown, Morayshire, for example, the walls of many of the cottages are composed of clay and straw reinforced with quite substantial beach-boulders.

In most stone-built structures of traditional character the masonry is either of 'drystone' construction—that is laid without mortar—or is bonded in mud or clay mortar only, for lime mortar was not generally used in the construction of buildings of this class before about the beginning of the nineteenth century. It was to these dwellings of unmortared or clay-mortared stone, with their somewhat gloomy external appearance that the term 'black house' (Gaelic, *taigh dubh*) came to be applied in contradistinction to the relatively spick and span 'white house' (Gaelic, *taigh-geal*) constructed in lime mortar, but in modern usage the former term is usually reserved for a particular type of building now found only in the Hebrides. The average wall-thickness of the traditional stone-built house of the Scottish mainland and the Northern Isles is in the region of 2 ft. 6 in., but in the Western Isles there exist buildings that show more primitive techniques of stone construction characterised by walls of exceptional thickness.

The most remarkable surviving examples of these archaic thick-walled dwellings are the 'bee-hive' shieling huts erected for the purposes of transhumance agriculture. The practice of moving stock to upland pastures during the summer months seems at one time to have been widespread throughout the Highland zone of Britain, as it was also in other western European countries, but in Scotland the custom persists today only in the island of Lewis. The arrangement was designed to give the cattle the benefit of the fresh hill pastures while at the same time keeping them away from the ripening crops around the township and allowing their winter grazings to recuperate; life in the shieling was looked forward to as a time of recreation, the women commonly employing themselves in butter- and cheese-making or spinning, and the men engaging in various outdoor pursuits or leading lives of leisure.

On the mainland shieling huts were frequently constructed of turf or wattle, as in the case of the 'scalan or houff made of divots and trees' that was recorded at Corgarff, Angus, in 1770. The shieling hut of the Western Isles (Gaelic, *bothan* or *b'oh*), however, was generally stone-built, the walls being constructed of drystone masonry covered externally with growing turf. The thickness of the walls was about 5 ft., and in some cases the stonework was built with an outer and inner face of boulders having a central earth core. The older form of bothan, which seems to have remained in general use in Lewis until about the beginning of the nineteenth century, was roughly circular on plan, and the dome-shaped roof was of corbelled stone—a technique of construction known to have been practised locally in many parts of Europe from prehistoric times onwards, as for example in the Early Christian oratories of Scotland and Ireland (p. 133), and in the modern 'bee-hive' huts of the Alberobello district of Italy. Huts similar in character to the Lewis shielings are said to have existed in Orkney within the recent past, while the remains of others survive on the island of St Kilda, where they were known as 'cleits' and were used chiefly as larders for drying and preserving sea-birds. A few ruinous bothans of early type still exist in Lewis, but most surviving examples are of fairly recent origin and, although noticeably thick-walled, are oval or sub-rectangular on plan and show evidence of timber-roof construction.

The other main variety of thick-walled dwelling found in the Western Isles is the Hebridean 'black house' (*178*), which seems formerly to have been widely distributed throughout the Outer and Inner Hebrides—and perhaps also further afield—but which is now found in considerable numbers only on the north-west seaboard of Lewis. The walls of the black house, like those of certain of the bee-hive shielings, are constructed with an earthen core; they are commonly 5 ft. or 6 ft. in thickness, but occasionally attain a thickness of as much as 8 ft. The roof is typically of collar-rafter construction and is thatched. Since the rafters are set upon the inner edge of the wall the remainder of the wall-top is exposed as a broad turf-covered scarcement, wide enough for children to play upon and for sheep to graze; access to this scarcement is usually provided by rough stone steps projected from the external wall-face. The nature of the roof construction is such that rain-water is shed directly into the earth core of the wall, through which it slowly percolates to the ground, thus compacting the hearting so that it forms an effective barrier against the fierce Hebridean winds. In some cases the stones of the inner wall-face are bedded on a slight incline so as to prevent water from penetrating the interior of the building. The external and internal corners of the black house are noticeably rounded, thus giving the building a sub-oval ground-plan—a feature which is also found in buildings with walls of normal thickness situated on the fringes of the main black house area.

To complete this brief survey of the structural characteristics of traditional buildings something more should perhaps be said about the main varieties of roof construction. In the first place attention may be drawn to certain differences in the geographical distribution of hip-roofed and gable-ended buildings. Hip-roofed structures are today found only in the Western Isles and in certain adjacent areas of the mainland such as the Ardgour peninsula of Argyll; elsewhere, from Shetland to the Borders, gable-ended buildings are almost universal. The factors that governed the evolution of this pattern of distribution are by no means easy to determine. In general, it might have been expected that the gabled roof would tend to occur in areas where timber-framed buildings of cruck construction had formerly been prevalent—for the end-pairs of a cruck framework themselves form structural gables—and that the hipped roof would be found in areas where it was customary to erect round-cornered stone-walled buildings, but the existing pattern of distribution lends only limited support to this hypothesis. It is clear, for example, that hip-roofed structures were at one time more widely distributed than they are today. Some of the surviving cruck-framed houses of the south-west Highlands, as at Bonawe and Auchindrain, Argyll, formerly had roofs of this type in which the hipped ends were supported upon crucks placed centrally in the end walls—a curious form of construction best explained as a hybrid combination of elements from both the timber-framed and the stone-walled building traditions. Again, the round-cornered stone-built Viking houses, and their early medieval successors, recently excavated at Jarlshof, Shetland, are thought to have been gable-ended, the roofs in some cases having been supported on double rows of interior posts.

The choice of one of these two main forms of roof construction, at any given time and place, may also have been influenced by various other factors. Properties of wind resistance, for example, must always have been considered of the utmost importance along the exposed north-western seaboard, and there is no doubt that the low rounded profile of the hip-roofed Hebridean house is ideally suited to local climatic conditions. The gable-ended house, on the other hand, could incorporate a more spacious roof-loft than the hip-roofed house, and its gable walls could conveniently embody the built-in flues that were introduced when the time came for the traditional open hearth to give way to the chimney fireplace.

The roof covering itself was generally of thatch, although there is evidence for the local use of other materials—flag-stone roofs, for example, may still be seen in Orkney, while the practice of pegging squared turfs root upwards to the rafters as a sole covering has been recorded in Shetland within the past generation or so. Techniques of thatching varied to some extent from one part of the country to another. Thus, in the Hebrides the main framework of rafters and purlins (often constructed largely of driftwood) was covered with a layer of branches followed by another of sods; the thatch itself, which might be of straw, heather, bent grass, or rushes, was laid upon the sods and secured with a network of heather- or straw-ropes weighted down with stones or attached to wall-pegs. Nowadays disused fishing nets or wire netting are often employed instead of rope. In Orkney the thatch was laid upon a web-work formed by threading straw-ropes, known as simmons, backwards and forwards across the purlins, the area between the lowermost purlins and the wall-head being covered with thin flagstones; the thatch was held on by ropes in the Hebridean fashion. Rope-thatching, in fact, seems to have been customary not only in the Western and Northern Isles, but also throughout the greater part of the Highlands. Elsewhere certain other techniques, such as scollop-thatching, in which the thatch is fastened down by horizontal rods pegged into a turf undercover, may have been practised.

Most Scottish thatching seems to have been of a pretty rough and ready character, and in many districts it was the practice to renew all or part of the thatch every year or so, and to employ the material as a fertiliser for crops, the accumulated soot content greatly adding to its value for this purpose. Before thatch ultimately began to give way to slate during the late eighteenth and early nineteenth centuries, however, various improved techniques of thatching were introduced. In the Kilmarnock district of Ayrshire, for example, thatched roofs were given outer coverings of lime mortar mixed with cut straw, while in parts of Aberdeenshire it was the custom to bed heather thatch in clay to promote adhesion, a life of up to 50 years being claimed for a roof of the former type and of up to 30 years for one of the latter. The practice of thatching is now confined largely to the Western Isles, but examples of thatched roofs may still occasionally be seen in other parts of the country, including the shores of the Moray Firth, the Strathmiglo district of Fife, and parts of Ayrshire and Roxburghshire.

Turning now to a consideration of different types of plan-form one is immediately confronted by the problem of the historical relationship of the round house to the rectangular house. Both types are known to have existed in western Europe from very early times, but the archaeological evidence—so far as it goes—suggests that throughout the greater part of Scotland the round house, of stone or timber, remained the dominant form until at least as late as the post-Roman period. The earliest rectangular houses so far identified are the Viking houses at Jarlshof, the oldest of which are ascribed to the early ninth century. But if, as has recently been argued, the introduction of cruck-framed buildings into Britain was due to Celtic peoples, the remains of rectangular houses of considerably earlier date may well await discovery in many parts of the country. Likewise, in those southern counties that formed part of the Anglo-Saxon kingdom of Northumbria from the seventh to the tenth century it is to be expected that evidence of other types of early rectangular timber-framed buildings may ultimately be forthcoming. The earliest of the Jarlshof houses had bow-shaped side walls and rounded corners, features that can be paralleled in another series of Viking houses of about the same period recently excavated at Birsay, in Orkney, as well as from other parts of the Norse world. The later houses at Jarlshof, dating from the Early Middle Ages, were more truly rectangular and had square corners, as did the contemporary Norse houses investigated in 1958–61 at Little Dunagoil, on the Island of Bute. The Viking houses at Jarlshof are evidently the direct ancestors of the traditional Shetland farmhouse, and the establishment of the rectangular plan-form in the Northern Isles may probably be attributed to the Norse settlers. The evidence so far available from the Western Isles suggests a rather different process of development, however, for although this area was subject to Norwegian rule from the early ninth century to the late thirteenth century the later pattern of building seems to owe as much to native as to Norse architectural traditions. Indeed, it is not improbable that the Hebridean black house, with its subrectangular plan and thick walls, represents an indigenous development from earlier stone-walled native buildings of circular form, such as the bee-hive hut.

When Captain Thomas, the Scottish antiquary, first drew attention to the bee-hive shielings of Lewis about a century ago he observed that in some cases several huts were grouped together to form an irregular composite dwelling comprising two or three intercommunicating apartments of which one was commonly some-what larger than the others (*177*). Sometimes additional chambers were contrived within the thickness of the walls to serve as sleeping places or churn-rooms. These composite bee-hive huts thus share many of the characteristics of the more primitive type of Lewis black house, from which they differ mainly in being shieling dwellings rather than permanent abodes, and in having corbel-roofed chambers of circular or oval form instead of timber-roofed ones of subrectangular plan. Captain Thomas also recorded one particularly elaborate group of nucleated bee-hive huts that had accommodated three separate families, each with its own series of rooms—a feature which can again be paralleled

177 Bee-hive shieling, Lewis

in an early type of black house, known as a 'creaga', which was inhabited by the several joint-tenants of a particular farm.

It is evident that in the case of the bee-hive hut, plan-form and roof construction are closely interrelated and constitute a limiting factor to the size of the chamber. It is unlikely that the maximum internal diameter of a bee-hive hut could ever have exceeded about 14 ft. (the dimension of the surviving cells (*188*) at Eileach an Naoimh, p. 133), and if bigger rooms came to be required they could most conveniently be provided by the construction of timber-roofed buildings of subrectangular plan. The suggestion that the Lewis black house may thus have evolved as a more spacious version of the primitive bee-hive dwelling gains some support from a consideration of the remains of early domestic structures recently recorded on the remote island of North Rona, some 45 miles beyond the Butt of Lewis. Here there may be seen several groups of dwellings in which the chief characteristics of both the bee-hive hut and the black house appear to exist in combination. Each group comprises a larger subrectangular building surrounded by and communicating with a series of inter-connected huts. The huts were evidently corbel-roofed, while the central buildings may have been timber-roofed in the middle and corbelled at the ends.

It must be added, however, that the characteristic nucleated plan of the composite bee-hive hut and the primitive black house of the Western Isles has Norse parallels in the medieval and later 'passage-houses' of Greenland and Iceland, where similar climatic conditions occur. This type of house, which appears to have evolved from the early Viking long house, comprised a number of apartments irregularly grouped around a long entrance-passage, but most excavated examples are more strictly rectangular in form than the Hebridean black house.

The most primitive form of Hebridean black house, of which examples today appear to survive only on the island of Lewis, comprises an irregular cluster of three separately roofed but intercommunicating buildings constructed alongside each other (*178*). The central building contains living quarters at one end and a byre at the other, both served by the same doorway. In most, if not all, inhabited houses byre and living quarters are separated by a stone wall, but this is a comparatively recent innovation, the byre having formerly been demarcated simply by a stone kerb and timber screen. The living quarters are usually subdivided by a light partition, the outer division comprising the kitchen and the inner the bedroom. It was formerly the custom to kindle the fire upon a stone hearth placed near the middle of the kitchen floor, whence the peat smoke drifted upwards through the thatch or found its way out through a smoke-hole placed a little to one side of the fire. A few houses still, in fact, retain hearths of this type, but most have now been provided with end chimneys. On one side of the central unit there is a combined stable and porch, which contains the main entrance-doorway, and on the other side a barn, and perhaps also a storeroom, the former usually entered from the byre and the latter from the kitchen. The barn is provided either with a back door or a vent-hole, and there is commonly an axial arrangement of openings throughout the building to promote a through draught for winnowing. The nucleated lay-out often makes it impossible to light the central unit except by means of small openings contrived at the base

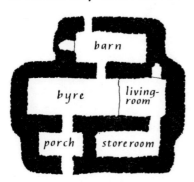

178 Black house, Lewis

of the thatch, and in older houses at least there is a complete absence of proper windows.

At a comparatively recent date a further stage in the evolution of plan-form appears to have taken place, namely the segregation of the various units of the nucleated black house to form a group of detached buildings (*184*). Thus, a number of simplified two-unit versions of nucleated dwelling exist in Lewis and Harris, while 'byre-houses' or 'long-houses' (that is to say buildings in which living quarters and byre are axially disposed beneath a common roof) standing in association with detached outbuildings may be seen throughout the Outer Hebrides. Many of these buildings preserve the chief structural characteristics of the Hebridean black house, being of thick-walled construction with exposed wall-tops (*185*). Elsewhere in the Western Isles, however, this type of construction is absent or uncommon, although the traditional Skye house (*186*), with its rounded corners and hipped roof, evidently reflects the influence of a similar building tradition. Although formerly the rule in these areas also, the byre-house is now the exception, the byre usually standing adjacent to, but detached from, the dwelling-house. The dwelling-house itself commonly incorporates a kitchen together with either one or two other main apartments. The entrance-doorway usually occupies a central position in one of the side walls and the entrance lobby often opens into a small additional room (Gaelic, *clòsaid* or *cùil*) large enough to accommodate a bed.

The vernacular buildings of the Northern Isles exhibit several different varieties of plan-form, all of which appear to be either of direct or indirect Norse origin. In some of the older buildings intercommunicating apartments are ranged alongside one another while in others, numbers of ancillary chambers project at right angles to the long axis of the principal range. Thus, a farm examined by Aage Roussell in 1934 at Effirth, on the mainland of Shetland, had the byre built alongside one end of the living quarters, with the barn (perhaps in this case an addition) placed in the re-entrant angle between them; entrance was obtained through the byre. In another instance, at Conglabist, in North Ronaldsay, Orkney, living quarters and barn were arranged lineally, while a pig-sty, stable and corn-drying kiln abutted one of the main side walls; the byre stood detached. Few if any of these structures were thick-walled enough to have allowed roof soakage to have been absorbed within the thickness of the walls, as in the Hebridean black house, and, despite the fact that buildings tended to be grouped in echelon, the problem of providing adequate drainage for contiguous roofs must have been a formidable one.

More typical of the traditional Shetland and Orkney farmhouse, however, is a linear arrangement in which the various units are placed end to end to form one or more ranges of intercommunicating apartments, according to the size of the farm. In its simplest form this lay-out corresponds very closely to that described by Dionyse Settle on the occasion of a visit to Orkney in 1577: 'Their houses are verie simply builded with pibble stone, without any chimneys, the fire being in the middest thereof. The good

man, wife, children and other of the familie eate and sleepe on one side of the house and
their catell on the other, very beastlie and rudely in respect of civilitie.' The dwelling-
house usually contains two main apartments, namely the fire-room (or but-end) and the
cellar (or ben-end), of which the former serves as a combined kitchen and living-room
and the latter as the householder's bedroom. In Orkney, at any rate, these two main
rooms are divided only by a dwarf-wall (known as a 'back') against which the kitchen
fire is kindled, and two small additional chambers frequently project beyond the rear
wall of the house, one of these being a bed-alcove and the other a storeroom, or 'ale-
hurry'. In some of the larger Orkney farms a number of the outhouses are grouped
together to form a second row of buildings running alongside the main farmhouse, the
intervening space between the two ranges being so narrow as to comprise a mere close
rather than a courtyard. Both in Shetland and in Orkney the outbuildings frequently
include a corn-drying kiln, of which two distinct types have been recorded in local
use (p. 254).

So far as the remainder of the country is concerned information about the internal
lay-outs of unimproved farmhouses and cottages has to be gleaned largely from documentary sources, for the effects of the agrarian revolution were felt much sooner and
more widely on the mainland than in the Northern and Western Isles and, except in
parts of the Highlands, comparatively few small rural buildings now retain any traditional characteristics. In general, however, it may be said that most farmhouses were
single-storeyed buildings of the 'long house' type, domestic quarters, byre and stable
all being accommodated under a single roof
(*179*, *187*). 'The byre and stable were generally
under the same roof, and separated from the
kitchen by a partition of osiers, wrought upon
slender wooden posts, and plastered with
clay', wrote the Rev. Patrick Graham of the
unimproved dwellings of Stirlingshire tenant-

179 Long house, Camserney

farmers in 1812, while a similar account of mid-eighteenth-century conditions in Ayrshire makes the point that is was customary for the cattle and the family to enter the
building by a common doorway. This latter arrangement, which seems at one time to
have been general, was vigorously attacked by the agricultural improvers, and the
practice of providing separate entrance-doorways to house and byre soon became
widespread. Thus, at the well-preserved Highland township of Auchindrain, in Mid-
Argyll (*203*), one of the earliest surviving houses—perhaps erected soon after the middle
of the eighteenth century—appears originally to have contained a single entrance
placed at the lower end of the kitchen, but this has subsequently been blocked up and
replaced by two inserted doorways giving access to house and byre respectively. The
later houses in the township have evidently been provided with separate doorways from
the first, but in all cases there is direct internal communication between kitchen and byre.

As in the Orkney farmhouses described above, the dwelling accommodation was commonly of 'but and ben' type, comprising an outer room, or kitchen, into which the outside door opened, and an inner room, which was used as a bedroom and storeroom. Some of the larger farmhouses, however, had three apartments, while others, situated in less prosperous parts of the country, had a single living-room only—an arrangement which prevailed almost universally in the cottages (or 'cot-houses') of farm labourers and the poorer tradesmen. Internal partition-walls were seldom employed, rooms customarily being divided from one another simply by a fixed piece of furniture such as a box-bed or dresser.

A number of farmhouses contained lofts, but two-storeyed buildings were almost unknown. One or two examples of early farmhouses with part upper storeys have been recorded in Orkney, however, and some Highland tacksmen (substantial leaseholders who farmed part of their lands themselves whilst sub-letting the remainder) certainly had two-storeyed dwellings. A surviving, but ruinous, example of a tacksman's house at Pitcastle, Perthshire (*192*), which may be as old as the seventeenth century, contains three living-rooms on the ground floor (*180*); the upper storey seems originally to have comprised a large common sleeping-room together with a small private bedroom, the former approached from a forestair and the latter from a narrow internal staircase. The byre and other outbuildings stood detached.

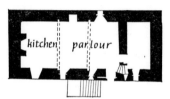

180 Pitcastle, Perthshire

The fireplace traditionally occupied a position in the centre of the kitchen floor the smoke being gathered into a wide canopied chimney constructed of wattle-and-daub or lath and plaster. An account of late eighteenth-century conditions in Peeblesshire, for example, refers to the 'round-about fire side— that is, a circular grate placed upon the floor about the middle of the kitchen, with a frame of lath and plaster, or spars and mats, suspended over it, and reaching within about five feet of the floor, like an inverted funnel, for conveying the smoke; the whole family sitting round the fire within the circumference of the inverted funnel'. By the end of the eighteenth century, however, the central hearth was being replaced by a fireplace situated in one or other of the end walls, the chimney itself being formed either as a projecting canopy or as an enclosed stone-built flue. Examples of both types of construction may be seen in a fairly well-preserved long house at Camserney (*179*), Perthshire, the central hearth in this case dating from the first period of occupation, when the family and cattle lodged under the same roof, and the end fireplaces (of which one has a canopied and the other a built-in flue) from a later period when the byre was converted into a separate dwelling-house.

Another traditional characteristic of the unimproved farmhouse and cottage was the built-in bed-recess—a feature whose antiquity is sufficiently established by the occurrence of massive stone-slab sleeping alcoves in the Neolithic huts at Skara Brae, Orkney.

In the older type of Hebridean black house, boot-shaped bed-recesses (Gaelic, *crubachan*) were contrived within the thickness of the walls, while in the Northern Isles the same purpose was commonly served by small projecting alcoves. On the mainland fixed box-beds of timber were in general use in the eighteenth and early nineteenth centuries, but it is difficult to know at what period such relatively sophisticated fittings were introduced into this class of building. Other domestic fittings were of the simplest description, the principal items of furniture invariably being a kitchen dresser and a bench. Windows were few in number and small in size, while doors were frequently hung upon wooden hinges of the type that is still to be seen in parts of the Western Isles.

Improved Farms and Cottages

It was one of the chief maxims of the agrarian reformers that well-housed tenants made better farmers than poorly housed ones. 'Nothing contributes more to the content and conveniency of a farmer, than good and well disposed buildings', wrote Dr James Anderson in 1794, 'it elevates his mind, gives him spirit to pursue his operations with alacrity, and contributes in many instances to augment his profits.' By this time a number of the more enlightened Scottish landholders had already begun to erect substantial farmhouses on their estates, and during the course of the next half century or so their example was followed by proprietors in most other parts of the country. A similar policy of improvement was adopted with regard to the dwellings of rural labourers and tradesmen, designs for all these classes of buildings being readily available through the media of illustrated agricultural journals and architectural pattern-books, of which large numbers were in circulation at this period.

Improved dwellings were invariably of stone and lime construction with roofs of slate or pantile, although thatch continued to be used in some places. Brick was seldom employed unless local conditions were exceptionally favourable—as, for example, in the Paxton district of Berwickshire, where a local laird had supported the establishment of a brick and tile works. The model usually adopted for improved farmhouses was the small laird's house or parish manse of the eighteenth century (p. 81), that is to say a plain rectangular block of two main storeys having a symmetrical plan focused upon a central staircase. Indeed, a number of houses originally occupied by bonnet lairds became farmhouses at this period, for while the agrarian revolution brought prosperity to the more progressive tenant farmers, it also led to the absorption of many of the small independent estates that had been so numerous at the beginning of the Georgian era.

Examples of improved farmhouses may be seen throughout the country (*194, 195*) and in most cases their lay-out corresponds to that of the Peeblesshire farms (*193*) described by the Rev. Charles Findlater in 1802. 'The best farm-dwellings in Tweeddale', he wrote 'are built in a style similar . . . to the dwelling-houses, or *manses* of the clergy. These latter are of the dimensions of from 34 to 40 feet in length, by from 19 to 22 feet in

182 Late eighteenth-century drawing of 'An Inn in Ross-shire'

181 Cruck-framed house, Camserney, Perthshire. Eighteenth century or earlier

183 Wattled barn, Balmacara, Ross and Cromarty. Nineteenth century

184 Houses with detached byres, North Uist. Eighteenth or nineteenth century

185 House and outbuilding, North Uist. Nineteenth century or earlier

186 House and peat-stack, Bernisdale, Skye. Nineteenth century or earlier

187 Houses, Lawers, Perthshire. Eighteenth and nineteenth centuries

188 Bee-hive hut, Eileach an Naoimh, Argyll

breadth, within the walls; the door is generally in the middle of the front, whence you enter upon a very small lobby and the staircase; on one hand is the kitchen, with a small division, probably taken off it, for a scullery and servant's bed; on the other hand, is generally the best room, occupying the breadth of the house for its length. When you ascend the stair to the second storey, the space above the kitchen may be equally divided, making two small sleeping apartments; and the space above the best room is unequally divided, affording a sort of drawing room, with a small sleeping closet. The garret space, under the roof, may be divided into a place for lumber in the one end, and the other end fitted up with a couple of beds, into what is called a *barrack* room. The farmer, having a greater number of servants than what are needed by the clergy man, is generally accommodated with a kitchen without the dwelling-house, which gives more room, though his dwelling-house is somewhat less than the manse.'

Many of these designs made provision not only for improved dwelling-houses, but also for the erection of farm offices upon a regular plan, a courtyard lay-out usually being found to be most convenient for this purpose (*196*). This type of arrangement had been advocated by agricultural writers, such as Lord Belhaven, as early as the end of the seventeenth century, but one of the first occasions upon which it seems to have been adopted in practice was in the erection of a model farm at Whim, Peeblesshire, by the Earl of Islay, afterwards third Duke of Argyll, in 1729–34. Although Lord Islay's scheme attracted considerable attention in its day as a pioneer experiment in the conversion of apparently barren tracts of country into cultivable land, the project was short-lived and nothing now remains of the early office buildings at Whim, while the 'farmhouse' itself (actually a small but well-appointed gentleman's residence) has been swallowed up within a later mansion.

In most parts of the country the regularly planned farm steading did not begin to appear until the last quarter of the eighteenth century. One of the first proprietors to adopt a comprehensive scheme of improvements was the eleventh Earl of Eglinton, who systematically rebuilt all the farm steadings on his Ayrshire estates soon after 1770. More controversial in their effects, perhaps, were the improvements carried out by the Marquess of Stafford on his northern estates during the first two decades of the nineteenth century through the agency of men such as James Loch and Patrick Sellar, but whatever may have been the shortcomings of a policy which could result in the Sutherland clearances, there can be no doubt that it revolutionised standards of rural and urban housing throughout that county. Most of the farm steadings erected by Lord Stafford in Sutherland were designed (perhaps by James Loch) in accordance with one or two standard lay-outs, and although many have since been altered to a greater or lesser degree, a number still preserve much of their original character. Two of the best examples are Cyder Hall and Inverbrora, erected in 1818 and 1820 respectively. The symmetrically planned courts of offices are very similar to one another in arrangement, but the plans of the detached dwelling-houses differ, Cyder Hall (*189, 190*)

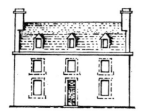

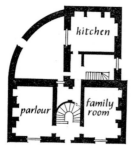

189 Cyder Hall Farm-
house, Sutherland

being a typical two-storeyed oblong block with a kitchen wing, and Inverbrora comprising a single main storey and a garret laid out on a miniature H-plan.

No survey of early planned farm steadings can omit some mention of the great court of offices erected for the fifth Duke of Argyll at Inveraray to a design in the Gothic style by Robert Mylne. Maam Steading (*197*), as it is called, was intended to be a two-storeyed courtyard building of circular plan measuring more than 200 ft. in overall diameter, and divided into two main segments by opposed entrance-gateways. The southern segment, comprising a model farmhouse and enclosing calf-sheds and stables, was never constructed, but the northern one, with its remarkable double barn and flanking cow-byres, was finished in 1790 and still stands in fairly good condition. One of the most ingenious features of the design was an arrangement whereby air could be circulated through open arcades on the ground floor, whence it rose through slatted floors to extensive corn-drying sheds on the upper storey. Almost exactly contemporary with Maam Steading are the two rectangular courtyard-plan farms of Rotmell and Blairuachdar on the Blair Atholl estate, Perthshire, both probably designed by George Steuart, a local architect much patronised by the fourth Duke of Atholl. A similar lay-out was followed in each case, but Rotmell is somewhat larger than its neighbour, and has been less altered in later times. The building is of two storeys and is executed in the classical style with considerable refinement of detail, the external elevations being arcaded, and the main courtyard front incorporating a pedimented arched entrance.

So far as cottages were concerned, the efforts of the reformers were concentrated primarily upon improvements in methods of construction and in standards of lighting and ventilation, rather than upon attempts to increase the average size of dwellings. Substantial lime-mortared walls, slated roofs, glazed windows and built-in fireplaces and chimneys were generally considered to be the most essential items. Plans were nearly always symmetrical, a typical lay-out for a two-roomed cottage comprising a room and kitchen flanking an entrance lobby, with a mid-partition formed by box-beds; in some cases an additional bed-closet, a scullery and an outside privy were constructed at the rear of the building. One-roomed dwellings continued to be erected for single labourers or childless couples, but the majority of cottages comprised two main rooms, either with or without a garret. Although no provision was now made for housing a cow or pig under the same roof as the householder, the reformers were insistent that each cottage should have its own garden—'no cottager should be without a garden, for it has been justly said, that a rood of land properly cultivated, will half maintain a careful

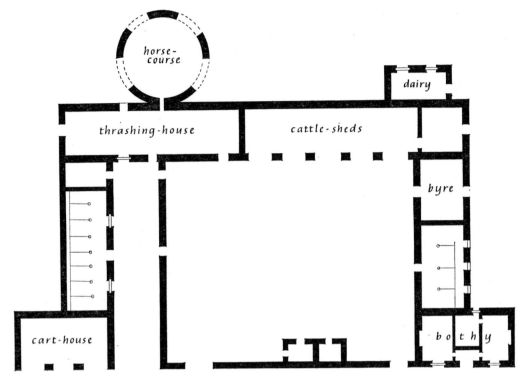

190 Cyder Hall Farm, Sutherland

family'. On grounds of economy the erection of individual dwellings was avoided wherever possible, the two most popular lay-outs being the double cottage and the long multi-unit row.

Some of the earliest improved cottages to have survived were those intended to house workers in small semi-industrial communities. Thus, at Torbrex, near Stirling, there may be seen numbers of eighteenth-century weavers' dwellings, of which one bears the date 1756 upon the lintel of the entrance-doorway. The village of Carlops, Peeblesshire, founded as a cotton-weaving centre by a local laird in 1784, retains several attractive weavers' rows of about this date, and there are others of the same period at Jericho, Angus. The Jericho cottages (*200*) are roofed with heavy stone slates of local origin (although others in the same neighbourhood are thatched), while some of those at Carlops were formerly pantiled. The original internal lay-out of a typical Carlops cottage appears to have comprised a kitchen and a combined workshop and parlour separated by a through passage; the partition walls are composed of panels of stone chippings set within stout timber frames—a form of construction known locally as a 'Galashiels partition'. This plan may be compared with that of a contemporary nail-maker's house at Chartershall, Stirlingshire (*201*), where there are two living-rooms, one on each side of the main entrance, while the workshop, which has its own external doorway, stands at one end of the building.

One of the first lairds known to have built improved dwellings for farm labourers and tradesmen was John Cockburn of Ormiston, who began to lay out the village of Ormiston, East Lothian, as a combined agricultural and manufacturing centre as early as 1735. Cockburn imposed stringent building regulations, even going so far as to forbid the erection of houses of less than two storeys in the main street of the village, but most proprietors were content to build single-storeyed dwellings. A few of the existing houses and cottages in Ormiston may belong to the initial period of expansion, while representative examples of farmworkers' dwellings of the later eighteenth century can be seen at Dunnichen, Angus, where George Dempster, one of the most eminent agriculturalists of the second generation of improvers, erected a number of slate-roofed double cottages in 1788. Not all landowners were as enlightened as these, however, and over the country as a whole progress towards better housing conditions was slow, even a relatively advanced county like East Lothian still standing in considerable need of improvement at the time of the preparation of the *New Statistical Account* in 1835–9.

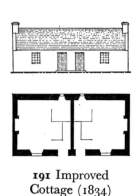

191 Improved Cottage (1834)

In some cases the co-operation of workers was sought by the award of money premiums for the erection of soundly constructed cottages—a method which seems to have been adopted with some success by the Marchioness of Stafford in Sutherland in about 1820. A few years later the Highland Society of Scotland offered a premium for an essay on 'the construction and disposition of dwellings for the labouring classes, calculated to combine salubrity and convenience with economy', and afterwards sponsored the publication of the prizewinning designs of the Edinburgh architect George Smith. Examples of the trim box-like little dwellings (*191, 202*) illustrated in this and other similar pattern-books of the period may still be seen in many parts of the country, disposed either individually or in neat estate villages.

Townships and Villages

So far as is known the traditional unit of rural settlement throughout the greater part of Scotland was the group-farm, held by several tenants in common and worked by their co-operative effort. The system of agriculture generally adopted in these circumstances involved the permanent cultivation of the 'infield', that is of the land within the immediate vicinity of the farm, and the alternate cropping and resting of the various portions of the larger but more distant 'outfield'. In order to ensure a fair and practicable allocation of land the arable was divided up into long narrow strips or 'rigs', half an acre or so in extent, and each tenant was assigned a number of strips in different

192 Tacksman's house, Pitcastle, Perthshire. Seventeenth century

193 Easter Happrew Farmhouse, Peeblesshire. *c.* 1800

194 Farm, East Kilbride, Lanarkshire. Early nineteenth century

195 Woodhead Farm, Fife. Early nineteenth century

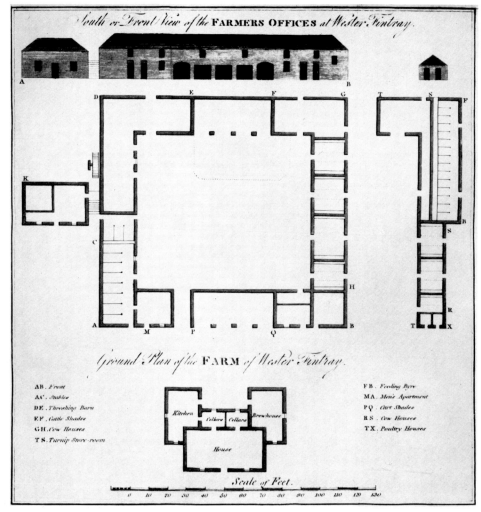

196 Wester Fintray Farm, Aberdeenshire. *c.* 1800

197 Maam Steading, Inveraray, Argyll. *Robert Mylne,* 1790

parts of the farm—a method of allotment known as 'runrig'. The buildings themselves were loosely clustered together without pretence to formal lay-out, each dwelling being sited in accordance with the local configuration of the terrain. As well as the dwellings of the tenant farmers, which were generally of long house type (p. 236), there were usually a number of cottages occupied by subtenants and tradesmen, together with barns, sheds, a corn-drying kiln and various small enclosures which served as stack-yards, stock-pens or gardens. In lowland districts this type of settlement was known simply as a 'ferm-toun', unless it happened to be grouped around a particular building of importance, in which case the term 'kirk-toun', 'castle-toun' or 'mill-toun' might be used. In Gaelic terminology the commonest name for a ferm-toun was 'baile', a term which occurs in many Highland place-names in the form of the prefix 'bal' or 'bally', while a kirk-toun was frequently known as a clachan.

So far as the Lowlands are concerned the effects of the agrarian revolution have been so widespread as to obscure virtually all traces of the traditional pattern of settlement. The sites of a number of 'deserted villages' are known, however, one of the few so far to have been investigated by archaeological excavation being the little township of Lour, Peeblesshire, where a number of stone- and clay-built houses are grouped around a small Border tower-house of the late sixteenth century.

In the Highlands the picture is rather different, for in many areas almost every glen harbours the remains of one or more farmsteads with their associated systems of cultivation. The existing buildings are invariably of stone and, in view of what has already been said about the date at which this form of construction appears to have been generally introduced in the Highlands (p. 224), it follows that few if any of them are likely to have been erected before the middle of the eighteenth century—although the townships themselves may have been in existence at an earlier period. This view has to some extent been confirmed by excavations recently carried out at the deserted townships of Lix, Perthshire, and Rosal, Sutherland, where in each case characteristic long houses yielded no occupation material of a date earlier than about 1800.

As might be expected Highland townships vary widely in the details of their lay-outs. At Rosal, for example, which is known to have supported some 15 families at the time of the clearances in 1814–20, three main groups of buildings are dispersed around the periphery of the arable land. The smaller, but much better preserved township of Auchindrain, Argyll (203), has a more centralised lay-out (198), the majority of the buildings clustering irregularly along the banks of a small burn that runs through the middle of the settlement. In other cases, as for example at Lix, linear or rectangular clusters can be recognised, such as might have arisen as a result of early attempts at agrarian improvement.

When, in the years after the Forty-five, the nucleated village did at last begin to usurp the traditional position of the ferm-toun as the principal unit of rural settlement, it was invariably as a result of planned development rather than through any process of

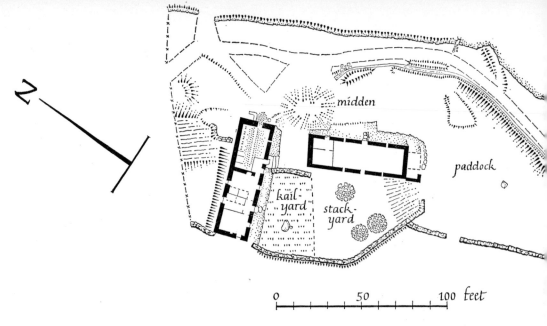

198 Auchindrain, Argyll

spontaneous growth. During the second half of the eighteenth century Scottish land-owners became increasingly convinced of the necessity of founding village communities, both to stimulate trade and industry in their localities and to re-settle that considerable proportion of the rural population whose traditional livelihood was being endangered by changes in agrarian economy. It has been estimated that more than 150 villages were founded in the period between 1745 and 1845, some as centres of domestic industry (usually associated with some branch of the textile trade), others as estate communities of farm labourers and tradesmen, and others again as fishing or harbour settlements.

The principles adopted in village planning were similar to those that governed the lay-outs of the new towns and burghs of the same period (p. 196). The two main essentials were a convenient situation with regard to water-supply, building-materials, and communications, and a plan of regular form that could be expanded in an orderly manner if need arose, 'so that' as one planner, the Rev. Robert Rennie, wrote in 1803, there is 'the appearance of a complete village, however small, and of a compact regular town however enlarged'. Most lay-outs were based either upon an axial main street or a central square, or upon some combination of these two features.

Archiestown ('Archie's Town'), Morayshire, founded by Sir Archibald Grant of Monymusk in about 1760 to re-house cottars cleared from surrounding ferm-touns, is a good example of a grid lay-out in which two main streets intersect at a central square. The village was partially destroyed by fire in 1783 and most of the existing rows of one- and two-storeyed houses, built of pink and yellow granite with neatly laid pinnings, evidently date from a subsequent reconstruction. Tomintoul, Banffshire (1775), has a similar lay-out, while Newcastleton, Roxburghshire (1793), an estate and hand-loom-weaving village established by the third Duke of Buccleuch, shows a more complex

248

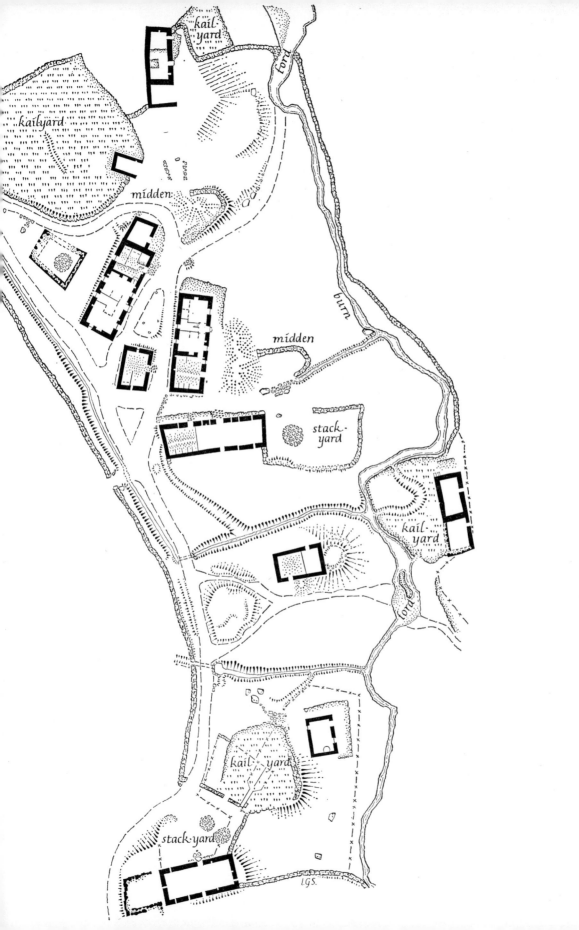

kail
yard

kailyard

ford

midden

burn

midden

stack-
yard

kail-
yard

ford

kail yard

stack-yard

I.G.S.

variant of the same theme in which the main street has a small square at each end as well as a larger one in the middle (*199*). More original, perhaps, was the scheme adopted by the fifth Earl of Elgin for the lay-out of his eponymous foundation of Charlestown, Fife, a village intended to house workers engaged in the local limestone industry. The plan was that of an elongated letter E, building being commenced at the middle stroke in the late 1760s and continued until the completion of the northern stroke some 50

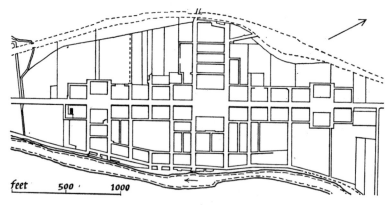

199 Newcastleton, Roxburghshire

years later. Yet another type of lay-out occurs at Eaglesham, Renfrewshire, where there is a triangular street-plan in which two principal thoroughfares flank a broad tree-covered green. Eaglesham was founded by the tenth Earl of Eglinton in 1769 as a centre for cotton spinning and weaving, and the unusually spacious lay-out together with the many well-preserved buildings of simple vernacular design make the village one of the most attractive of its kind.

Among the coastal villages mention may be made of the British Fisheries Society's twin foundations of Ullapool, in Wester Ross (*169*), and Tobermory, on the island of Mull (1788), and of the rather earlier settlement of Crovie, Banffshire, fostered by its proprietors the Gardens of Troup. This last is interesting for its complete lack of any formal lay-out, the sinuous cliff-bottom site being so narrow as to leave no space for a proper access roadway to the houses, the majority of which present one gable wall to the sea whilst abutting the other against the sheer cliff-face. Two of the most notable early nineteenth-century foundations were Brora (1811–13) and Helmsdale (1814), both established on the Sutherland estates of the Marquess of Stafford, the former as a coalmining and salt-producing centre and the latter as a herring-fishing port. Each was laid out on a regular grid-plan and provided with an improved harbour, that at Brora being linked to the coal-pits and salt-pans by a railway more than half a mile in length.

200 Weavers' cottages, Jericho, Angus. Late eighteenth century

201 Nailmakers' houses, Charters-hall, Stirlingshire. 1782 and later

202 Crofter's house, Clachtoll, Sutherland. Early nineteenth century

203 Auchindrain Township, Argyll. Eighteenth and nineteenth centuries

204   Horizontal water-mills, Shetland. Nineteenth century or earlier

205   Preston Mill, East Lothian. Eighteenth century and later
206   Corn-drying kiln, Kirkabist, Orkney

207   Tangy Mill, Argyll. Late eighteenth or early nineteenth century
208   Wheel-house, North Bellsdyke Farm, Stirlingshire. Early nineteenth century

Mills and Kilns

The most primitive type of water-mill recorded in the British Isles, the 'horizontal mill', was nothing more than a mechanised version of the ubiquitous hand-operated rotary quern. The method of operation was extremely simple, as befitted a contrivance serving small peasant communities in which each householder was accustomed to grind sufficient meal to meet the needs of his own family. From a dam constructed across a small stream water was diverted along a lade to the mill-house, where it drove a horizontal wooden paddle-wheel. A vertical spindle rising from the paddle-wheel passed through the lower millstone and engaged the upper one, thereby causing it to rotate. The grain was fed into the eye of the upper millstone from a pyramidal-shaped box, known as a hopper, and, in order to ensure an even flow, the spout of the hopper was continuously vibrated by means of a string attached to a 'clapper' stone, which rested loosely upon the upper millstone—a device whose acoustic effects were echoed in the popular name of 'Clack Mill'. The mill-house itself (204), usually a small stone-built structure of subrectangular plan, comprised two chambers, the lower one housing the water-inlet and paddle-wheel, and the upper containing the working area.

This type of mill appears to have originated in the Middle East at a very early period, and to have reached parts of northern Europe by about the beginning of the Christian era. No horizontal mills have so far been recorded in England, but they were fairly common in Ireland and in northern and western districts of Scotland, where they remained in general use until comparatively recently. Ruinous mill-houses may still be seen in considerable numbers in Shetland and the Outer Hebrides and, less frequently, on the mainland as far south as the Mull of Kintyre, while a complete example in full working order is preserved under state guardianship at Dounby, in Orkney.

The other main type of water-mill, incorporating a vertical wheel and geared horizontal shaft, appears to have been invented in Classical Italy, and was first introduced into Britain about the eighth century. The supervision and maintenance of the efficient but comparatively complex mechanism of the 'vertical mill' was a task for a specialist, while—in medieval western European feudal society at any rate—its high initial cost brought it under manorial control, thus giving rise to the system of 'thirlage', by which a lord's tenants were bound to have their grain ground at the lord's mill. In medieval and post-medieval Scotland this type of corn-mill was probably to be found chiefly in southern and eastern districts of the country, and in the burghs, but existing examples, most of which are of eighteenth-century or later date, are more widely distributed. Preston Mill, East Lothian (205), Tangy Mill, in Kintyre (207), and Perth City Mills, may be mentioned as interesting and well-preserved specimens of their class.

Notwithstanding the notorious windiness of the Scottish climate, relatively few windmills seem ever to have been erected in that country—a state of affairs which is probably to be explained by the fact that in most areas it was a fairly easy matter to harness water power. Such wind-driven corn-mills as did exist appear for the most part to have been of the tower type, in which the main body of the mill is immovable and only the upper portion of the structure turns with the sails. Tower mills (replacing the traditional rotating 'post-mills') were invented in the Low Countries about the beginning of the seventeenth century, but most surviving Scottish examples, none of which remains in working order, are of rather later date.

The third main source of energy used to supply rotary power for agricultural purposes was the domestic animal, usually the horse or ox. The majority of animal-powered machines incorporated some form of horizontal wheel or axle rotated about a central pivot, the equipment either being attached directly to the animal—as in the gorse-crushing, or whin-mill—or worked by means of gears—as in the case of mills used to drive farm implements. In both cases the machinery was of fairly simple design such as could be operated either in the open air, or in outbuildings of very modest size. The most interesting architectural manifestations of the horse-mill are the 'horse-gangs' or 'wheel-houses'—usually single-storeyed buildings of circular or hexagonal plan (*208*)—that form such a familiar feature of lowland farms. Most of these horse-gangs were constructed in the late eighteenth or early nineteenth century for the purpose of housing gear-turning wheels to drive threshing-machines; with the introduction of steam power they soon became obsolete, and few examples now remain in working order.

The two varieties of kiln that are most likely to be met with in country districts are those constructed for corn drying and lime burning respectively. Corn-drying kilns, in which grain was dried preparatory to grinding, were formerly in use in many parts of Scotland, particularly in those areas where grinding was done by means of hand-querns or horizontal mills. The most common form of kiln was a small free-standing construction comprising a storage chamber and a cone-shaped drying chamber served by a low-level horizontal flue. The structure was usually built on sloping ground so that the outer end of the flue, where the fire (usually of peat) was kindled, was accessible externally; the grain was spread for drying upon a wooden rack laid across the mouth of the chamber. In some areas, however, it was customary to construct the kiln at one end of the barn and to serve it from an internal fireplace by means of a comparatively short flue. Numbers of quite elaborate kilns of this type survive on Caithness, Orkney (*206*), and South Shetland farms, while in North Shetland there may be seen small box-shaped kilns, similar to those found in Norway and the Faroe Islands.

The small individual lime-kiln built to produce lime for local agricultural or building purposes was similar in design to the cone-shaped corn-drying kiln described above, except that it lacked a flue. To operate the kiln alternate layers of limestone and brush-wood fuel were thrown into the chamber from above and the fire was kindled within a low opening at the base. Lime-kilns of this type may be seen in most parts of the country where limestone outcrops occur, the majority of the existing examples evidently being of eighteenth- or nineteenth-century date.

FURTHER READING

GENERAL

The only publications that attempt to present a comprehensive survey of Scottish historic architecture are the regional *Inventories* of the Royal Commission on Ancient and Historical Monuments (Scotland). These volumes are still in course of publication, the areas so far covered being: Berwickshire (1915), Caithness (1911), Clackmannanshire (1933), Dumfriesshire (1920), East Lothian (1924), City of Edinburgh (1951), Fife (1933), Kinross-shire (1933), Kirkcudbrightshire (1914), Midlothian (1929), Orkney and Shetland (1946), Outer Hebrides (1928), Peeblesshire (forthcoming), Roxburghshire (1956), Selkirkshire (1957), Skye and the Small Isles (1928), Stirlingshire (1963), Sutherland (1911), West Lothian (1929) and Wigtownshire (1912). The earlier volumes are summary in approach, and those published before 1951 take no account of buildings of a date later than 1707. Useful general introductions to the subject are provided by G. Scott-Moncrieff's *The Stones of Scotland* (1938) and W. Douglas Simpson's *The Ancient Stones of Scotland* (1965), while M. W. Barley's *The House and Home* (1963) illuminates the relationship of the Scottish material to the development of British architecture as a whole.

Information about the opening-hours of buildings that are regularly open to the public may conveniently be found in two annual publications, *Historic Houses, Castles and Gardens in Great Britain and Ireland* (Index Publishers) and *Seeing Scotland* (National Trust for Scotland).

Excellent short guide-books are available at the majority of sites and monuments under the guardianship of the Ministry of Public Buildings and Works.

National Monuments Record of Scotland maintains an extensive archive of published and unpublished information relating to historic buildings, including a collection of plans, drawings and photographs. This material may be consulted by members of the public at the Record's offices at 52–54 Melville Street, Edinburgh 3.

CHAPTER I: CASTLES, TOWERS AND PALACES

Cruden, Stewart *The Scottish Castle* (1960).
MacGibbon, D. and Ross, T. *The Castellated and Domestic Architecture of Scotland* (1887–92).
Mackenzie, W. Mackay *The Medieval Castle in Scotland* (1927).
Salmond, J. B. *Wade in Scotland* (1938).
Simpson, W. Douglas *Scottish Castles* (1959).

CHAPTER II: LAIRDS' HOUSES

MacGibbon, D. and Ross, T. *The Castellated and Domestic Architecture of Scotland* (1887–92).
Tranter, N. *The Fortified House in Scotland* (1962–).

CHAPTER III: COUNTRY MANSIONS

Fleming, John *Scottish Country Houses and Gardens open to the Public* (1954).
Fleming, John *Robert Adam and His Circle* (1962).
Hannan, Thomas *Famous Scottish Houses* (1928).
Summerson, John *Architecture in Britain 1530–1830*, 4th edition (1963).

CHAPTER IV: ABBEYS AND CHURCHES

Cruden, Stewart *Scottish Abbeys* (1960).
Hay, George *Architecture of Scottish Post-Reformation Churches 1560–1843* (1957).
Lindsay, Ian G. *The Scottish Parish Kirk* (1960).
MacGibbon, D. and Ross, T. *The Ecclesiastical Architecture of Scotland* (1896–7).

CHAPTER V: BURGH ARCHITECTURE

[Cant, R. G.] *Old St. Andrews* (1945).
Cant, R. G. and Lindsay, Ian G. *Old Glasgow* (1947).
Cant, R. G. and Lindsay, Ian G. *Old Stirling* (1948).
[Cant, R. G. and Lindsay, Ian G.] *Old Elgin* (1954).
Edinburgh Architectural Association *Edinburgh, An Architectural Guide* (1964).
Lindsay, Ian G. *Old Edinburgh* (1947).
Lindsay, Ian G. *Georgian Edinburgh* (1948).
Walker, David M. *Architects and Architecture in Dundee 1770–1914* (1955).
Young, Andrew Mclaren and Doak, A. M. *Glasgow at a Glance* (1965).

CHAPTER VI: INDUSTRIAL ARCHITECTURE

Cadell, H. M. *The Story of the Forth* (1913).
Fell, Alfred *The Early Iron Industry of Furness and district; with an account of Furness ironmasters in Scotland, 1726–1800* (1908).
Pratt, E. A. *Scottish Canals and Waterways* (1922).
Smiles, Samuel *Lives of the Engineers* (1861).

CHAPTER VII: SMALL RURAL HOUSES, FARMS AND VILLAGES

Grant, I. F. *Highland Folk Ways* (1961).
Roussell, Aage *Norse Building Customs in the Scottish Isles* (1934).
Sinclair, Colin. *The Thatched Houses of the Old Highlands* (1953).

A comprehensive list of books and articles relating to vernacular architecture in Scotland was published by the Vernacular Architecture Group in 1964.

INDEX

The numerals in bold type refer to the figure numbers of the illustrations